Slaughterhouse Blues

The Meat and Poultry Industry in North America

SECOND EDITION

DONALD D. STULL
The University of Kansas

MICHAEL J. BROADWAY
Northern Michigan University

Case Studies on Contemporary Social Issues:
John A. Young, Series Editor

WADSWORTH
CENGAGE Learning·

Australia • Brazil • Japan • Korea • Mexico • Singapore • Spain • United Kingdom • United States

WADSWORTH
CENGAGE Learning·

Slaughterhouse Blues: The Meat and Poultry Industry in North America, Second Edition
Donald D. Stull and Michael J. Broadway

Senior Publisher: Linda Schreiber-Ganster

Acquisitions Editor: Erin Mitchell

Editorial Assistant: Mallory Ortberg

Media Editor: Bessie Weiss

Marketing Manager: Andrew Keay

Marketing Coordinator: Jack Ward

Marketing Communications Manager: Laura Localio

Cover Direction, Production Management and Composition: PreMediaGlobal

Art Director: Caryl Groska

Manufacturing Planner: Judy Inouye

Rights Acquisition Specialist: Tom McDonough

Cover Image: *Meat&Poultry* magazine

For product information and technology assistance, contact us at **Cengage Learning Customer & Sales Support, 1-800-354-9706**.

For permission to use material from this text or product, submit all requests online at **www.cengage.com/permissions**. Further permissions questions can be emailed to **permissionrequest@cengage.com**.

Library of Congress Control Number: 2011943456

ISBN-13: 978-1-111-82878-3

ISBN-10: 1-111-82878-4

Wadsworth
20 Davis Drive
Belmont, CA 94002-3098
USA

Cengage Learning is a leading provider of customized learning solutions with office locations around the globe, including Singapore, the United Kingdom, Australia, Mexico, Brazil, and Japan. Locate your local office at **www.cengage.com/global**.

Cengage Learning products are represented in Canada by Nelson Education, Ltd.

To learn more about Wadsworth, visit **www.cengage.com/ wadsworth**.

Purchase any of our products at your local college store or at our preferred online store **www.cengagebrain.com**.

Printed in the United States of America
1 2 3 4 5 6 7 16 15 14 13 12

✳

For our families, who sustain us in all things,
for the men and women who make our meat,
and for the communities that sustain them

My gal she bring me chicken,
My gal she bring me ham,
My gal she bring me everything,
An' she don't give a damn.

> "Chain Gang Blues," Howard Odum and Guy Johnson,
> *Negro Workaday Songs*, 1926

But he said unto them, I have meat to eat that ye know not of.

> John 4:31

You have just dined, and however scrupulously the slaughterhouse is concealed in the graceful distance of miles, there is complicity.

> Ralph Waldo Emerson, "Fate," *The Conduct of Life*, 1860

Contents

Figures and Tables

FIGURES

TABLES

✳

Series Foreword

ABOUT THE SERIES

This book series explores the practical applications of anthropology in understanding and addressing problems faced by human societies around the world. Each case study examines an issue of socially recognized importance in the historical, geographical, and cultural context of a particular region of the world, while adding comparative analysis to highlight not only the local effects of globalization, but also the global dimensions of the issue. The authors write with a readable narrative style and include reference to their own participation, roles, and responsibilities in the communities they study. Their engagement with people goes beyond observation and research, as they explain and sometimes illustrate from personal experience how their work has implications for advocacy, community action, and policy formation. They demonstrate how anthropological investigations can build our knowledge of human societies and, at the same time, provide the basis for fostering community empowerment, resolving conflicts, and pursuing social justice.

ABOUT THE AUTHORS

Donald D. Stull is professor of anthropology at the University of Kansas, where he has served on the faculty since 1975. He received his doctorate from the University of Colorado, Boulder, in 1973, and a master's degree in public health from the University of California, Berkeley, in 1975. Stull formerly served as editor of *Human Organization*, the journal of the Society for Applied Anthropology, and coeditor of *Culture & Agriculture*. Since 1987, his research has focused on the meat and poultry industry's impact on growers, workers, and host communities. He has received the Omer C. Stewart Memorial Award for exemplary achievement from the High Plains Society for Applied Anthropology; the Irvin

E. Youngberg Award for Research Achievement in the Applied Sciences from the Kansas University Endowment Association; and the Sol Tax Distinguished Service Award from the Society for Applied Anthropology. Stull was made an honorary citizen of Garden City, Kansas, in 2001 and was presented with the key to the city in recognition of the value of his work for that community.

Michael Broadway is professor of geography and dean of the College of Arts and Sciences, Northern Michigan University. He holds degrees in education and geography from Nottingham University and London University and received his Ph.D. in geography from the University of Illinois at Urbana-Champaign in 1983. Before joining the faculty at Northern Michigan in 1997, Broadway taught at the State University of New York at Plattsburgh, Wichita State University, and the State University of New York at Geneseo. It was during his time in Kansas that Broadway developed his interest in the meat industry, and he has gone on to study its impact upon communities and the environment in the United States, Canada, and the United Kingdom. Broadway was an expert witness in a court case against one of the leading meatpacking companies in the late 1990s. His research was the subject of a Canadian Broadcasting Corporation documentary that aired on "The National" in 1998. He was awarded a Fulbright Research Chair to the University of Alberta in 2006 and received Northern Michigan University's Excellence in Scholarship Award in 2007.

Stull and Broadway have written numerous journal articles and book chapters together. With David Griffith, they edited *Any Way You Cut It: Meat Processing and Small-Town America*, published by the University of Kansas Press in 1995.

ABOUT THIS CASE STUDY

The relationship of food production to other aspects of culture has always attracted the attention of social scientists. This case study tells how the modern system of meat and poultry production has altered our very way of life. The authors take the reader on a journey through factories, farms, and communities to explore how corporate-driven forces cause air and water pollution, threaten the health and safety of workers, deny farmers the means to control their own livelihood, and alter the ethnic makeup and class structure of rural towns. They also recount how their work has helped communities resist and mitigate the negative impacts of rural industrialization, and illustrate how your own food choices have far-reaching political, economic, environmental, and social consequences. This second edition provides poignant examples and statistics indicative of present trends in industrial meat production.

John A. Young
Series Editor
Department of Anthropology
Oregon State University
john.young835@gmail.com

✳

Preface

M eat. In the King James Bible, meat refers to food of any kind, and as late as the medieval period, "white meat" meant milk and cheese, not chicken. Only in recent times has the word been used primarily to denote the edible flesh of mammals (and distinguished from fish and poultry). The term may have lost its inclusive Old English meaning, but meat remains the most esteemed of foods in Western society. A meal is not a proper meal without it.

Not everyone eats meat, of course. Adam and Eve were vegetarians, and not until after The Flood did God give humans permission to consume the flesh of animals (Genesis 9:2–4). Until recently, anthropological notions of the role meat eating played in human evolution were not all that different from the biblical one. Although current thinking no longer attributes the technological and biological advances that characterize the appearance of *Homo sapiens* to hunting, and thus meat eating, there is no doubt that humans eat more meat than any other primate. And some anthropologists argue that cooking, specifically the cooking of the flesh of animals, is what distinguishes humans from other animals (Fiddes 1991:15; Wrangham 2009).

Maybe cooking (and eating) meat is what made (and makes) us human, maybe not. In any event, meat eating is increasingly under attack, from those who say it is bad for our health to those who say it is bad for our planet to those who argue that humans do not have the right to slaughter and consume other animals. For these and other reasons, the number of persons in affluent Western countries who avoid some or all forms of meat is increasing. Yet, paradoxically, in the developing world rising per capita incomes are correlated with increasing meat consumption.

Most of us come to know meat only through the grocery store or the restaurant. But meat must be made, and it can only be made by the slaughter of animals. Indeed, the Judeo-Christian tradition forbids the eating of animals that die by other than human hands (Leviticus 17). For Jews and Muslims, tradition dictates that the slaughter of domesticated animals be accomplished by an officially authorized and supervised slaughterer, who ensures that the animal is conscious when its throat is severed by a single knife stroke (Davidson 1999).

Most of us have no compunctions about eating meat, but few relish the thought of where that meat comes from or how it was transformed from "animal to edible" (Vialles 1994). Death and dismemberment are never pleasant to witness, and while they are essential in the making of animals into meat, most of us would just as soon know as little as possible about the whole process.

This seems like a good place for a confession. We are both eaters of animal flesh—beef, pork, mutton, lamb, poultry, fish—we love them all. In fact, we met over cheeseburgers, big juicy ones, if memory serves us. It was Wichita, Kansas, August 1986. We knew little—and cared even less—about the meat and poultry industry. We had been invited to lunch by a mutual friend—Ken Erickson, then refugee services coordinator for southwest Kansas—to consider a study of the Vietnamese refugees who were coming to Garden City—four hours to the west—to work in its two beef plants.

Serendipity isn't given near enough credit in the shaping of human destiny. But those cheeseburgers changed our professional lives, and we have hungrily studied the people and places that produce our meat and poultry ever since.

We became perhaps the first social scientists to systematically study the modern meat and poultry industry and its impact on workers and the communities where its plants are located. Our research has taken us to rural communities across the United States and Canada, and our publications have informed scholars, journalists, industry insiders, community leaders, and general readers. Since we wrote our first article together in 1990, scholarly and journalistic writings on the meat and poultry industry have mushroomed. Still, our work remains the broadest in geographical coverage and the deepest in research experience on this subject.

Slaughterhouse Blues is our attempt to pull together what we have learned about the meat and poultry industry and its consequences for growers and production workers, communities, and consumers. We discuss in depth each major sector of the meat industry—beef, pork, and poultry—and present the results of our research in several states and provinces in the United States and Canada. We combine macro- and microlevel analyses with geographic and anthropological perspectives. Drawing upon extensive ethnographic materials, we often quote directly from interviews and fieldnotes. We like to think our presentation is balanced, but after so many years of study we have reached certain conclusions and taken definite positions. For research to be useful, we believe it must be put to use, and we have worked with local governments and community groups as well as union and industry representatives to apply our knowledge. In short, we have tried to tell readers what we know, how we learned it, and what we have done with that knowledge.

Canada and the United States are urban societies and, despite our collective dependence upon agriculture, most North Americans have lost any connection to their agrarian heritage. Yet, if we do not understand where our food comes from and how it gets to our table, who produces it and at what cost, we stand to jeopardize the very food supply that sustains us. Over the course of the last century, the meat and poultry industry has reshaped North American agriculture and its rural communities. In the process, it has significantly altered what we eat and how.

We may or may not be what we eat, but what we eat has real consequences for workers, communities, and the environment. Whether we eat meat or not, knowing more about the meat industry's impact on our diet and our lives behooves us all. This book is our attempt to identify some of the ramifications of North Americans' seemingly insatiable appetite for meat.

Preface to
the Second Edition

By the time we finished writing the first edition of this book in 2003, we had spent almost 20 years studying this industry. *Slaughterhouse Blues* was supposed to encompass all we had learned on the subject before we looked around for something new to study. It hasn't turned out that way.

The past decade witnessed many changes for meat and poultry. Companies that were industry powerhouses when we began our research no longer exist and new ones have taken their place. The United States and Canada have suffered from mad cow disease, and meat recalls are becoming commonplace. Vocal criticisms by scholars and journalists, demonstrations and undercover videos by activists are putting the industry under pressure to modify how animals are raised and slaughtered. Fast food giants like McDonald's and expanding grocery chains such as Whole Foods are insisting on more humane treatment and slaughter of animals. Consumer demand for organic and "natural" foods is rapidly growing.

Food, as a subject, has become immensely popular over the past decade. Organic. Natural. Grassfed. Free range. Factory farm. Local. These terms are no longer the sole purview of "foodies"; they pop up in the everyday conversations of everyday Americans and Canadians. North Americans are also asking more of their food. They want it to taste better and be safer, to be better for them and for the environment. Nowhere is this trend more obvious than in animal agriculture and meat processing. The general public is increasingly concerned about how the animals that give us our meat, dairy, and eggs are treated—in life and in death.

Dramatic changes swept over the North American meat and poultry industry in the first decade of the twenty-first century, and the places we studied in the 1980s and 1990s remain under its influence. We continue our fieldwork in several of them: Garden City, Kansas; Brooks, Alberta; Webster County, Kentucky.

What those changes have meant for producers, workers, and host communities, combined with new public sensibilities that are reshaping the industry, prompted us to revise and expand *Slaughterhouse Blues*. The second edition incorporates new research and broadens the scope of the book. Every chapter was edited, updated, and several, including the conclusion, were substantially revised. We have added a new chapter on animal rights and welfare, as well as new material on mad cow disease and the federal crackdowns on unauthorized immigrants in several meat and poultry plants. Some material from the first edition does not appear in this edition. For example, the earlier discussion of Guymon, Oklahoma, was eliminated because we were unable to update our earlier work. Tables and figures from the first edition were updated or eliminated. New figures have been added, as well as new photographs.

We have now studied the meat and poultry industry for almost three decades. In the decade since *Slaughterhouse Blues* first appeared, our knowledge has increased and our sensibilities have expanded. After reading this book, we hope you can say the same.

Invariably, the first question we are asked after we talk about our research is: "Do you still eat meat?" We do, but our research has definitely altered our eating habits. Over the years, we have become what Michael Pollan calls "conscientious omnivores." We eat less meat and more or less of some kinds than we used to; we avoid the products of certain companies. In short, we are thoughtful about what we eat and where it comes from. That said, like any good fieldworkers, we eat anything that is put in front of us by anyone who is kind enough to feed us.

All of us are eaters. We believe informed eaters will become conscientious eaters. And we believe conscientious eaters will help improve the agricultural and industrial system that brings food to our tables.

ACKNOWLEDGMENTS

Social science research is a collaborative enterprise, founded on trust and reciprocity, and dependent on the goodwill and generosity of those who share their knowledge and their lives with investigators. We have studied the meat and poultry industry and its impact on people and places for nigh on 30 years. After so long a time, and after working in so many places, we have amassed professional and personal debts well beyond enumeration and repayment. We cannot begin to acknowledge all who are deserving of our recognition, and we herewith apologize to everyone who we should thank but simply cannot because of the limitations of space and memory.

We are indebted to the following institutions and individuals for supporting our research and the writing of this book: The Ford Foundation's Changing Relations Project; the Aspen Institute; Wichita State University; the State University of New York at Geneseo; the Canadian Studies Program, Canadian Embassy, Washington, D.C.; the Foundation for Educational Exchange between Canada and the United States of America; Terry Seethof, Associate Provost, Northern Michigan University; Susan Koch, Provost, Northern Michigan University; the

Kansas University Endowment Association; and the University of Kansas for grants from its General Research Fund and sabbatical leaves.

Of the many people who have been so hospitable and so patient with us during our research, we are especially grateful to Gary Bright, Danny and Cindy Coffman, Marcial Cervantes, Keith Downer, Bobbie and the late R.L. Dunville, Jerry and Debbie Dunville, Roger Epp, Ed Fitzgerald, Jose and Hilda Flores, Ellen Goddard, Bob Halloran, James Hawkins, Tom Henry, Lorine Hewson, David Kattenburg, Paul and Joanne Kondy, Greg Lauby, Barry and Lana Love, Ian MacLachlan, Joyce and Laine McGaughey, Robin Marsh, Dennis Mesa, James Mireles, Karen Munro, Milt Pippinger, Bill Podraza, Marcus Qualls, Mary Regan, Lee Reeve, Amy and Jeff Richardson, Roberta Rogers, Levita Rohlman, Penney Schwab, Dwight and the late Blondell Simpson, Bill, Jeannine, Brian, and the late Olivia Stull, Roxy Thompson, and Dave Whitson.

To our mothers, Marjorie Stull and Phyllis Broadway, we owe debts beyond measure, but here we wish to thank them for sharing some of their memories. For sharing her home and her marvelous cooking with her wayward nephew, Frances Horner commands never-ending gratitude and devotion.

Several people kindly read and commented on portions of this book as we wrote it: Aloma Dew, Kerry Feldman, the late Bill Hatley, Roger Horowitz, Paul Kondy, John Massad, Michael Paolisso, Penney Schwab, Marjorie and the late E.B. Stull. But the one who labored longest and hardest with us in this vineyard was Laura Kriegstrom Stull, who read every word—many, many times— and offered valuable editorial commentary and advice.

Aloma Dew's labor and leadership on the Sierra Club's campaign to raise public awareness of the environmental costs of concentrated animal feeding inspired us to write Chapter 10. Many long conversations and lengthy e-mail exchanges with Erik Marcus convinced us of the need to add a chapter on animal rights and welfare. He has been a valuable source for and critic of our work. Steve Bjerklie, Bill Bullard, Mike Callicrate, Rich Dunville, Roger Horowitz, Kaleb Kentner, Robin Marsh, Richard Pantoja and Miranda Nelson, and Penney Schwab provided valuable source material, as did Aloma Dew, Frances Horner, and Blondell Simpson. Bill Hatley and Paul Kondy kindly helped us get some of our facts straight.

Steve Bjerklie provided photos from *Meat&Poultry*'s files from the time when he was the magazine's editor. Adam Reynolds also allowed us to use some of the images from his photo essay on Garden City. Mary Brohammer and Melissa Filippi-Franz transcribed taped interviews.

Laura Kriegstrom Stull drew the maps, designed the graphics, formatted the final manuscript, suggested photo layout, prepared the photographs, recommended the cover design, and otherwise helped us make this an attractive book.

Lin Gaylord and Erin Mitchell of Wadsworth welcomed our suggestion for a second edition of this book. Series editor John Young not only encouraged the second edition, he read and commented on each chapter.

To all these generous and talented people—and more—we offer our thanks, a thousand times over. And we absolve them of any errors or omissions in this work, for which we are solely to blame.

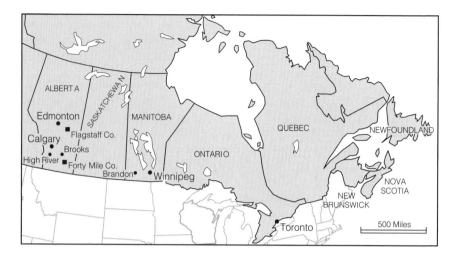

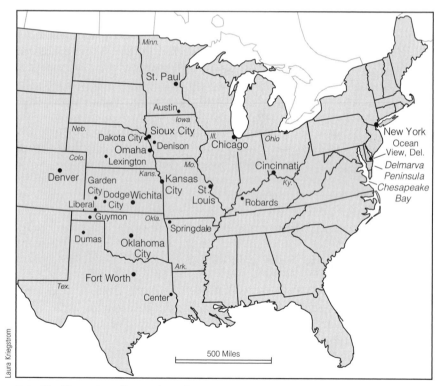

F.1 Significant Canadian and U.S. locations in the text

Laura Kriegstrom

Introduction

THE TOUR

The doors to the guard station were marked in Spanish and Vietnamese—but not in English. The uniformed guard behind the glass window said to sign in. Then a guide let us inside a high chain-link fence and down a long walkway and into the plant. From there we walked through the cafeteria and into a training room where he gave us brand-new white hardhats and smocks along with yellow foam rubber earplugs. As we clumsily adjusted the plastic headbands inside the hardhats, buttoned up our smocks, and removed the earplugs from their plastic envelopes, a middle-aged Anglo man dressed in a golf shirt, polyester western dress jeans held up by a trophy buckle, and snakeskin boots began to speak:

> Welcome to IBP. IBP is the largest beefpacking company, and this is the largest and most sophisticated plant in the world. Please do not talk to the employees, for their safety and yours, since they are operating machinery and using knives. And please stay together for your safety. Because of the high noise level, and since you'll be wearing earplugs, we won't be able to answer your questions in the plant, but we will return here after the tour and you can ask questions then.

Our guide was Vietnamese, in his early thirties. We followed him through two heavy swinging metal doors and out onto the "killfloor," where we gazed upon a moving row of dead cows, suspended upside down on meat hooks, their tongues hanging out, their limbs jerking. As they passed by, quivering like monstrous red and black shirts being called up at the dry cleaner, an Anglo man clipped off their hooves with a tool resembling large pruning shears, while above us on a catwalk a Latina slapped plastic sheets onto their skinned rumps.

Forty-five minutes later, back in the training room, we removed our earplugs and took off our smocks and hardhats, still dazed by what we had just experienced. The man in the snakeskin boots, who turned out to be the personnel manager, asked if we had any questions. For almost an hour, he cheerfully answered our questions, taking great pleasure in his statistics, and in our wonder at "the Cadillac of all packing plants."

> Here at the Finney County plant, we kill between 30,000 and 32,000 head of cattle a week. Many feedyards in this area have a capacity of about 40,000 head, so we empty the equivalent of about one feedyard per week. Every day we receive 101 trucks of live cattle and load out one truck of boxed beef every 22 minutes of every day, seven days a week. From hoof to box, the longest a cow will stay in this plant is six days; the prime time is two to three days.
>
> The number of head we can process depends on whether we're doing "bone-in" or "bone-out." Bone-out is largely for institutional buyers, such as hospitals and restaurants, and requires more cuts because most of the bones are removed. It is heavy work—and hard. We can do about 350 head an hour on bone-out. Bone-in is mainly what the housewife will buy at the local grocery store, and it moves a lot faster—400 head an hour or more. They do 240 cuts of meat here; nine of ground beef alone!
>
> Right now, this plant has 2,650 employees and an annual payroll of $42 million. Each job is ranked, and paid, according to importance and difficulty. There are seven levels. Starting pay for someone just off the street with no experience on a level-1 job is $6.40 an hour in processing, $6.70 in slaughter. The base for level-7 employees is $9.40 in processing, $9.58 in slaughter. After six months you get an automatic 50 cents raise and another 72 cents at the end of one year. We have profit sharing and yearly bonuses. IBP is self-insured. We offer an excellent insurance package—health, dental, vision, retirement, disability, alcohol and drug abuse coverage. Line workers are eligible for coverage after six months.
>
> Absenteeism normally averages 1.7 percent. We compensate for absenteeism by having more workers on a shift than we absolutely need. If too many show up, we assign the extra workers to different tasks, which helps them qualify for more than one job, or we experiment with new techniques.

The man in the snakeskin boots spewed his statistics with ease, and he neatly sidestepped a question about worker turnover. Instead, he informed us that

> More than a thousand of our workers have been in this plant for two or more years. As plants get older their workforce becomes more stable. Most workers stay on the same job for about a year. By then they are getting bored and usually bid to another job.
>
> We have an internal job posting system here at IBP. Current employees are given the opportunity to apply for and fill jobs before we hire from outside. New hires are placed wherever the need is greatest. After the initial 90-day probationary period, you can bid on

other jobs and move around the floor. The more jobs you are qualified for, the more competitive you are for supervisory jobs. Each supervisor oversees 45 employees and has a trainer working under him. Although it helps, supervisors don't have to be qualified on the jobs they oversee. We look around the plant for workers who show real promise—leadership, potential, interpersonal communication skills. The supervisor runs his own business out there; he is responsible for his crew's production and is given daily reports on its output.

We stress safety here. We spend $1 million a year on training and employ 28 hourly trainers. Each new hire receives three days of orientation, then comes back each day for 30 minutes of stretching exercises until he gets into shape to do his job. Depending on their job, each worker may wear as much as $600 worth of safety equipment—hardhat, earplugs, cloth and steel-mesh gloves, mail aprons and leggings, weight-lifting belts, and shin guards. Knife users normally carry three knives. Each one is owned by IBP and has its own identification number. The workers use the same knives as long as they work here. They grow very attached to their knives; they know their feel, and this helps them do a better job. Knives are turned in at the end of the day for sharpening and are picked up at the beginning of the next shift. They also carry sharpening steels with them and sharpen their knives while they work.

"With all those knives, they must cut themselves a lot?" one of us asked.

"The most common injuries are punctures, not lacerations," he replied.

These wounds usually occur when a knife slips and pokes the other hand. Such injuries are usually caused by workers not wearing their safety equipment. But we've had very few such injuries so far this year. In fact, we won the President's Award for the best safety record of any IBP plant.

The list of products we produce at this plant is almost never ending. We separate the white and red blood cells right here in the plant, and each is used for different things. Blood is used to make perfume. Bone meal is used as a feed additive. Kodak is the biggest buyer of our bone gelatin, which is used in making film paper. Intestines are used to string tennis rackets. The hairs from inside the cow's ears are used for paintbrushes. Spleens are used in pharmaceuticals.

Processing begins at 6:05 A.M. Slaughter starts an hour later. Workers get a 15-minute break after about two-and-a-half hours and a 30-minute lunch break after about five-and-a-half hours. The day shift, we call it A shift, ends at 2:35. B shift begins at 3:05. In between shifts we do a quick, dry cleanup. From midnight to 6:00 A.M. we contract out for a wet cleanup, which holds down bacteria.

Our heads were swimming. We wanted to know so much more, but we were exhausted from trying to absorb it all and remember even a fraction of the facts and figures he glibly tossed back in response to our questions. The man in the snakeskin boots made no attempt to hurry us, and he seemed a little disappointed when we could no longer think of anything more to ask. As we uneasily shuffled in tacit recognition that this adventure was about to end, someone asked, "Do you get any flak from the animal rights people?"

"Not really," he quipped. "Most people enjoy a good steak."[1]

• • •

And so began our research on meatpacking and meatpacking workers. What left us in awe on that June day in 1988, as we followed our guide through a confusing maze of men, machines, and meat, was remarkably similar to what Upton Sinclair had witnessed more than 80 years earlier in the packinghouses of Chicago.

> It was all so very business-like that one watched it fascinated. It was pork-making by machinery, pork-making reduced to mathematics. And yet somehow the most matter-of-fact person could not help thinking of the pigs.... Then the party went across the street to where they did the killing of beef—where every hour they turned four or five hundred cattle into meat.... This made a scene of intense activity, a picture of human power wonderful to watch.... The way in which they did this was a sight to be seen and never forgotten; they worked with furious intensity, literally on the run.... It was all highly specialized labor, each man having his task to do; generally this would consist of only two or three specific cuts. (DeGruson 1988:28–32)

Upton Sinclair did his research for *The Jungle* in 1904, but were he to visit one of today's packinghouses he would be struck with how little the industry—its work or its workers—has really changed. Knockers still start the killing, but now they use a stun gun instead of a sledgehammer. Splitters are still the most expert and highly paid workers on the killfloor, deftly cutting carcasses in half with band saws from moving platforms, where once they used massive cleavers. And, just as they did a century ago, today's stickers and gutters, tail rippers and head droppers, chuck boners and short ribbers still wield razor-sharp knives as they turn 400 cattle an hour into meat.

Meatpacking plants remain massive factories, employing hundreds or even thousands of workers, but instead of the Lithuanian, Serbian, and Polish workers of Sinclair's day, today's packinghouses are crowded with immigrants from Mexico and Guatemala, refugees from Myanmar and Somalia. Immigrants are still attracted to packinghouse jobs because command of English is not required, and because the wages they earn on "disassembly" lines are better than they can earn elsewhere in North America—or in the jobs they left behind.

Companies still "make a great feature of showing strangers through the packing plants, for it is a good advertisement" (Sinclair 1985:43). And somewhere in between pointing out the "wonderful efficiency" of the plant, the unbelievable speed with which they kill and disassemble cattle, and the "many strange and unlikely products [that come from] such things as feet, knuckles, hide clippings, and sinews" (Sinclair 1985:50), the guide will chuckle and say, "They don't waste anything here. IBP markets every part of the cow but the moo. My father used to work at IBP before me, and he used to tell me that the little toy boxes that moo were made by IBP." The group will laugh, and the tour guide will smile to himself that we should take this ancient witticism as his own.

STUDYING THE MEAT AND POULTRY INDUSTRY—AND WHY

When Upton Sinclair wrote *The Jungle* at the beginning of the twentieth century, cattle were raised on the grassy plains and prairies of North America and shipped by railroad to be slaughtered in packinghouses in the stockyard districts of Chicago, St. Louis, Toronto, New York, and other major cities. The United Nations now stands on the site of an old meatpacking plant; the Kansas City and Omaha stockyards have been razed; and the Fort Worth stockyards have been transformed into chic boutiques and upscale restaurants. The largest Home Depot in Canada now stands on the grounds of Toronto's meatpacking district.

Urban stockyards and packinghouses are no more. In their place, giant modern meat processing plants have sprung up throughout rural North America, from beef plants on the plains of Kansas and Alberta, to pork plants in North Carolina and Manitoba, to chicken plants in Maryland and Kentucky.

This book tells the story of the modern meat and poultry industry in North America, of its impact on farmed animals, on those who turn those animals into meat, and on the communities where they live and work. It is also a story of discovery by a cultural anthropologist and a social geographer as they seek to understand the social and economic forces at work in modern food production and how their research might be best put to use in the service of the communities and the people they have studied.

In the mid-1980s we began studying Garden City, Kansas, as part of a national research project on immigration funded by the Ford Foundation. Our team consisted of five anthropologists and a social geographer, and we lived and worked in Garden City on and off for two years. We have returned repeatedly over the years to conduct research, provide technical assistance, and visit friends.

It soon became clear that any understanding of the social processes at work in Garden City required an understanding of the beef industry itself. Michael Broadway's role as a geographer was to explain the presence of the new immigrants in the community and to document the social and economic changes that accompanied the arrival of the beef industry. Michael explored the evolution of the industry, collected data on its changing structure, and even interviewed the founder and chief executive officer (CEO) of a major beef company.

Don Stull was the team leader and, like Michael, his research focused on beefpacking and cattle feeding. He was to study ethnic relations in the workplace, but the packinghouses refused to cooperate. Participant observation is the hallmark of ethnography, and ethnographers actively participate in the lives of those they study. So how could he learn about the ways packers relate to their coworkers without ready access to the killfloor and the processing line?

Don subscribed to *Beef Today*; toured the plants every chance he got; attended workers' compensation hearings, which offered detailed job descriptions and graphically illustrated why meatpacking is among America's most dangerous industries. He enrolled in Meat and Carcass Evaluation at Garden City Community College to learn more about the industry, make contacts, and gain regular entry to the "cooler," where carcasses are graded. Don helped his instructor tag carcasses for Beef Empire Days as the dead animals snaked along the chain, being skinned and gutted before entering the cooler. He rode with friends on the Santa Fe work train to pick up tallow and hides at IBP. He interviewed packers, feedyard managers, meat inspectors, and others who work in the meat and cattle industries.

But Don did most of his research on work in Tom's Tavern. There he could meet a cross-section of Garden City—packinghouse line workers and supervisors, farmers and ranchers, feedyard pen riders, doctors and lawyers, railroad engineers and truck drivers—the unemployed and the well-to-do; whites, blacks, Hispanics, and an occasional Vietnamese; old-timers and newcomers alike. Lacking access to the packinghouses, Don found that Tom's offered the best opportunity to talk candidly with workers. In its relaxed atmosphere, people talked openly and often of their work. Don became one

Laura Kriegstrom

FIGURE I.1 Don Stull (center) talks with Joyce McGaughey, owner of Tom's Tavern, and her son Laine while doing fieldwork in Tom's.

of Tom's regulars, playing Trivial Pursuit and hearts with a circle of devotees, shuffleboard and pool with friends and acquaintances. On Thursdays—payday at the packinghouses—he helped tend bar from midnight till closing at 2:00 A.M., waiting on, talking with, and listening to thirsty line workers coming off B shift. On Sunday—"zoo day," so called because it was the only day off for many workers—he worked from 10:00 P.M. to 2:00 A.M.

Meatpacking and meatpacking workers were only part of the story. We were also interested in learning how Garden City had dealt with the unique challenges posed by an influx of new immigrants and rapid population growth. This involved interviewing teachers, school principals and administrators, police officers, health care providers, clergy, city officials, business owners, and everyday citizens.

As our initial fieldwork came to a close in the fall of 1989, we wondered whether what we were discovering in Garden City was also occurring in other industry towns. Beginning in the 1990s we embarked on a systematic investigation of beef, pork, and poultry processing plants and their impact on workers and communities throughout North America—from Oklahoma to Alberta, from Kentucky to Manitoba. Along the way, other social scientists have joined our quest to understand the meat industry and influence its direction. In what has become an extended natural experiment, the ethnography of Garden City has evolved into the ethnology of the meat and poultry industry and its host communities.

This book integrates what we have learned about the meat and poultry industry in the course of three decades of research. It traces our involvement in studies of how this industry alters the communities where its plants are located. It is, after all, in the business of turning farm animals into meat, and we have also learned about raising and slaughtering cattle, hogs, and chickens. Our story is not only about who grows these animals and who turns them into meat, but also how the industry treats growers, workers—and the animals themselves. As applied social scientists, our goal has been to make our research useful to the people who are its subjects, to the industry that has captured our interest for so long, and to the general public.

• • •

Chapter 1 traces the emergence of industrialized agriculture in North America after World War II, paying particular attention to the changing structure and geographical location of beef, poultry, and pork production and processing since the 1960s. It also examines how industrial agriculture has inextricably altered rural landscapes and dinner tables, and considers how changes in household structure and the role of women in the workforce have affected the demand for whole and processed food.

Chapter 2 presents an overview of the beef cattle industry, beginning with the emergence of the "cattle kingdom" on the Great Plains after the War Between the States. Until the 1960s, most cattle were fattened in the Midwest's Corn Belt and slaughtered in cities such as Chicago and Kansas City. In the second half of the twentieth century, cattle feeding and beef processing relocated to the High Plains of the United States and Canada. Production and processing concentrated in the hands of a handful of multinational conglomerates, which went about aggressively restructuring the industry and its workforce.

Modern poultry production is the model for what has come to be called "factory farming." Born on the Delmarva Peninsula in the 1920s, specialized production of "eating chickens"—commonly called broilers—spread to Georgia and Arkansas during World War II. In the 1990s, chicken processors expanded into new territories. One of those was Kentucky. Chapter 3 presents the history of modern poultry production and the effects of a Tyson Foods chicken plant on agriculture in the area surrounding Don Stull's hometown in western Kentucky, where he has been conducting research since 1998.

Chapter 4 examines hog production and pork processing, which have emulated changes in the poultry industry. Just as the centers of gravity for beef and poultry production and processing have shifted, so too has pork, which has concentrated and relocated into new territories in the United States and Canada, even as its production processes have restructured and vertically integrated.

By law livestock must be handled and slaughtered humanely. Public perceptions of what constitutes humane treatment of animals are changing, however, as animal welfare and animal rights have become global issues. Chapter 5 explores the philosophical underpinnings of the animal rights movement, the growing influence of People for the Ethical Treatment of Animals and Temple Grandin, and how an embattled meat and poultry industry is responding to growing pressure to modify how it raises and slaughters animals.

Packinghouses early in the twenty-first century are a far cry from those early in the twentieth. But for all their computerization and laser technology, their robotics and ergonomics, the knife, the meat hook, and the steel are still the basic tools of the trade. Today's plants remain, like the ones they replaced, rigidly organized, labor-intensive factories that use disassembly lines to turn animals into meat. Chapter 6 begins with an overview of working conditions at the beginning of the twentieth century, known to many readers through Upton Sinclair's famous novel, *The Jungle*, and then briefly reviews union efforts to improve wages and working conditions in the meat and poultry industry. The chapter closes with a glimpse at what it is like to labor in the factories that produce the meat and poultry that grace our tables.

Chapter 7 takes the reader onto the plant floor as it explores labor relations in one of these modern meat factories from the vantage point of Don Stull's 1994 participant observation in a packinghouse we call Running Iron Beef.

In December 1980, what was at the time the world's largest beef processing plant opened a few miles west of Garden City, Kansas. Three years later another beef plant opened on the other side of town. On Christmas night 2000, that packinghouse burned, putting more than 2,000 out of work and ending Garden

City's two decades of population and job growth. The authors began studying Garden City in the mid-1980s, documenting its transformation from a predominantly Anglo American community to the first majority-minority city in the state. Chapter 8 presents the social, economic, and cultural changes that have beset Garden City over the past three decades, along with the community response to those changes.

Chapter 9 discusses the authors' efforts to help communities throughout the United States and Canada plan for and mitigate the negative consequences of meat and poultry processing plants and the lessons we have learned about applying social science knowledge at the local level.

When we began studying the meat and poultry industry in the mid-1980s, few people knew of—or cared about—its environmental consequences. But community opposition to factory farms and meat processing plants has been mounting across North America. Chapter 10 examines the environmental issues surrounding the production and processing of chickens in Kentucky and hogs in Canada.

Industrialized agriculture has changed the face of rural North America forever. The imperative of being the lowest-cost producer means that processors have moved to rural locations and forced farmers to adopt factory techniques. Given the constant search for lower-cost production sites, agribusiness will continue to confront rural communities with the Faustian bargain of economic development at the expense of social and environmental disruption. Most North Americans have blithely signed on to this agreement in exchange for ample and consistent supplies of food at relatively low prices.

Meat and poultry processors offer rural communities a similar bargain: the creation of jobs, not only in their plants, but in related industries and services. Some argue that the jobs and tax revenues these plants bring are essential if rural communities are to survive, but the plants also bring high population turnover, relatively low wages, and working conditions that remain among the most hazardous in manufacturing. In addition, packinghouse towns suffer from elevated rates of crime, shortages of affordable housing, increased enrollment and turnover in schools, and greater demand for health and social services. Companies do little, if anything, to help communities meet the challenges presented by their workforces. Is this how it must be?

In Chapter 11 we consider human consequences associated with agricultural industrialization and various attempts to address the model's deficiencies. We begin by reviewing one of the most infamous outcomes of the drive to increase productivity—"mad cow disease." We explain its origins and outline some of its impacts in Britain and the United States. The bounty produced by agricultural industrialization is at the heart of another societal impact—the rise in obesity in North America. Increasing worker productivity through faster line speeds is associated with the rise in pathogen contamination and meat recalls, while the industry's failure to offer an attractive work environment is central to the packers' knowingly or unknowingly hiring unauthorized or illegal workers. The chapter concludes with a discussion of alternatives to the industrial model and suggests that two food systems might be evolving—one that promotes sustainably produced foodstuffs but is not affordable for all, and the other, an industrial system that produces cheap food and externalizes its production costs upon the environment, growers and workers, and communities.

NOTE

1.   The information presented in the question-and-answer period after the tour is from several sessions over more than a year (Stull fieldnotes June 17, 1988; July 10 and 22, 1988; and May 5, 1989). Although it did not come in a single session, or in such a flowing narrative, most is from the man in the snakeskin boots. Supervisors, line workers, and industry observers at times have disputed some of these facts and the conclusions drawn from them. Wages, number of employees, and other "facts" come from 1988–1989 and have changed since then. We present more recent figures in Chapter 6. "The Tour" is slightly modified from an earlier publication (Stull 1994:44–48).

1

✳

Setting the Table

At the beginning of the twentieth century, land-hungry homesteaders flocked to the Canadian prairies, creating a vibrant rural landscape of farms and ranches, small towns and villages, just as homesteaders had settled the Midwest and the Plains of the United States in the nineteenth century. But even as family farming was blossoming on both sides of the border, it was sowing the seeds of its own demise.

In the early 1900s, farmers began increasing output and income by investing in machinery and fertilizer. These investments, coupled with improvements in seed quality and livestock, raised yields and ultimately lowered commodity prices, forcing farmers either to increase production by purchasing more inputs, such as seeds and fertilizer, or to quit farming. Since the 1930s, millions of families across North America have abandoned farming. In their place today are highly specialized and capitalized farms that produce one or two commodities, often under contract to agribusiness giants such as Tyson, Smithfield, JBS, and Cargill. These transnational corporations, not family farmers, determine how and where most of our food is produced.

This shift in power from producers to processors reflects a change in consumer demand for food, from fresh seasonally based produce at the beginning of the twentieth century to highly processed convenience foods a century later. Innovations in refrigeration, packaging, and transportation made this transition possible by allowing processors to gain year-round access to different sources of produce and enabling them to operate their plants more efficiently. At the same time, societal changes have reduced the time spent in the kitchen.

One hundred years ago, a typical woman in the United States spent an average of 44 hours a week preparing meals and cleaning up after them. By the 1950s, this figure had dropped to fewer than 20 hours (Bowers 2000). And with the rise of two-income families, single-parent households, and increased participation by women in the labor force, Americans devote even less time to food preparation. Early in the twenty-first century, full-time, working women spent on average 38–46 minutes a day preparing food, compared with just over 70 minutes for non-working women. Single working women spent about 15 minutes less per day

Michael Broadway

FIGURE 1.1 Tyson Foods trailers outside a warehouse in Chicago's stockyard district.

preparing food than married or partnered working women (Mancino & Newman 2007). Food companies have responded to these societal changes by further processing agricultural products and supplying consumers with ready-to-eat meals and restaurants with prepared portions. A visit to any supermarket or restaurant kitchen confirms these trends.

MORE INPUTS, FEWER FARMS

Agriculture is presently in the midst of its third revolution (Troughton 1986). The first revolution originated in Southwest Asia about 10,000 years ago and was associated with the development of seed agriculture, the domestication of animals, and the invention of the plow. Agriculture offered a distinct advantage over hunting and gathering because it could support many more people on less land. Agriculture ultimately formed the economic basis for permanent settlements, and complex urban centers emerged in both the Old and New World.

Industrialization emerged in Western Europe in the late eighteenth century, and with it a second agricultural revolution that replaced subsistence agriculture with a system based upon creating surpluses and profit. Fast-growing urban populations created a commercial market for food, and farmers responded by boosting output. They began purchasing fertilizers, improving field drainage, and incorporating new horse-drawn machinery. The feudal system of communal land holdings had already been replaced with individual farms, and Europeans exported this model of small family farms throughout much of the world. This second agricultural revolution cemented agriculture's ties to industry. Farmers purchased machinery and other inputs, and in the process replaced labor, improved productivity, and created surpluses for trading (Bowler 1992).

Agricultural industrialization—the third agricultural revolution—originated in the United States at the beginning of the twentieth century, and is characterized by mechanization, chemical farming, and food manufacturing (Ibid.: 11). It aims to sell crops and livestock at the lowest possible cost by creating economies of scale, purchasing inputs from other segments of the economy, and substituting capital for labor (Symes & Marsden 1985). Mechanization replaces humans and animals with tractors, combines, sprayers, and other machinery. These and other innovations boost productivity and reduce the demand for farm labor, leading to out-migration from rural areas, as fewer farm workers are needed. In 1910, 54 percent of Americans lived in rural areas and 33 percent of workers were employed in agriculture (U.S. Census 1913, 1914). In 2009, only 16 percent lived in rural areas and fewer than 2 percent worked on farms and ranches (USDA ERS n.d.).

Chemical farming relies on inorganic fertilizers, fungicides, and pesticides to increase crop yields. Developed on a large scale in the 1950s, the use of such chemicals, combined with improvements in seed quality, dramatically improved crop yields. In 1950, the average yield for an acre of corn was 38 bushels; in 2009, it was a record 165 bushels (USDA National Agricultural Statistics Service n.d.). The use of biotechnology to develop genetically modified organisms (GMOs), or transgenic plants, such as Monsanto's Roundup Ready™ soybeans, marks the latest phase in this development. Genetically modified soybeans and corn were widely adopted by American farmers in the late 1990s, but foods made from these crops have proved controversial. GM crops are engineered to resist diseases and pests and provide higher yields. They reduce production costs and the need for herbicides and pesticides. There are, however, grave concerns about the risks of genetically modified food and feed grains for human health and the environment. Opposition to GM foods has been especially pronounced in Europe. The rise in the popularity of organic foods, including meat and dairy, is in part a reaction to public concerns about what critics call Frankenfoods.

Food manufacturing is the most recent stage of the third agricultural revolution. It involves adding economic value to agricultural products through processing and packaging and as its importance has risen, farmers have received a dwindling proportion of the final sale price. The share of the food dollar that goes to the farmer decreased from 33 cents in 1960 to just 19 cents in 2006—the remainder is absorbed by processors, wholesalers, distributors, and retailers (Hofstrand 2008). This means that increases in consumer food prices rarely benefit farmers, who are at the beginning of the production process. And because farmers generally have limited options for marketing their crops and livestock, they are often forced to accept lower prices, making it even harder for them to profit from their labor.

The farm is no longer at the center of the production process; instead, it is one component in a complex agribusiness system that consists of five separate but connected sections: agricultural inputs, farm production, processing, distribution, and consumption. Each section is, in turn, affected by the physical environment, government policies, trade agreements, and the availability of credit and finance. In the beef industry, for example, cattle feeding is just one part of a food network in which agribusiness supplies producers with seeds, fertilizers, and pesticides to grow feed grains, as well as antibiotics and hormones to keep animals healthy and accelerate maturation, while specialized facilities, often owned by these same companies, slaughter and process the animals. The more a company can dominate this network, the greater its ability to control costs and increase profits. This strategy, known as vertical integration, is most evident in the poultry industry, where companies like Tyson control each step of the production process, from when the egg is hatched to when it appears as a boneless chicken breast in a restaurant kitchen or supermarket.

EAT IN OR EAT OUT?

Processing and adding value to raw commodities is, in part, a response to changes in the demand for food. Women have traditionally been responsible for meal preparation, and as more women have entered the labor force they have less time to cook. Increases in divorce and children born out of wedlock have produced a surge in single-parent households, while persons living alone now account for more than one in four households. As a result, Americans eat fewer meals at home and spend less time preparing them. Found in over 90 percent of American homes, the microwave oven has provided a technological "fix" for those without the time—or inclination—to cook (Bowers 2000). Meanwhile, supermarkets offer an array of processed foods, such as Jimmy Dean's Scrambled Eggs with Bacon and Cheese, Diced Apples & Seasoned Hash Browns: "From the freezer to table in just 3 minutes, this protein packed entrée is a delicious way to jump start your day" (Sara Lee Corp. n.d.). ConAgra's Healthy Choice® brand offers more than 50 different ready-to-eat convenience meals, including Fresh Mixers™ where "everything's in one compact container: sauce, pasta or rice, and strainer. So you can make it fresh from your desk, with no refrigeration or freezing necessary" (Healthy Choice n.d.).

Supermarkets have adapted to these changes. Late-afternoon shoppers at Wegmans' in suburban Rochester, New York, cruise the aisles amid aromas of freshly prepared meals ready to take home to the oven, microwave, or dinner plate. As demand for easy-to-prepare meals has risen, so, too, has the proportion of the food dollar spent eating out—from 26 percent in 1960 to 49 percent in 2009 (USDA ERS 2010). This trend translates into demand for more processed and prepared meals in restaurants. McDonald's relies on Tyson to supply it with prepared portions of Chicken McNuggets and on ConAgra, through its Lamb Weston subsidiary, to supply it with French fries. Nearly a third of Tyson's $27 billion in 2009 sales went to the food service industry in the form of prepared food items such as battered and breaded chicken and fully cooked dinner meats (Tyson Foods 2009).

AGRICULTURAL INDUSTRIALIZATION

Bowler (1985) identifies three structural forces behind agricultural industrialization: intensification, concentration, and specialization. *Intensification* occurs when farmers increase their purchases of nonfarm inputs (fertilizers, machinery, agrichemicals) to improve yields. For livestock producers, advances in selective breeding have reduced the time it takes an animal to reach its slaughter weight, which, in turn, allows farmers to increase their output. One of the unintended consequences of intensification, however, is that production costs increase faster than the prices farmers receive for animals and crops. This situation is exacerbated by relative declines in commodity prices, which put pressure on farmers to increase output levels even more, and the cycle repeats itself.

Critics charge that one factor promoting intensification is government price support programs that guarantee commodity prices. The 2002 Farm Security and Rural Investment Act, commonly called the Farm Bill, provided farmers with $73 billion in price supports over six years; most major commodities such as corn, rice, cotton, and sugar are part of this program (Chite 2008). In signing the 2002 bill, President George W. Bush noted, "Americans cannot eat all that America's farmers and ranchers produce. And therefore it makes sense to sell more food abroad."

But guaranteeing commodity prices and selling subsidized surpluses abroad leads to similar demands from farmers in other countries and the production of more food, which eventually depresses prices. Soon after President Bush signed the 2002 Farm Bill, Canadian farmers demanded that their government provide them with $1.3 billion (Canadian) a year to deal with the impact of the new legislation (Edmonds 2002). Subsidies also disrupt agriculture in the developing world, since poor countries often import subsidized commodities and in the process, put their own farmers out of business.

Concentration means fewer but larger units use economies of scale to produce a greater share of the output of a particular product or commodity. Producing calves on a ranch with 500 cows costs nearly 50 percent less per cow than on a ranch with fewer than 50 cows (Lamb & Beshear 1998). Similarly, production costs on farms with more than 3,000 hogs are estimated to be nearly a third less per hog than on farms with fewer than 500 hogs (Drabenstott 1998). These economies of scale have led to the loss of hundreds of thousands of cow-calf and hog operators (Figure 1.2), leaving the largest producers in control of most production. For example, 99 percent of the 10 million hogs grown in North Carolina in 2007 came from farms with 1,000 or more hogs, and 44 percent of the state's hog production came from just two counties (USDA NASS 2009).

Processing firms increasingly contract with producers to provide them with livestock. In the early 1980s, less than 5 percent of U.S. hogs went to market under some type of contract; in 2008, more than 88 percent were committed to packers through direct ownership or contract arrangements (Lawrence, Grimes, & Hayenga 1998; USDA GIPSA 2010). Large producers want the certainty that comes from a guaranteed market, while processors want the certainty of a guaranteed supply to run their operations efficiently. This system favors large

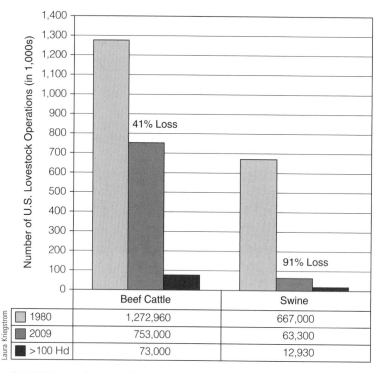

FIGURE 1.2 Loss of U.S. beef and swine operations, 1980–2009.
SOURCE: USDA-NASS; R-CALF USA.

producers, sometimes referred to as "factory farmers," since processors do not want the added costs of dealing with many small suppliers.

Some family farmers have tried to survive by banding together in cooperative arrangements (Grey 2000). Many others have sold out. Fewer farms mean fewer links to the local economy, since large factory farms tend to purchase inputs from outside the local area, which fuels further loss of capital from rural areas (Ikerd 1998). When farm families fail, grain elevators, local businesses, and schools soon follow.

Specialization is the natural outgrowth of intensification and concentration, as farmers focus their expertise, land, and labor on a narrow range of commodities (Bowler 1992). This means growing fewer farm products on each farm and in each region. U.S. cattle feeding operations have gravitated to the High Plains of Texas, Kansas, and Nebraska. The abundance of feed grains in these states helped increase their share of U.S.-fed cattle production from 40 percent in 1980 to 55 percent in 2010 (USDA NASS n.d.). A ready supply of corn, the primary feed for hogs, shifted the center of pork production from western Ohio to eastern Nebraska by the mid-1980s. Iowa is still first in hog production, but changes in how hogs are raised and resulting environmental concerns have driven industry expansion to North Carolina, Oklahoma, and Utah. U.S. poultry production more than doubled between 1980 and 2009, with most of the growth occurring in an arc from East Texas to North Carolina. The region's mild climate provides year-round growing conditions and low heating and cooling costs for the chicken houses. A preponderance of small marginal farms is key in attracting the poultry industry into this region (Broadway 1995).

The structural forces of agricultural industrialization are also at work in Canada. Cattle feeding expanded in Alberta because of the availability of surplus feed grains. The province increased its share of Canadian-fed cattle from 47 percent in 1984 to 68 percent in 2010 (Canfax 2001, 2010). Quebec and Ontario have historically been at the focal point of Canada's hog production. But in the mid-1990s, the province of Manitoba emulated North Carolina by allowing pork processors to contract for supplies with individual producers. As a result, Manitoba's share of Canadian pork production rose from 17 percent in 1996 to 29 percent in 2009 (Canadian Pork Council n.d.). A system of supply management restricts imports and establishes provincial production quotas and prices in Canada's poultry industry. This system ensures industry stability by linking the distribution of poultry production to population. In 2009, Ontario and Quebec accounted for 59 percent of Canada's population and 59 percent of its poultry output (Statistics Canada n.d.a).

CONSEQUENCES OF AGRICULTURAL INDUSTRIALIZATION FOR THE MEAT AND POULTRY INDUSTRY

All three components of agricultural industrialization are manifest in the North American meat and poultry industry. *Growers,* now the preferred name for farmers, specialize in a single species, using custom-built cattle feedlots, hog barns, or chicken houses, and incorporating off-farm inputs. Each specialized facility confines animals to restrict their movements and maximize weight gain. They add hormones and antibiotics to the animals' feed to promote growth and prevent disease. In the poultry and pork industries, large processors, called *integrators,* own the animals and contract with growers to raise them until they reach their slaughter weight. Then, the company transports them to its processing plants. This system has serious consequences for farmers, rural communities, the environment, and consumers.

Contracting versus Farming

The U.S. poultry industry pioneered vertical integration in agribusiness, and its "success" has become a model for the pork and beef industries. Tyson Foods, the largest poultry company in the United States, contracts with about 6,000 "family farms" to grow its chickens (Tyson Foods 2009). Growers receive compensation primarily based on "feed-conversion ratio," and their goal is to grow birds to slaughter weight as quickly and with as little feed as possible. If Tyson is not satisfied, it may cancel its contracts with growers, leaving them with no way to pay off their loans on chicken houses and equipment. Smithfield, the largest U.S. pork processor, is also the nation's biggest producer of hogs. It owns more than 1.1 million sows in 12 states, which gave birth to nearly 20 million pigs in 2009 (Smithfield n.d.).

Four companies—Tyson, JBS, Cargill, and National—controlled more than 76 percent of U.S. beef slaughter in 2007 (USDA GIPSA 2010). And the beef companies are poised to follow in the footsteps of poultry and pork by owning their own cattle and contracting with feeders to raise them. Critics argue that cattle secured with forward contracts and those already owned by the packers, called captive supply, allow them to drive down prices for independent producers who are dependent on markets controlled by a only few buyers (Domina & Taylor 2010). Efforts to prevent such practices have consistently failed in the U.S. Congress, despite the overwhelming support of producer groups such as the National Farmers Union, R–CALF USA, the Organization for Competitive Markets, and the National Coalition for Sustainable Agriculture. The National Cattlemen's Beef Association and the American Meat Institute, the principal lobbying organizations for the meatpackers, oppose the ban. They argue that the contract system benefits producers, processors, and consumers, since it provides Americans the "most abundant and most affordable meat supply in the world" (American Meat Institute n.d.).

Contracting has put many small, independent livestock producers out of business and has led to calls for a system of sustainable agriculture that considers the ecological and social impacts of production. Such a system would rely "more on people, including the quality and quantity of labor and management, and less on land and capital" (Ikerd 1998:158).

F I G U R E 1.3 The Kansas City Stockyards stand empty the day after they closed in 1991. These stockyards have since been razed.

Packers Say Good-bye to the City

Processing companies that now dominate the beef and pork industries have closed older packinghouses in urban centers and constructed large slaughter and processing plants close to livestock supplies in rural areas. IBP, Inc., now owned by Tyson Foods, began this process in 1960, when it opened a plant about 80 miles northwest of Des Moines in the small town of Denison, Iowa. At the time, most hogs and cattle were shipped to stockyards in large cities, such as Chicago, Kansas City, and Toronto, and then slaughtered in adjacent multispecies plants. Locating packing plants near supplies of fed cattle lowered procurement and transportation costs. Worker productivity rose with the construction of single-species slaughter facilities and a disassembly line that made each worker responsible for a single task.

IBP introduced boxed beef at its new Dakota City, Nebraska, plant in 1967. Instead of shipping sides of beef, the carcass is "fabricated" into smaller cuts, vacuum packed, and shipped out in boxes. Demand for this boxed beef was strong, and the company built new plants in small towns on the High Plains. Old-line urban plants had difficulty competing with this lower-cost competitor and their owners declared bankruptcy or sold out. ConAgra bought Armour, and Cargill purchased Missouri Beef Packers Excel Corporation and renamed it Excel. These new companies followed IBP's example by cutting wages and building plants in small towns near their cattle supplies.

Since the communities that hosted the new plants lacked workers to run them, companies recruited new immigrants and refugees in large numbers. As a result, packinghouse towns have been subject to rapid growth as well as ethnic, cultural, and linguistic transformation.

Michael Broadway

F I G U R E 1.4 The Africa Super Market sells halal meats and other goods to Brooks, Alberta's growing Muslim population, many of whom work at the local beef plant.

Hog processing was concentrated in the Midwest until the 1980s, when the industry moved into North Carolina and then, into Oklahoma. The major processors at the time—IBP, ConAgra, Cargill, and Smithfield—adopted beefpacking's rural industrialization strategy, with similar consequences for host communities (Grey 1995).

Poultry plants share many characteristics with their counterparts in the red meat industry: they are located in small towns, the work is tedious and dangerous, and the pay is low. African American women provided most of the labor in these plants until recent years, when companies started recruiting Latino immigrants and refugees to replace them, and in the process transformed many small southern towns (see Fink 2003).

Competitive pressures also forced the restructuring of Canada's red meat industry (MacLachlan 2001). During the 1970s and 1980s, old urban plants closed from Vancouver in the West to Charlottetown in the East, and a new generation of single-species plants with large slaughter capacities sprang up in small towns on the Canadian prairies. Cargill opened a beef plant in High River, Alberta, in 1988. Six years later, IBP bought Lakeside Packers of Brooks, Alberta, doubled its slaughter capacity, and added a boxed-beef plant. At the close of the 1990s, Maple Leaf Foods opened a large pork plant in Brandon, Manitoba.

What's that Smell?

Nitrogen and phosphorous are the principal components of manure, and they cause problems when they enter water systems in large quantities. When they

FIGURE 1.5 Canada Packers Meatpacking Plant, St.-Boniface, Manitoba, Canada, closed in 1987 and has since been demolished.

Michael Broadway

F I G U R E 1.6 In 1999, Maple Leaf Foods opened a plant in Brandon, Manitoba, that has the capacity to slaughter 108,000 hogs per 6-day week.

hold large numbers of animals, feedlots, hog barns, and chicken houses produce massive amounts of manure, which can pose a threat to the environment.

Classified according to the minimum number of animals a facility has on site—700 dairy cows, 1,000 beef cows, 30,000 broilers, 2,500 hogs—concentrated animal feeding operations, commonly known by their acronym as CAFOs, have become the norm for producing livestock (Gurian-Sherman 2008). For example, hog operations with 5,000 or more animals accounted for 62 percent of U.S. production in 2009, up from just 18 percent in 1993 (USDA NASS n.d.). Problems arise from the excessive size and density of operations. In Arkansas, 20 percent of the 1.2 billion broilers produced in 2007 came from just two counties, Benton and Washington, in the northwest corner of the state. The biggest problem created by CAFOs is manure disposal. Typically, farmers apply manure to fields before planting, but if applied at levels above the nutrient absorption rates of soil and crops, the potential for runoff and subsequent ground and surface water pollution increases. According to the EPA, there are approximately 15,500 confined animal feeding operations in the United States.

Feed People, not Cows!

The export of the North American model of meat production to the developing world has been widely criticized. Advocates for the world's poor argue that feeding grain to animals instead of humans makes little sense (Lappé, Collins, &

Rosset 1998). But as developing countries become richer, their citizens eat more animal protein, and local farmers are changing from food production to feed production. The poor and small landowners feel the consequences of the reduction of food crops most severely.

Amazonian rainforests are being cleared at an alarming rate to provide cattle pasture and to grow feed grain (Pearce 2004). In Brazil, the cost of black beans, a staple of the poor, rose sharply when farmers started growing soybeans for domestic and European cattle feeders. These large farms displaced thousands of small farmers, many of whom migrated to the Amazonian states of Acre and Rondonia, where they cut down the rainforest, planted crops, then moved on after the soil was exhausted (Lappe, Collins, & Rosset 1998). During the past two decades, Brazil's beef cattle herd increased by nearly 150 million head—80 percent of this growth occurred in Amazonia (Friends of the Earth 2010). Cattle have become the most appealing and profitable way to earn a living for large ranchers and small farmers alike. Owning cattle brings prestige, and *cauboi* (cowboy) culture, *contri* (country) music, and rodeos are now part of Brazilian popular culture (Hoelle 2011:38).

Deforestation has also made Brazil the world's largest beef exporter. Between 1988 and 2008, the value of the country's beef exports increased sixfold to exceed $4 billion (FAOSTAT n.d.). Using data from a 2006 agricultural census, researchers at the Swedish Institute of Food and Biotechnology found that beef ranches are responsible for 70 percent of forest cleared in the Brazilian Amazon. While such ranches produce only 6 percent of Brazilian beef, that 6 percent accounts for 60 percent of Brazilian beef's carbon footprint, which is double the world average (Friedland 2011). The European Union is the biggest recipient of Brazilian beef exports, and environmental groups have demanded restriction of Brazilian meat imports to conserve the rainforest (Friends of the Earth 2010). Soon after the 2009 release of the Greenpeace publication, *Slaughtering the Amazon*, JBS S.A. announced it would no longer purchase cattle from newly deforested areas of the Brazilian Amazon, a policy that was also adopted by Walmart. Despite its pledge, in 2011 Brazilian authorities announced they were seeking $1.2 billion in fines against JBS and other companies for buying beef grown in illegally deforested areas or using slave labor (Channelnewsasia 2011).

The livestock industry has come under attack for its contribution to climate change. In 2006, the UN's Food and Agricultural Organization (FAO) published *Livestock's Long Shadow: Environmental Issues and Options*, which blamed the industry for 18 percent of greenhouse gas emissions. This finding was challenged by the U.S. beef industry, which cited EPA data indicating that the entire U.S. agricultural sector accounted for just 6 percent of the country's greenhouse gas emissions (National Cattlemen's Beef Board 2009).

What's for Dinner?

Rising affluence during the twentieth century increased North Americans' meat consumption, even as meat preferences were also changing. Per capita

TABLE 1.1   U.S. Per Capita Consumption of Meat, 1910–2008 (selected years)*

Year	Beef	Pork	Chicken	Other[†]	Total
1910	51.1	41.2	10.4	21.2	123.9
1930	33.7	41.1	11.1	20.2	106.1
1950	44.6	43.0	14.3	23.4	125.3
1970	79.6	48.1	27.4	22.3	177.4
1990	63.9	46.4	42.4	30.7	183.4
2008	61.2	46.0	58.8	30.9	196.9

*Pounds per capita, boneless trimmed equivalent.
[†]Veal, lamb, turkey, fish, and shellfish.
SOURCE: USDA Economic Research Service, Food Availability Spreadsheets.

consumption of beef peaked in the United States at just under 89 pounds in 1976 and has been trending downward ever since (see Table 1.1).[1] The same trend occurred in Canada (MacLachlan 2001). These reductions in beef consumption are due, in part, to medical reports that a diet rich in animal fat and cholesterol increases risk of heart disease and stroke, government recommendations that consumers choose a diet low in saturated fats, and popular diatribes against the beef industry, such as Jeremy Rifkin's (1992) *Beyond Beef* and Howard Lyman's (1998) *Mad Cowboy*. Interestingly, pork has not been subjected to the same medical and public scrutiny as beef, and consumption has remained largely unchanged during the past century (see Table 1.1). Americans' taste for veal and lamb has dramatically declined over the past century, but their taste for turkey, fish, and shellfish has grown. The biggest change in U.S. meat-eating habits has been the explosive growth in consumption of chicken. These trends have been duplicated in Canada (MacLachlan 2001).

Meeting changes in demand has meant expanding and quickening the pace of meat production and processing. Critics charge that faster production line speeds translate into a greater likelihood that meat will be contaminated by manure and by the contents of animals' stomachs. According to the U.S. Centers for Disease Control, one in six Americans—48 million people—contract a foodborne illness each year. Of these, 180,000 are hospitalized and 3,000 die (Associated Press 2011). The most common meat-borne pathogens are *Campylobacter*, *Salmonella*, and *Escherichia coli* O157:H7. *Campylobacter* is a bacterium found in the intestines of healthy birds, and it is present in most raw poultry. The intestines of most animals contain *Salmonella* bacterium, while *E. coli* O157:H7 is a bacterial pathogen found in cattle. Public awareness of *E. coli* O157:H7 stems from an incident in 1993, when four children died and 700 people were hospitalized after eating contaminated Jack-in-the-Box hamburgers (Schlosser 2001). Since then a number of highly publicized meat recalls in the United States and Canada have led government regulators to require that safe cooking and handling instructions accompany the purchase of fresh meat. On January 4, 2011,

President Barack Obama signed the Food Safety Modernization Act. Under this law, the Food and Drug Administration must increase inspections of U.S. and foreign food facilities and will, for the first time, be able to order recalls of tainted foods. Unfortunately, the new law exempts meat, poultry, and processed eggs, which are regulated by the U.S. Department of Agriculture (Associated Press 2011).

Antimicrobials and antibiotics[2] promote growth and prevent disease in livestock. The European Union prohibits nontherapeutic agricultural use of antimicrobials, such as tetracycline, penicillin, and streptogramin, which are used to treat human illnesses. The World Health Organization (WHO) and the U.S. Centers for Disease Control (CDC) agree that the use of antimicrobials for livestock is an important cause of antibiotic resistance in food-borne illness and a substantial contributor to the emergence of antibiotic-resistant diseases in humans. Antibiotics and antimicrobials are used extensively in U.S. agriculture. The Union for Concerned Scientists estimates that 24.6 million pounds of antimicrobials are given to poultry, hogs, and cattle for nontherapuetic purposes every year in the United States. The Animal Health Institute, which represents companies that make animal medicines, argues that the figure is much lower—17.8 million pounds for both therapeutic and nontherapeutic uses in all animals. Whichever figure is closer to the truth, agricultural use of antimicrobials dwarfs the 3 million pounds used each year in human medicine (Mellon, Benbrook, & Benbrook 2001:xii–xiii).

No one opposes the use of antimicrobials to treat sick animals, but groups such as the Union for Concerned Scientists and the Pew Campaign on Human Health and Industrial Farming say they should not be "given to healthy food animals on industrial farms ... to promote growth and to compensate for the effects of overcrowding and unsanitary conditions" (Schoenborn 2010). But efforts to restrict antimicrobial use in animal agriculture have thus far failed. Producers, industry groups, and the American Veterinary Medical Association have opposed federal restrictions, arguing that "broad bans are not based on science" and they would have far-reaching consequences for human as well as animal health (Fyksen 2010).

Responding to public concerns, in 2007 Tyson Foods began advertising that its chickens are "raised without antibiotics." But it soon came to light that it was injecting eggs with antibiotics, including one used to treat humans for urinary tract and blood infections, and the USDA forced the company to stop labeling its chickens as antibiotic-free. Several of Tyson's competitors, including Perdue and Sanderson Farms, filed a class-action suit based on this violation, which Tyson settled for $5 million in early 2010 (Gutierrez 2008; Animal Welfare Approved 2010).

CONCLUSIONS

Industrialization has transformed agriculture. Its goal has become the production of large quantities of uniform products at the cheapest possible price. Under this regime, producers purchase more inputs to increase output, which ultimately lowers commodity prices and forces "inefficient" producers out of business. Under this "survival of the fittest" model, the spoils have gone to the biggest producers. By 2007, just 57,000 farms out of 2.2 million (or less than 3 percent) accounted for 60 percent of agricultural sales, and the only kind of farms recently gaining in numbers have been those with sales of more than $500,000 (USDA NASS 2009). Small independent producers are an endangered species.

Large transnational corporations determine methods and places of production for cattle, hogs, and poultry by owning the animals themselves, contracting with large producers, slaughtering and processing the animals, and branding their products for retail sale. This system has proved highly profitable for processing companies. Smithfield Foods (n.d.) has seen its pork sales soar from $4.5 billion in 2000 to more than $12 billion in 2009; during the same period it recorded a net profit of over $1 billion. It achieved these successes while the number of independent hog producers plummeted. Tyson (2009) saw its sales increase from $4 billion in 1991 to more than $27 billion in 2009. And like Smithfield, Tyson has increased its share of the meat and poultry market by buying out competitors. In 2001, it purchased IBP, the world's largest red meat processor, to enhance its "value-added protein portfolio" and become the world's largest meat and poultry producing company.

Most dramatic has been the meteoric rise of JBS-Friboi. Founded in 1953, it was a family-owned company little known outside of Brazil a decade ago. But in the first decade of the twenty-first century, it went on a buying spree. It grew from a private company worth $1 billion to a publically traded company worth $40 billion by aggressively acquiring feedyards, packing plants, and chicken processors in Italy, Argentina, and Australia. Among its acquisitions were Swift and Pilgrim's Pride in the United States. Now the world's largest supplier of beef: it slaughters 90,000 cattle a day, employs 125,000 workers, of whom 75,000 are in the United States, and exports to 150 countries (Forero 2011).

The next three chapters of this book provide historical analysis of the evolution of the beef, pork, and poultry production systems in North America and how Smithfield, Tyson, and other companies have attained their dominant position in the industry. The remaining chapters consider the consequences of this production system for producers, processing workers, animals, communities, and consumers.

NOTES

1. Data on meat consumption can be misleading, depending on how it is measured. For example, according to the 2010 Statistical Abstract of the United States (U.S. Census Bureau 2009), beef consumption in 2007 amounted to 62 pounds per capita (boneless trimmed weight), and the equivalent figure for chicken was 60. By contrast, the 2009 Agricultural Statistics (U.S. Department of Agriculture) lists beef consumption at 93 pounds per capita (carcass weight equivalent or dressed weight), and chicken is listed at 101 pounds per capita (ready-to-cook basis) for 2007. We use boneless trimmed equivalent, which we believe is the most accurate measure of actual consumption. Regardless of the measure, trends are clear. Overall meat

consumption continues to rise in the United States, fueled by increased chicken consumption.

2. "Antibiotic growth promoters stimulate an animal's growth by improving weight gain and feed conversion efficiency as a result of their effect on the microflora of the gut. Antimicrobials kill or inhibit the growth of micro-organisms (bacteria, fungi, protozoa, and viruses). They include antibiotics, disinfectants, preservatives, and other substances such as zinc and copper" (Report of the Policy Commission on the Future of Farming and Food 2002:102).

2

✳

From Roundups to Restructuring: The Beef Industry

A BRANDING ON THE FLYING V

I arose at 5:00 A.M., well before sunup. Chet had already rounded up the horses, and, with his wife Kris, was putting homemade cinnamon rolls in the oven. It was Kris's first branding, and she was nervous about whether she had made enough food and whether it would be the right kind—not a repeat of what had been served earlier that week at a neighbor's place. Reed, Chet's 15-year-old son, and the hired man came in from the bunkhouse, and we ate rolls and drank coffee while the hired man talked of earlier brandings when the fog was so thick riders passed each other—and the cattle—unseen. It was only the first of many stories of brandings, ranch work and life, local characters, and hilarious antics that would be told and retold throughout the day.

Neighbors began arriving shortly after 6:00, their pickups hauling horse trailers with mounts already saddled. As the men got out of their trucks, often with sleepy-eyed but eager children in tow, they checked with Chet to see what they would be doing and what equipment was needed. Some looked the part in well-worn black Stetsons; pearl-buttoned western shirts; faded Wranglers held up by trophy buckles and tucked into underslung, high-heeled boots; chaps and spurs, often decorated with their brands or initials. Others wore "gimme" caps, Lees, buttoned-down sport shirts, and ropers—"cowboy tennis shoes." Several had yellow slickers tied behind the cantles of their saddles in case of rain. All wore jackets against the early morning chill. In all, about 20 men showed up—the women would come later to help Kris get dinner ready for the men when branding was done.

When everyone was there—horses unloaded, saddles adjusted, instructions given—15 riders, including two preteen girls complete with braces, loped off into the early morning light, up a draw and over a sandhill. Five men and two old cow dogs followed in two pickups. In the lead was Chet: "It isn't couth to rope at your own branding." He would stay afoot, manage things, and do some of

27

the dirtier work. In the cab with him was Pat—tall, thin, young, his dusty black hat settled down on his ears. They carried branding irons and other necessaries. In the second pickup came Chet's uncle Norm, another elderly gentleman, and me.

The Flying V is a cow-calf operation, located in the breathtaking, treeless expanse of the Sandhills of western Nebraska. The ranch covers 52 or 53 sections, Norm wasn't sure exactly. (A section is one square mile, 640 acres.) It is owned by a family that lives in town, about an hour south of the ranch, but Norm's family has managed it since his father's time. The ranch is divided into two operations—Chet manages one, encompassing about 16,000 acres, his brother manages the other. Half the cattle—about 900 head—belong to the ranch owners; the other half to Norm and his sons. Chet's hired hand runs a few head. Most are Black Angus, with a few Black Baldies (Angus-Hereford cross), or Black Whiteface, as they are called up here.

After 15 minutes, we drove down into a pasture surrounded by low rising hills, where a portable corral had been set up the afternoon before. While we waited for the riders to drive the "mama cows" and their calves into the corral, Chet opened up bags of yellow ear tags, black plastic ear hormone implants that get put on with the ear tags, and loads for the vaccine guns. Before long the first riders appeared, stretched in a straight line behind the herd. Occasionally, a stray would break loose and a rider would chase it back in the bunch. When all the calves were in the pen, and the gates closed, the men dismounted and stood in a line in front of the herd, which had begun mooing and bawling in a strangely melodic cacophony. This sound continued until each bunch was completely branded and let loose, mamas and their calves free to graze together once again.

F I G U R E   2.1 Driving cattle into branding pens on the Flying V, May 1992.

Chet and Pat drove a few mama cows out of the corral with buggy whips, while the truck bearing the branding irons and the stove to heat them backed into the corral. The men unloaded and heated up a butane tank and stove. More pickups arrived, bringing kids and adults. Everyone pitched in—the only people who did not do anything to speak of were me, a 3-year-old who stood in the truck bed beside me, a man in a weathered cowboy hat, boots, and overalls, and his granddaughter. (I volunteered to help, but they must have figured I would be more trouble than I was worth.)

For the young ones, it was a time to learn, and to show what they were made of. During the branding and at dinner afterward, men talked about how "stout" certain youngsters were and how well they "rastled" the calves. Norm's son Todd, in his late thirties and wearing a beat-up straw hat, good-naturedly made sure the kids stuck to the rastling. They got right into it, and the consensus was that they did a "right good job" of it. Pride goes with getting in there and getting dirty, and at one point an old-timer turned approvingly to a 12- or 13-year-old girl and said, "You know, you've gotta have shit on you to get any dinner." She had nothing to worry about, and she proudly threw dirt on her jeans to "wash" off the dung.

This branding was little different from those of a century earlier (cf. Ward 1989:59–62), except for basic changes in technology—a butane-fueled fire, rather than one of wood; plastic ear tags instead of markings made with a knife; and hormone implants. Some outfits try to recreate the old days, and one farther north takes out a chuckwagon for two or three days, brings in cowboy poets (and cowboy wannabes), and uses a wood fire to heat branding irons.

Don Stull

FIGURE 2.2 Paul Kondy heeling a calf at the Flying V branding.

Four teams worked systematically and efficiently. Riders rode into the herd, picked a calf, and let their catchrope sail. Calves were usually "heeled"—roped around their hind feet and dragged out to two rastlers, who worked in tandem—it might take three to immobilize the calf if kids helped with the rastling. Then, they branded, tagged, vaccinated, and, if it was a male, castrated the calf.

The butane stove was set up behind the pickup in the middle of the corral: Pat worked one side; Norm worked the other. A half-dozen branding irons, each about four feet long and bearing the "flying V" ($\tilde{V}$), were lined up on the stove's grate. When the irons were hot, the branding began. It takes an experienced hand to put a brand on right, and Norm and Pat were very careful. The calves were always branded in the middle of the ribs, for both the brand and its placement are necessary to establish ownership. As they applied the iron to the calf, white smoke rose from its side, occasionally erupting into a bright red flame. The smell of burning hair floated on the still morning air.

Neither the iron men nor the rastlers were in any way cruel, and they always tried to be gentle and soothing to the calf. Never did I hear anyone curse in anger. Yes, the calves experienced pain, but only minimally and briefly. The calves were likely more frightened by all the strange activity and because they were separated from their mothers. After their release, they ran out of the corral gate to rejoin their mothers, soon to recover.

Chet and Red castrated the bull calves, one on each side of the truck. Scott applied yellow ear tags to each animal, while other men stood on each side of the truck vaccinating them—giving one shot in the hind leg, another in the neck, and forcing two pills down the throats of some animals with a long plastic applicator. Virgil, a freckled old hand in his sixties, and Becky, a pretty short-haired woman in her thirties, sat on folding chairs in front of me cleaning calf testicles and putting them in a bucket of water. Though slightly bloody, this is a coveted job, since it is done sitting down. Becky was clearly enjoying herself and joked easily with the men about her job.

Chet and Red did all the castrating, but generally others traded off—rastling sometimes, roping sometimes. Done from atop a horse, roping is the most prestigious job at a branding, less strenuous than rastling and much more romantic.

By 9:00 A.M., they had branded the first bunch, and pairs of riders loped over the surrounding hills and through draws to gather the next bunch of cattle to be branded. It was up to those of us in the trucks to load up the corral panels and haul them to the next site, set up the corral, and wait for the riders to bring in the cattle. I finally got to earn my keep, helping dismantle, load, unload, and reassemble the metal panels of the corral. This job is not popular, and the riders headed out soon after branding the last calf, leaving those behind to joke about their hasty departure.

We branded two more bunches that morning—about 600 calves in all. As Chet said afterward, "It doesn't seem to matter how many head you do, we always seem to finish up around noon." This has something to do, I'm sure, with the fact that a big dinner, and the women, are waiting back at the house. Anyway, they had run out of ear tags and drinking water. By now it was probably 80 degrees, and everyone was down to shirtsleeves and some to T-shirts.

Don Stull

FIGURE 2.3 Branding a calf on the Flying V.

With all the dust swirling, it had been thirsty work, and most of the men were parched. The riders loped off, and the rest of us rode back in the trucks. Chet wasn't going to bother loading up the corral panels—they would do that tomorrow. Right now a cold beer and dinner were on their minds.

Cars were lined up in front of the house by the time we got there, and it was filled with wives and mothers and daughters—from Norm's 94-year-old mother on down—who had come to help prepare and share in the meal. Card tables were set up in the living room and food filled every available surface in the kitchen. Most of the men were nowhere in sight. Paul, who had invited me to the branding, and Kim—a tall, bearded, quiet man in a beat-up black hat and a T-shirt extolling Angus cattle—and I were the first through the line. We loaded our plates with green salad, pot roast, baked ham, lasagna, and dinner rolls, leaving the chicken and dumplings and several other dishes to others. I followed them out to a large prefab metal building, where most of the men were congregated on metal folding chairs at several long tables borrowed from the Baptist church. Entering the side door, we passed large pots of coffee and iced tea and three coolers—one filled with beer, one with soft drinks, and one with ice.

At the first table sat Chet, his brother Scott, Pat, and one or two others. A frosty, half-empty quart bottle of Old Grandad sat in front of Scott, and men occasionally came over to take swigs. They clustered in groups of three or four, drinking beers, talking over the morning's work, telling stories of past brandings.

By ones and twos the men went into the house and returned with heaping plates of food. Dinner stretched on into the afternoon—the men talking a little, drinking a little, eating a little, going back for seconds and dessert. Talk was leisurely and comfortable, revolving around a shared past—a men's group trip to Mexico to repair a church; gathering cattle in blinding snow with a wind chill of 70 degrees below zero. They laughed at retellings of a local legend already in the making—a branding a few days ago got rowdy and one prankster pulled out electric shears and cut off another man's hair. Before long, every man there looked like a skinhead. Then, they drove into town and went through the pool hall, shearing everyone in sight till somebody finally cut the electrical cord. Pat's ill-fitting hat attested to his involvement.

Gradually, the men took their leave; Virgil had a yard to mow; others had chores too. Besides, there was a branding at a neighbor's place tomorrow, and more to follow in the days ahead. The cycle of early days and big noon dinners with too many leftovers was beginning to take its toll.

After everyone but Scott left, we cleaned up the tables and folded the chairs, to be returned to the church the next day. Scott, Paul, and I lingered, swapping tales in the shade of the barn. Chet fed the chickens, and Reed and the hired man drove off in a pickup, while Kris napped. Chet joined us about 4:30 in the afternoon and we talked on until 6:00. They tried to talk Paul into going to the branding tomorrow, but his aching muscles said "no." Chet invited me to stay on—and I would have loved to—but I didn't want to wear out my welcome. They should have saddled me up a horse, they reckoned, but just didn't think of it. I guess they had decided I wasn't a total rube after all.

A little after 6:00 P.M., Scott said he had better get on home, and I followed him in my car back out to the highway. As I started the long drive back to Kansas, I remembered Becky's comment as she sat in the corral, her long fingernails bloody from cutting calf testicles, soon to become prairie oysters, out of their sacks: "This is really a social event." It is, in fact, a ritual of both renewal and passage, one that brings neighbors together each spring, after a long winter of cold and isolation. They come together to help one another; to share tools and labor; to visit and retell tales over good food and drink; to demonstrate their common bond and community—and thereby reaffirm a living heritage.

As the Busch beer commercial said, "It doesn't get any better than this," and for them it probably doesn't. They remain practitioners of the most romantic and most American of all occupations—it is not a job, but a way of life. Much is drudgery, hard and dangerous, but at this time at least, it is a joyous celebration of a treasured way of life. And I felt incredibly lucky to have taken part in it (Stull fieldnotes, May 13–14, 1992).[1]

THE CATTLE KINGDOM

Today's beef cattle industry got its start in South Texas. After the War Between the States ended in 1865, what Walter Prescott Webb (1981) calls the "cattle kingdom" spread rapidly out of the brush country, or *brasada*, of South Texas onto the Great Plains. From 1866 to 1880, more than 4 million head of Longhorn cattle were driven along the Chisholm and Western Trails to Kansas towns such as Abilene, Ellsworth, Hays, and Dodge City, and then shipped by rail to be slaughtered in Chicago and cities farther east. Others were driven to the emerging cattle ranges of New Mexico, Colorado, Oregon, and the Northern Plains of the United States and Canada along the Western and the Goodnight-Loving Trails (see Figure 2.4).

The spread of beef cattle throughout the Great Plains and intermountain West is one of the great stories in American history. In little more than a decade, men, horses, and cattle became the undisputed masters of what had once been called the Great American Desert. In reality, it was a vast empire of grass (Dale 1965).

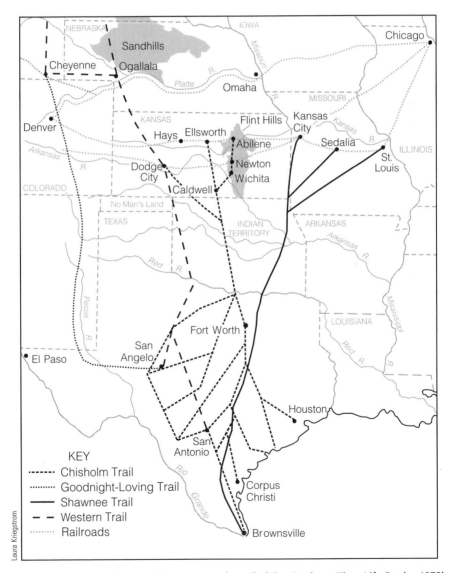

F I G U R E 2.4 Nineteenth-century cattle trails (*The Cowboys*, Time-Life Books, 1973).

The era from the close of the Civil War until the late 1880s has been immortalized as the age of the open range. In those days, land and grass were free, water belonged to first-comers, and all a man needed to set himself up in the business was some cattle, enough common sense to handle them, and the courage to protect them. Such a man was Doc Barton. In February 1872, Doc, his brother Al, and 14 drovers left South Texas driving 3,000 Longhorns up the Pecos Trail. In July, they set up camp under a cottonwood tree along the old Santa Fe Trail, where Garden City, Kansas, now stands. That fall they established ranch headquarters in a sod "dugout" built into the bank of the Arkansas River. From there Doc Barton's cattle, marked with his OS brand on the left side and a crop off the right ear, ranged south through No Man's Land (the Oklahoma Panhandle) and the Texas Panhandle to the Red River, a distance of about 250 miles (Blanchard 1989:45–52).

In the early 1880s, yearlings could be bought for $4 or $5 a head, fattened on free grass for another dollar, and sold for $60 or $70 profit. But the Homestead Act passed in 1862, and cheap land, tales of bountiful harvests, and incentives offered by the railroads attracted settlers. The first piece of barbed wire was sold in the United States in 1874, and the open range gave way to fenced range.

Doc Barton lost 1,200 cattle in the blizzard of 1886, which decimated herds throughout the Plains. A year later, the best grass-fed Texas steers brought only $2.40 a hundredweight (cwt)—a mere $28.80 for a 1,200-pound steer, which after expenses would bring the owner $5–$9, depending on where it was sold.

The open range and with it the golden age of the cowboy disappeared by the turn of the twentieth century, but cattle ranching remains vital to the economies

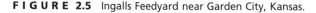

FIGURE 2.5 Ingalls Feedyard near Garden City, Kansas.

and cultures of western North America. Beef production is the largest segment of the American agricultural economy. In 2008, 757,000 farms and ranches raised beef cattle, but big spreads like the Flying V make up less than 1 percent of these operations. Nine out of 10 beef producers had fewer than 100 head and four out of five had fewer than 50 head (Ellis 2009).[2]

HOME ON THE RANGE: THE SHORT, HAPPY LIFE OF A BEEF COW

Calves are weaned at 300 pounds or so. Until they reach "feeder" weight, 600–900 pounds, when they go to feedyards, they graze in pastures or on corn stubble in the fall and wheat before it ripens in the spring. Farmers or ranchers may "background" their animals, placing them in pens where they are "broken to the bunk" (feed trough) by slowly shifting their diet to feed grains in preparation for their feedyard diet.

The Flint Hills run through the eastern third of Kansas. They are all that is left of the tallgrass prairie, which once stretched as far to the east as Indiana and across the plains from Texas to Canada. In the summer, the region's bluestem grasses offer some of the best pasturelands in North America, but in winter the grass is dormant and of little food value. As a result, the region is home to thousands of "transient" cattle each summer (Hoy 1997). In spring, "stockers," weighing 300–600 pounds, arrive by truck from cow-calf operations across the country to fatten on the region's lush pastures for a few months before being shipped to feedyards, most in the southwest part of the state, where they are "finished" in final preparation for slaughter.

Cattle may come to the feedyard from anywhere and at any time. Weighing from 400 pounds (light feeders) to 800 pounds (heavy feeders), they journey to feedyards in "bull wagons"—18-wheeled stock tractor-trailers. "Bull haulers" stop only for gas and meals from the time they pick up a load of cattle in a Flint Hills pasture—or on a farm or ranch in Texas, Kentucky, or Florida—until they reach the feedyard, many hours later. Shipping is hard on cattle. They lose 5 to 6 percent of their body weight ("shrink") during transport over long distances and 2 to 3 percent on short hauls. And when cattle lose pounds, their owner loses dollars (Raab 1997:18).

Commercial feedyards buy cattle, while "custom feeders" finish someone else's cattle. Feedyards are really "bovine hotels": they house the cattle in metal-fenced pens, feed and water them, doctor them when they are sick, and market them to packing plants when they are "finished." Like hotel guests everywhere, cattle pay room and board, through a markup on the price of feed and medicine, or through a "yardage fee"—a flat fee per day—or both.

It takes one human to care for about 1,000 head of cattle in a feedyard. A 30,000-head yard typically employs three or four cowboys, or "pen riders," four or five maintenance men, four or five workers in the feed mill, a secretary, a manager, a couple of people to scrub and maintain the water tanks in each

Don Stull

F I G U R E 2.6 Cattle feeding at the bunk, Lexington, Nebraska.

cattle pen, and feed-truck drivers. And there are plenty of odd jobs that always need doing.

Cattle are fed twice in the morning and once in the afternoon. The daily ration—mainly corn, with alfalfa and corn silage for roughage—is carefully calibrated to maximize "rate of gain." Trucks drive in alleys between the pens, automatically dispensing a measured ration into concrete feed bunks. Feedyard cattle eat somewhere between 24 and 32 pounds of feed a day, depending on the amount of moisture in the ration and the weather. They gain about three pounds a day—more for steers, less for heifers.

A steer eats 30 pounds or so, and gains only three pounds, so he produces 27 pounds of waste each day. Not only is manure an effective fertilizer, it is also free. Liquid manure mixed with water is pumped onto fields during irrigation; solid manure is spread on fields. Some feedyards stockpile excess manure and give it away or pay someone to haul it away.

Cattle remain in feedyards until they reach slaughter weight, optimally between 1,200 and 1,300 pounds. Buyers from the packing plants bid on "show pens" of "fat cattle," offering so much per hundredweight for all the animals in the pen. Once the seller agrees to the price, the buyer sets a date and time for delivery to the packinghouse. Cattle are usually picked up at the feedyard early in the morning. They are driven out of their pens, down the alleys that divide them, and into a bull wagon like the one that brought them there four or five months earlier. Price is based on the weight of the loaded trucks before they leave the feedyard. When the packinghouse pays the feedyard for its cattle shipment, it deducts its costs and fees, and writes a check for the balance to the owner.

At least, that's how it used to work.

In 2005, company buyers who bid on pens of live cattle and paid their owners in cash bought half the cattle slaughtered in Kansas. Accurately judging the quality and percent of red meat an individual animal will yield by looking at a pen of live cattle is not easy, even for the most experienced cattle buyer. Carcass-based pricing eliminates the guesswork. Final price is based on the weight and quality of meat and byproducts each carcass yields. The base price is adjusted up or down according to formulas or grids specified by the company, which charges the seller for the costs of transporting the animals to the packing-house and their slaughter. In 2005, not quite half of cattle slaughtered in Kansas were marketed under a carcass-based pricing formula. But five years later, Kansas packinghouses paid cash for only 39 percent of their cattle, while those bought on a carcass-based pricing formula had increased to 54 percent. The cash market has declined in the other major beef slaughter states as well (Bullard 2010:55).

Not only are meatpacking companies changing how they pay for the cattle they slaughter, they are also extending their control of the market through what is called "captive supply." Packers procure cattle through forward contracts, which call for delivery at a specified future time for a specified price. They also own some of the cattle they slaughter outright, finishing them in their own feed-yards. JBS, the world's largest beefpacker, owns Five Rivers Cattle Company, the world's largest cattle feeding company, with a combined feeding capacity of almost one million head in eight states. Cargill owns the third largest cattle feeder in the United States. Because packinghouses purchase cattle from feedyards within a 300-mile radius, even cattle feeders who sell on the cash market may have only one bidder on their cattle, who offers a take-it-or-leave-it price. More than half, perhaps as much as 80 percent, of the cattle now slaughtered in the United States are procured through captive supply: either through forward con-tracts, formula pricing, packer ownership, or feeders who have only one viable buyer (Domina & Taylor 2010:3).

GO WEST, YOUNG STEER, GO WEST

Cattle feeding in the manner and on the scale described in this chapter is of recent origin, but cattle feeding itself has a long history. Cattle are fed to increase their weight as rapidly as possible and to improve the quality of their meat. Today's steers are only 15–18 months old when they "go to town," as the trip to the slaughterhouse is sometimes euphemistically called. Cattle were also fed in the eighteenth and nineteenth centuries to convert surplus crops into a market-able commodity and to fertilize fields. Until railroads came west and refrigerated boxcars were invented in the 1870s, livestock and whiskey were about the only ways farmers on the frontier could turn their surplus grain into cash. Cattle could walk to market, and a few barrels of good corn whiskey brought a handsome return in the city.

The perceived wisdom in the cattle business was that young cattle—three years old and under—lacked flavor, so cattle usually did not go to market until they were four or five years old. But in the early 1900s, the Swensons of the famous SMS ranch in Texas began pushing their cattle to maturity in less than two years. Soon other cattlemen decided to feed young animals too. But not until chain grocery stores emerged as a major meat market in the 1940s, and began demanding top quality corn-fed beef, did "baby beef" become the standard of the industry.

The Plains of North America are not blessed with an abundance of rivers, lakes, and streams. Not until the windmill became readily available in the 1870s could farmers and ranchers be assured a steady supply of well water for their stock and themselves. Nearly a century later another innovation—center pivot irrigation—turned the Texas and Oklahoma Panhandles, southwest Kansas, and much of central and western Nebraska into a new corn belt—and one of the most productive agricultural areas in the nation. This new technology allowed farmers to tap the Ogallala Aquifer, a huge underground reservoir, and enabled them to bring marginal land under cultivation. Soon they were producing mountains of grain, and before long western cattlemen realized it would be far more profitable to keep their grain and the animals it fed at home rather than ship them east to the Corn Belt.

In 1960, half the grain-fed cattle in the United States were in the old Corn Belt—Ohio, Indiana, Illinois, Wisconsin, Michigan, Minnesota, Missouri, and Iowa. Less than one-fourth were in the Plains—the Dakotas, Oklahoma, Nebraska, Texas, and Kansas. Thirty years later, those numbers were reversed—55 percent of the cattle on feed were in the Plains and only 21 percent were in the old Corn Belt. Texas, Nebraska, and Kansas had become the top three cattle-feeding states (Krause 1991:5). They still are.

FROM HOGSHEADS TO DISASSEMBLY LINES: THE RISE OF THE MEATPACKING INDUSTRY

Grazing their cattle, hogs, and sheep on open range, stockmen were at the forefront of the American frontier as it advanced in the eighteenth and nineteenth centuries. But the slaughter, butchering, and processing of livestock—meatpacking—was an urban enterprise.

Commercial meatpacking began in the American colonies in 1660, when William Pynchon of Springfield, Massachusetts, bought hogs, then slaughtered and packed them for the West Indies trade. Before mechanical refrigeration appeared, most meatpacking took place in the winter, and the means to preserve meat from spoilage were primitive. Beef did not preserve well, so cattle were slaughtered year-round as needed for fresh meat. Pork was "packed"—cured, salted, and stuffed into large barrels known as hogsheads.

In the colonial period, every city had its own slaughterhouses. Then, as now, large concentrations of livestock—and their slaughter—offended the sensibilities of city dwellers, and commercial meatpacking moved ever westward. The first commercial pork packing plant was built in Cincinnati, Ohio, in 1818. Thirty years later, Cincinnati's 40 plants were sending pork and lard to the eastern seaboard and beyond (Skaggs 1986:33–44).

Chicago's first slaughterhouse was built in 1827. Located in the midst of what was becoming the nation's primary cattle feeding area, and linked to the eastern seaboard by the Great Lakes, the Erie Canal, and later the railroads, Chicago soon became the nation's most important meatpacking center. Livestock pens and slaughterhouses were consolidated on the city's southern boundary as the Union Stock Yards in 1865. The Yards, as they were known, held 200 horses, 21,000 cattle, 22,000 sheep, and 75,000 hogs, as well as hotels, saloons, restaurants, and offices. Workers lived nearby in an area called Back of the Yards (Ibid.:45–48).

In the latter half of the nineteenth century, technology transformed meatpacking from a small-scale, localized, and seasonal activity into a national industry dominated by a handful of giant companies. First, came expansion of the railroads, which tied the nation together. Then, came the invention of an efficient refrigerated rail car in 1879, which enabled meatpackers to ship carcasses instead of animals. Three beef carcasses could be shipped in a refrigerated car for what it cost to ship one live steer by rail. Lured by the promise of cheap western cattle, tax abatements, and greater profits, Chicago's meatpacking giants began building slaughterhouses in cities throughout the Midwest and the Plains (Skaggs 1986:97).

On the eve of World War I, Chicago was still the largest producer of red meat in the United States, followed, in order of volume, by Kansas City, Omaha, St. Louis, New York, St. Joseph, Fort Worth, St. Paul, Sioux City, Oklahoma City, Denver, and Wichita (Ibid.:98). At the turn of the twentieth century, "trust" referred to a combine of large companies that conspired to divide markets among themselves, fix prices, and control wages and labor conditions (Skaggs 1986:7). Five companies—Swift, Armour, Morris, Cudahy, and Wilson—formed the Beef Trust. In 1916, the Big Five, as these companies were also known, killed nine out of every 10 cattle and eight of 10 hogs in the 12 major meatpacking cities (Horowitz 1997:13).

Railways and refrigeration transformed meatpacking from a local and seasonal small business enterprise into an industry that distributed its product year-round and nationwide. But meeting the demands of a growing and urbanizing nation required a steady supply of workers. In 1870, there were only 8,366 packinghouse workers in the United States, including 202 women and 258 children under age 16. They earned an average of $305 for the three months or so they worked each winter. By the turn of the century, meatpacking employed 68,500 workers, of whom 3,000 were women and 1,700 were children. Their earnings had risen to an average of $488, but they worked all year long (Skaggs 1986:108–109).

F I G U R E 2.7 Early twentieth-century postcard of the Swift & Company Beef Dressing Department, Chicago.

Butchering is a skill, requiring precision to kill, eviscerate, skin, and bone an animal without damaging its hide or its meat. Into the 1880s, "all-round" butchers killed and cut up animals. They were paid by the head and worked at their own pace. But if the tasks required to slaughter and butcher an animal could be divided, the pace of work could be increased, more animals could be processed, and more profit could be made.

"Disassembly" lines appeared in Cincinnati's pork packinghouses in the 1830s and were refined in Chicago. Animals were driven up a runway to the top floor of the slaughterhouse, several stories above ground. As the animal was killed and disassembled, gravity brought hides, intestines, and other parts of the animal to lower floors through chutes. Trolleys, hooks attached to rollers on overhead rails, moved the carcass down the line, where crews of workers performed their assigned tasks. In 1908, the introduction of a conveyor system, using an "endless chain," brought animals directly to the workers. The speed of the chain, which the floor supervisor set by moving a lever, determined the pace of work (Barrett 1987:23–26).

With division of labor came "deskilling." Each task in the complicated process of slaughtering and butchering an animal was separated and assigned to a single worker. Although tasks at critical junctures in the process still demanded considerable skill, workers no longer dictated their own pace, and jobs became ever simpler. Splitters, who used giant cleavers and later saws to split the carcass down the middle of the backbone, were the most skilled workers on the kill-floor, and the best paid. But their skill was restricted to a single task, and it paled in comparison to the many skills of butchers from an earlier day. And if workers could stand the stench and keep up with the chain, they could learn most any job in a packinghouse—and learn it quickly.

BEEFPACKING MOVES TO THE COUNTRY: RELOCATING AND RESTRUCTURING THE INDUSTRY

The companies that created the meatpacking industry at the turn of the twentieth century are gone. Tyson, JBS, and Cargill have replaced the industry's original Big Five by dramatically cutting costs and increasing productivity.

Plant capacity is key to cutting costs: the cost of slaughter is reduced by nearly one-half at a plant that operates at 325 head an hour compared to one that processes only 25 head an hour. But reducing costs through economies of scale is not enough. Since live animals lose value through shrinkage, bruising, and crippling during shipping, fat cattle are rarely trucked more than 150 miles to slaughter.

Shipping costs have also been reduced at the other end. No longer do processors ship carcasses to wholesalers or retailers as hanging sides of beef. Workers now remove fat and bone at the plant and truck meat in boxes directly to retail outlets. Aside from the cost of the animal, the single largest expense in meatpacking is labor. Meatpacking companies have succeeded in driving down wages and crippling once-powerful unions.

These changes, which rocked the meatpacking industry, and ultimately led to the demise of its original Big Five, began in 1960, when Iowa Beef Packers, Inc., opened a one-story plant in the small town of Denison, Iowa. Twenty years later, the company's name had been changed to IBP, and it had become the leading producer of red meat in the world and the pacesetter for the entire industry.

NOTES

1. When I returned to the Nebraska Sandhills in 2003 for a branding on the Lazy 5, Chet was no longer with the Flying V. The ranch's owner had passed away, and his widow and stepson put its administration in the hands of a corporation. This did not sit well with Chet, who was the third generation of his family to manage the ranch. At about the same time, his marriage to Kris was breaking up. Chet was unwilling to work through the managerial transition on the Flying V, so he quit and opened up a small business in a nearby community. Pat and Todd were managing the Flying V ranches (Stull fieldnotes May 29, 2003).

2. Nevertheless, the number of small cattle producers is falling rapidly, while the number of large operations is rising. Figure 1.2 shows this trend quite dramatically.

3

✳

Chicken Little, Chicken Big:
The Poultry Industry

DOWN ON THE FARM

Mother and Frances shared a laugh about Birdie, a "Banty" (Bantam) hen they used to haul around in their little red wagon when they were girls. They pulled the wagon up and down the front walk, and sometimes Birdie would lay an egg for them. Mother also remembered a mean old rooster. She had to pass through the chicken yard—and by Old Red—on the way to the outhouse. Once when Old Red attacked her, she picked up a tobacco stick that stood by the gate and "hit him right between the eyes—like David killed Goliath—and Old Red fell over dead with one flop!"

Grandmother didn't scold her, but Mother knew she wasn't happy since Grandmother then had to scald the rooster to get his feathers off and cook him. "I used to hate to go to the outhouse because of that rooster. Maybe he's why I'm still always constipated," Mother laughed (Stull fieldnotes, September 17, 1998).

POULTRY PRODUCTION AND CONSUMPTION IN
THE EARLY TWENTIETH CENTURY

Chickens were part of daily life for every farm kid who, like my mother and aunt, grew up in the 1920s. Their mothers raised the birds for their eggs and meat. There was a chicken house inside a large fenced chicken yard behind my grandparents' house, and Grandmother sold eggs to the egg man who came by every week or so. For Grandmother and farm wives all across America, "egg money" was about their only independent source of cash. Grandmother used it to buy an occasional luxury item, and in lean times egg money might have to

Michael Broadway

FIGURE 3.1 Hens in a farmer's chicken house.

pay for clothing or groceries, such as coffee and sugar. But more often it went to treats for her children when they went to town on Saturdays—and later for her grandchildren.

I spent summers on my grandparents' farm, and I always looked forward to helping my grandmother shell corn to feed the chickens in the morning. I also liked gathering eggs, though I was a little afraid of the roosters and the hens when they were sitting in their nests in the chicken house. A fried chicken dinner was a treat, even into my teenage years in the early 1960s. After all, it was a lot of work—the chicken had to be killed; the feathers, head, and feet removed, and then the carcass eviscerated before cooking—and few things smell worse than scalded chicken feathers.

Chickens, like cattle, came to the Americas with the first European colonists. The birds are small and easy to transport, and they require little care. They eat virtually anything, reproduce quickly, and offer a ready source of fresh meat and eggs (Gordon 1996:56). Until well into the twentieth century, every American farm had a small flock of chickens. Farmers and their families bartered or sold surplus eggs, and once a hen grew too old to lay, she was eaten or sold in town. Tender meat came from cockerels, young roosters culled from the flock each spring and sold to brokers, who sent them off to big-city hotels and restaurants. What passed for eating chickens in those days—tough old hens and cockerels—were a byproduct of egg production and were not readily available to most people (Williams 1998:7–9).

Its scarcity made chicken a delicacy. If you had gone shopping in Chicago in 1914, and then stopped for lunch at the exclusive Blackstone Hotel, you might have dined from a menu that offered:

Crabmeat Supreme	$0.60
Prime Rib	$1.25
Imported Venison Steak	$1.50
Broiled Lobster	$1.60

But if you really wanted to indulge yourself, or impress your dinner companion, you could have ordered:

Chicken	$2.00! (Snow 1996:5)

All of that was about to change.

MRS. STEELE'S CHICKS: THE BIRTH OF THE MODERN POULTRY INDUSTRY

America's broiler industry began on the Delmarva Peninsula, a 200-mile finger of flat farm country extending from the northern border of Delaware through the Eastern Shore of Maryland to Cape Charles, Virginia. Bounded on one side by the Atlantic Ocean and on the other by Chesapeake Bay, Delmarva has remained rural and agricultural despite its proximity to some of the largest urban centers on the eastern seaboard.

In the spring of 1923, Mrs. Cecile Steele of Ocean View, Delaware, ordered 50 chicks from a hatchery a few miles down the road to replenish losses to her small flock of laying hens. The hatchery misread her order and sent her 500 chicks. Instead of sending them back, she built a small shed and raised them as "broilers" (young chickens grown to be eaten). Eighteen weeks later, the 387 survivors weighed more than two pounds each, and she sold them for the princely sum of 62 cents a pound to a local buyer, who shipped them to northern cities for the restaurant and hotel market (Williams 1998:11–12).

The next year Mrs. Steele ordered 1,000 chicks, and her husband left his job with the U.S. Coast Guard to raise chickens. By 1926, they were growing 10,000 birds at a time. It didn't take long for word to spread. In less than a decade, the Peninsula was producing 7 million broilers a year. But along with this dramatic increase in production came a sharp decline in the price growers received for their birds. In 1934, chicken farmers were paid 19 cents a pound, live weight—less than one-third the price Mrs. Steele received in 1923. As prices and profits fell, farmers searched for ways to reduce production costs and the time it took to "grow out" their birds, while simultaneously increasing the size of the birds they marketed (Gordon 1996:60; Williams 1998:20).

Chickens mature quickly, and experiments in chicken genetics and nutrition offered rapid results. By the mid-1930s, breeders were developing chickens that grew bigger and faster, and nutritionists were experimenting with improving feed efficiency. These innovations paid off handsomely. In 1927, Delmarva broilers went to market at 2.5 pounds in 16 weeks; in 1941, they averaged 2.9 pounds after only 12 weeks. Over that same period, the amount of feed it took to produce a pound of chicken meat fell by half a pound (Williams 1998: 26–28).

Corn is the main ingredient in chicken feed, and as more farmers began growing broilers, demand for chicken feed rose rapidly. Companies like Pillsbury and Ralston Purina opened feed mills and began selling premixed chicken feed. They also funded research on poultry nutrition.

Humans are not the only animals that like the taste of chicken—so do rats and raccoons, foxes and chicken hawks. To protect them, farmers usually kept chickens in a fenced yard and at night brought them into a shed, called a chicken house. But as broiler flocks climbed into the thousands, and as farmers began growing them throughout the year, something had to change.

Chickens, like humans, need vitamin D to ensure proper bone growth, and they need sunlight to synthesize vitamin D on their own. As long as chickens had to spend at least part of their time outside, death loss from predators, weather, and disease presented a serious problem. And the more chickens move around, the longer it takes them to reach market weight. The first major breakthrough in chicken nutrition came with the discovery that by adding cod liver oil (and later purified vitamin D) to their feed, growers could raise chickens entirely indoors (Gordon 1996:60). Chicken yards and wooden sheds gave way to long, low, metal buildings in which thousands of birds are grown completely indoors.

Chickens mature in a fraction of the time it takes for cattle and hogs, and, as the saying goes, armies march on their stomachs. In 1941, the year the United States entered World War II, the Delmarva Peninsula produced two-thirds of the nation's broilers—77 million. This fact, coupled with the Peninsula's proximity to seaports, placed a premium on its broilers. The armed forces' insatiable appetite for chicken meat also created opportunities for other areas to expand broiler production (Williams 1998:37).

Responding to increased wartime demand, Delmarva farmers raised 90 million broilers in 1942; far ahead of Arkansas's 11 million and Georgia's 10 million (Williams 1998:38). In that same year, the War Food Administration placed price controls on chickens and commandeered the Peninsula's broilers for the armed forces. As a result, the center of broiler production shifted to Georgia and Arkansas, as urban markets looked elsewhere for chickens, which, unlike beef and pork, were not rationed during the war (Gordon 1996:66). Soon chickens from Georgia, Arkansas, and North Carolina were replacing Delmarva broilers in New York and Philadelphia.

Broiler production expanded rapidly after World War II, and the "broiler belt" stretched from the Delmarva Peninsula through North Carolina, Georgia, Alabama, and Mississippi to Arkansas and East Texas. As the broiler belt was wrapping itself around the South, the industry was pioneering what some claim is "the most advanced form of food production in the entire world" (Williams 1998:ix) and others decry as "industrial agriculture" (Heffernan 1984).

INDUSTRIALIZING, INTEGRATING, AND MARKETING THE CHICKEN

By the late 1950s, the structure of the modern poultry industry was in place, and the stage was set for the appearance of the giants of today's industry. In 1935, John Tyson began buying surplus chickens from Arkansas farmers and hauling them to Kansas City and St. Louis. Soon, he bought a hatchery so he could sell baby chicks to farmers. By the late 1940s, he was supplying chicken feed to farmers from his own mill, and in 1958, he built his first processing plant in Springdale, Arkansas. In the 1920s, Arthur Perdue began raising laying hens and selling eggs on his farm near Salisbury, Maryland. In the 1940s, he started hatching and raising broilers. His son, Frank, took over the business in 1950 and signed contracts with farmers to grow broilers. He built a feed mill and, in 1968, purchased a chicken processing plant, making Perdue Farms, Inc., a fully integrated firm (Long 1991:D-30; Williams 1998:98–99). Men like John Tyson and Frank Perdue "started in their backyards and built regional and national operations that contributed to the industrialization of the nation's poultry industry. Each managed the production of fertile eggs, hatching of chicks, milling of feeds, raising, slaughtering, processing, and marketing of the product within a single company" (Morrison 1998:146).

By combining production, processing, and distribution in the same firms, the poultry industry achieved complete vertical integration (Heffernan 1984:238). It also developed close working relationships with poultry specialists and university agriculture extension agents, whose job it is to provide farmers with the latest research findings. Poultry companies funded university research on avian genetics and nutrition, while extension agents worked directly with company servicemen to increase grower efficiency and expand markets. The interests of poultry companies, university researchers and extension agents, and retailers converged in a national campaign to create "the chicken of tomorrow."

The poultry research director for A&P Food Stores, then the leading retail poultry distributor in the United States, told a Canadian poultry convention in 1944 that "what the poultry industry needs is a better meat-type chicken similar to the broad-breasted turkey." He was widely quoted, and in 1946 A&P joined with the U.S. Department of Agriculture, poultry companies, and university extension services to form the National Chicken of Tomorrow Committee. Its task was to find the ideal broiler.

State and regional contests in 1946 and 1947 winnowed the competition to 40 breeders, who submitted their eggs for the national contest in the spring of 1948. The chicks from these eggs were raised under controlled conditions at the University of Delaware Extension Station. The winner of the National Chicken of Tomorrow contest was announced on June 23, 1948. It was a red-feathered Cornish-New Hampshire crossbreed developed by the Vantress Hatchery & Poultry Farm in Marysville, California. The runner-up was a White Plymouth Rock from Arbor Acres Farms near Hartford, Connecticut. The press proclaimed "the chicken of tomorrow" a "breakthrough for American agriculture" (Bjerklie 1993:24; cf. Horowitz 2006).

The University of Arkansas hosted a second contest in 1951. It even built a new facility to grow out the birds. Climaxing a week of festivities, Vice President Alben Barkley announced the results of the competition to a crowd assembled in the university's football stadium. Vantress Hatchery & Poultry Farm won again, and Arbor Acres Farms was again the runner-up. Ironically, the runner-up, not the winner, ultimately became the chicken of tomorrow. Arbor Acres' White Plymouth Rock became the industry's standard in part because of its white plumage, which processors preferred over the dark-plumed birds of Vantress, because stray white feathers were not as easily seen on plucked birds. Ann Arbor Farms went on to become the largest broiler breeder in the world, accounting for nearly 40 percent of the U.S. supply and a third of the world's supply. Continued modification of its genetic stock has produced a bird that maximizes rate of growth, feed conversion, and "liveability" (Bjerklie 1993).

In 1968, Perdue Farms became the first poultry company to "brand" its product. Beginning with radio commercials and expanding to television in 1971, the company embarked on a major campaign to convince American shoppers its chicken was worth paying more for. With its president, Frank Perdue, telling television viewers that "it takes a tough man to raise a tender chicken," Perdue Farms quickly rose from twelfth to fourth among poultry companies (Williams 1998:103–105).

Rapid and dramatic changes in poultry production and processing after World War II, combined with aggressive marketing, transformed chicken from an expensive delicacy, reserved for Sunday dinner or special occasions, into an everyday, inexpensive meat. At market in 1923, Mrs. Steele's chickens cost almost $8 a pound live weight in today's dollars—no wonder the average American ate only 14 pounds of chicken a year. Today, the descendent of one of those birds weighs more than twice as much, grows to maturity in less than half the time, and sells for less than $1 a pound fully dressed and ready to cook. Is it any wonder that "chicken" has replaced "beef" as the most likely answer when Americans ask, "What's for dinner?"

Chicken's short "generation interval" from conception to consumption, as well as vertical integration, enabled poultry companies to rapidly respond to changes in the market and gave chicken a clear advantage over beef and pork. As chicken became cheaper, it also gained a reputation as being leaner and, therefore, healthier than beef and pork, fueling the meteoric rise in chicken consumption in the 1980s and 1990s.

CONTRACT GROWING AND FACTORY FARMING

By the late 1950s, a contract system was taking shape that promised to reduce risk for growers and maximize profits for companies. The poultry company provided the farmer with day-old chicks from the hatchery, as well as feed, medications, and technical assistance. In turn, the farmer provided fully equipped chicken houses, utilities, and labor. The company also expected the farmer to dispose of dead birds and manure. In return, the farmer received a guaranteed payment, which was often tied to the feed-conversion ratio—the less feed it took to grow the bird to market weight, the better (Morrison 1998:146; Williams 1998:50–51). By the early 1960s, the independent chicken farmer, who raised his own birds and made his own decisions about how best to do it, had been transformed into a chicken grower who signed a contract to raise the company's birds according to its specifications.

As poultry companies achieved vertical integration, farmers' ability to market their eggs and birds vanished. These firms, now called integrators, owned not only the broilers they supplied to contract growers, but the eggs that hatched the birds, the feed that went into them, and the plants that processed and then sold them to grocery stores. By the early 1980s, 95 percent of the broilers sold in the United States were grown under production contracts with fewer than 40 companies (Heffernan 1984:238). For growers, contracts offered a guaranteed income from their flocks and took the risks out of raising chickens, save one— the company did not have to renew the grower's contract.

BIG CHICKEN COMES TO ROOST IN KENTUCKY

Industry expansion during the 1970s and 1980s saturated the old broiler belt with chicken houses, and concerns mounted about the industry's treatment of its growers and processing workers, as well as environmental problems associated with disposal of manure and dead birds. Poultry integrators moved into new territories. One of those was Kentucky.

Kentucky is within a day's drive of 70 percent of the U.S. population and is crisscrossed by interstate highways (Ulack, Raitz, & Pauer 1998:3). Its low educational and income levels, coupled with declines in its major industries, coal and agriculture, held promise for a readily available supply of workers for processing plants and growers to supply them. Adding to its appeal were an abundance of corn and water, generous tax incentives, minimal environmental regulations, and an absence of rural zoning. As if those enticements weren't enough, the poultry companies received $165 million in state and local tax credits and incentives (Associated Press 2000).

If Kentucky had much to offer the poultry industry, chickens were attractive to many Kentucky farmers as well. Tobacco—the state's primary cash crop—was under increasing attack, and tobacco farmers were being encouraged to find alternative crops (Stull 2000). The state's farms are small, 151 acres on average in 1998, of which only a third was in harvested cropland (Ulack, Raitz, & Pauer 1998:159), making them ideal for poultry production. Take Shawn[1] for example. Together, he and his semi-retired father had about 750 acres, scattered over several farms. They erected six broiler houses on about 30 acres of a hilly 130-acre farm. Shawn decided to grow broilers because 750 acres was not enough ground to support their two families on what they could make from corn, soybeans, cattle, and tobacco, and they were unable to rent enough additional acreage to make a profit.

Chickens appealed to Kentucky's farmers because they are raised inside massive houses, which eliminate weather as a factor in production, and growers are guaranteed a minimum price per pound for each bird they grow out. Poultry companies also promised easy financing for minimal investment, coupled with attractive incomes in exchange for a modest amount of labor.

These factors led to an astonishing increase in Kentucky's production of chickens: soaring from 1.5 million broilers in 1990 to 307 million in 2009. Absent at the beginning of 1990, Kentucky now boasts four large processing plants, two primary breeder hatcheries, six feed mills, three layer complexes, and 2,800 chicken houses on 850 farms in 42 of Kentucky's 120 counties. In less than two decades, chickens flew past Kentucky's traditional agricultural powerhouses of horses, cattle, and tobacco to become the state's leading farm commodity. Kentucky now ranks seventh among the states in chicken production (Keeton 2010:6; USDA NASS 2010).

Tyson's processing plant in Robards, Kentucky, originally built by Hudson Foods, opened on July 9, 1996. The first chicken houses to serve this plant were completed in September 1995. Four years later, Tyson's plant received chickens

FIGURE 3.2 A complex of 16 broiler houses, each home to more than 25,000 birds, in McLean County, Kentucky. The buildings with the open doors store chicken litter until it is spread on fields.

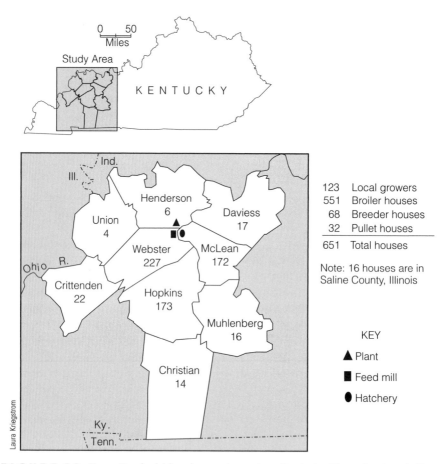

FIGURE 3.3 Tyson Foods chicken houses in western Kentucky (Tyson Foods n.d.:6).

from 124 growers who operated 667 chicken houses in 10 counties: 32 pullet houses, 68 breeder houses, and 567 broiler houses. Of those houses, 572 (86 percent) were located in three adjacent counties immediately to the south of the processing plant. The greatest number, 227, were in Webster County (Tyson Foods n.d.:6).[2] (See Figure 3.3.) The plant employed more than 1,500 workers to slaughter and process two million chickens a week (Stinnett 1996b). At this rate, 80 broiler houses, each home to about 25,000 birds, were being emptied every week.

OLD MACDONALD TAKES A FACTORY JOB: HOW CHICKENS ARE GROWN, 1998

Bill's two breeder houses sit long, low, and shiny at the edge of a cornfield. The door opens into an anteroom where he stores stacked trays of eggs at a constant 62 degrees, awaiting pick up for delivery to the hatchery.

Laying hens and roosters come to Bill at 20 weeks of age—10,700 hens and 980 roosters for each of his two houses. They are trucked in from pullet houses in the next county where they have been raised from day-old chicks, originally driven up from Alabama. The "working life" of a breeder hen is only 45 weeks; after that Bill says she is "destined for the soup can." Roosters fight and kill one another over "their hens" and must be periodically replaced. They also attack humans. When entering the laying area, you always knock on the door to avoid startling the chickens, and you walk slowly. Even so, roosters sometimes fly up on Bill's back and attack him. Hens are aggressive, too, and peck at your legs as you stand in the house. But more than the frequent pecking, what a first-time visitor notices most is the sound—a constant cacophony of clucking hens and crowing roosters.

On each side of the floor, where the chickens move freely about, is a row of metal cubicles running the full length of the house. They are positioned on both sides of a conveyor belt covered with a removable roof. To lay their eggs, hens enter the small compartments, where they rest on nothing but the bare metal. The compartments are slanted slightly inward, ensuring that eggs will roll through a rubbery fabric flap down onto the conveyor belt.

Twice a day, Bill's daughters stand in the anteroom, turn on the conveyor belt, and collect the eggs as they come out of the laying area onto a metal-frame work station. They place good eggs in the storage racks for later pickup, and cull dirty, small, misshapen, and double-yoked eggs. Bill receives 32 cents per dozen for regular eggs and 10 cents a dozen for culls.

On average, a hen lays an egg every 23 hours for five or six days, and then does not lay any eggs for one or two days. As hens get older, they lay less often, and by 45 weeks their productivity is below acceptable levels. Bill's two breeder houses combined generate about 18,000 eggs per day when the hens are at their laying peak, but toward the end of their 45-week laying period they will produce only 10,000 to 11,000 eggs.

Bill and his daughters each take a third of the income from their operation. The daughters gather eggs twice daily, which takes them a total of four to five hours. Bill takes care of the houses and the flocks, which he figures requires three hours a day for each house.

Bill's eggs spend 21 days in careful monitoring at the hatchery, a climate-controlled concrete and glass building located on a two-lane road a few miles from the processing plant. On the day they hatch, the chicks are placed in cardboard trays and driven in a white school bus to a broiler house.

Broiler houses are 43 feet wide and come in two lengths: 510 feet and 460 feet. The longer ones house about 27,000 birds, the shorter ones 24,000. Screened windows, which can be opened for light and ventilation, run down both sides of the houses, but they are usually covered with dark curtains, at Tyson's instructions, to keep the birds calmer. Large exhaust fans at one end of the house kick on periodically for ventilation and to suck out the smell of ammonia that can become stifling as the flock matures. Next to each house are two large metal bins for automatically dispensing feed into round red plastic trays, divided into compartments, much like a school cafeteria tray. Two rows

Don Stull

FIGURE 3.4 Hens lay eggs inside metal cubicles that run along both sides of the breeding house. From these "nests," eggs roll through a rubbery flap down onto a conveyer belt and into an anteroom where they are sorted.

of brooders (heat lamps), feed trays, and plastic water lines, which dispense water through metal nipples, run the full length of the house.

Attached to each house is a small control room containing all the switches, knobs, and electrical breakers needed to run it. Temperature regulation is key to flock survival, and the control panel sets and maintains house temperatures at 85 to 88 degrees for days 1 through 3; 85 degrees for days 4 through 7; and down to 65–70 degrees by the time the flock reaches 42 days of age.

As the birds age, the feed ration changes in both consistency and content. Initially, feed has the consistency of a fine powder, but as the birds grow its form changes to pellets. By the end of the grow-out cycle the ration consists almost entirely of corn, and the birds are emptying one six-ton feed bin each day. Birds should put on a pound of weight for every 1.9 pounds of feed. Broilers should weigh about 5.6 pounds at seven weeks, when they are ready for slaughter.

Growers get paid according to what economists call a "tournament pay system" (Taylor & Domina 2010:3). Tyson sets the base price per pound live weight, and makes adjustments in pay according to performance (feed conversion and death loss) as measured against other growers whose birds are slaughtered at that plant in the same week.

Constructing a broiler house costs between $125,000 and $140,000 and must be built to company specifications. Breeder and pullet houses can cost even more. A grower with six broiler houses could easily have $1 million invested in the houses, equipment, and wells needed to supply water to the houses. Approved growers can borrow up to 110 percent of the cost of their houses on their loan, usually set to mature in 10 to 15 years.

Breeder and pullet growers usually erect only two houses, whereas broiler growers usually build at least four, and sometimes as many as 16 houses in the same complex. Sam has 16 broiler houses. "I'm not really a farmer," he confided, and he never intended "to get into the chicken business." But he jumped at the chance when MetLife and John Hancock offered to loan him $2.4 million for $1,000 down, and their financing arrangement even included his $1,000 deposit.

Sam and his daughter, who attends night classes at a nearby community college, manage the operation. It takes four full-time workers to run the 16 houses, and at peak times—the week before the flock goes out and the week after when they are cleaning the houses—it takes eight workers. Sam's operation needs every bit of the 14 to 18 days between flocks to get everything done.

Integrators claim that each broiler house will provide gross annual revenues of $27,000 to $31,000 and generate profits of $3,000 to $7,000. Of more immediate concern to growers, annual net cash inflow over the 10-year life of the initial loan averages only $1,070 per house (Gibson 1998:9). But none of these figures take into account the cost of growers' labor or any help they may hire.

Laura Kriegstrom

FIGURE 3.5 Don Stull stands between feeding trays and a water line inside a broiler house.

Shawn "walks" his six houses first thing each morning and works in them until he knocks off for dinner about 11:00 A.M. He may walk the houses again in the afternoon. Shawn pays his hired man $6.00 an hour and lets him live rent-free in a small trailer a hundred yards or so down the gravel road that leads to the houses. Shawn figures that it takes two workers about four hours each day to take care of six broiler houses. Shawn's father, wife, and two young children pitch in when he needs extra hands.

For the first few days, the chicks need special attention. As Shawn walks the house, chicks bunch up and run, almost in waves, from one side of the house to the other, or seek darker areas in the corners where they feel more secure. Bucket in hand, he picks up dead birds and culls diseased ones, which he dispatches with a blow from a tobacco stick or smashes underfoot. Once having filled a bucket, Shawn empties it into a large blue freezer that sits outside one of the houses. Periodically, Tyson picks up his dead birds and takes them to its "protein plant" for rendering.[3]

Hanging on the door inside each house is Tyson's broiler mortality sheet, which lists the grower's name, house number, number of birds placed in the house, and the date delivered. Rows for each week allow the grower to record the number of culls and the number of dead birds by day. The Tyson field representative, or flock manager, comes by once a week and records the weekly total, as well as the mortality percentage for that week: 25,980 chickens delivered on August 11; 1.1 percent death loss for Week 1; 1.8 percent for Week 2; 2.1 percent for Week 3; 2.3 percent for Week 4.

His flock manager told Shawn his flock would be picked up at 51 days. The catching crew in this case consisted of seven men, six Mexican immigrants to catch and an Anglo American supervisor who drove a forklift. Catchers work at night when the birds are calmer. Using knee-high plastic barriers and folding plastic fences for catch-pens, while wearing white cotton stockings and gloves to protect their arms and hands, the men scoop up five birds in one hand, four in the other, then sling them into cages. Catchers move with remarkable ease, joking and laughing as they take a moment to rest once they fill a coop of cages and the forklift driver whisks it outside and onto a waiting semi-truck. Each semi holds 22 coops, each divided into 50 cages that hold nine birds each; it takes three semi-loads to empty a house. The crew can finish catching a house in about three hours, and it catches three houses a night.

Ten days or so later, Tyson mailed Shawn a settlement ranking report, which justified the size of the accompanying check. The report specified the numbers for chicks initially delivered, birds picked up, birds dead on arrival at the processing plant, birds condemned because of disease, average weight of the healthy birds, feed-conversion and calorie-conversion ratios. The most important number on Tyson's report, however, is the grower's rank in relation to the others whose birds the company caught in the same week. This ranking determines how much the grower is paid per pound and whether he makes money, breaks even, or loses money. Tyson guarantees four cents a pound, but most growers say they need at least five cents to do better than break even.

So it was in the fall of 1998. Tyson's Kentucky plant was barely two years old, and most of its growers had been in operation not much more than a year. They generally agreed with the pullet grower who said:

> I think it has been great. It's contributed to the decline of the unemployment rate. It's brought a lot of dollars in here…. Our grain farmers are getting prime money for their grain…. The wages paid out and the spinoff dollars … have tremendous effect on the country around here. It's a heck of an improvement. (Stull interview, November 24, 1998)

THE SKY IS FALLING

"A heck of an improvement." Perhaps. But by 2005, a decade after the plant opened, many growers did not think so. Tyson lets growers keep all the money from the first flock—minus costs for electricity and water—so, as one local skeptic put it, "they get dollar signs in their eyes." But beginning with the second flock, loans start coming due, and the reality of income, expenses, and cash flow became increasingly apparent.

Shawn made $36,000 on his first flock, more than most people in the county make in a year. Then, energy prices soared in 2001. Shawn spent $2,800 on electricity per flock for his six houses that summer and $25,000 to heat his flock that winter. Many of the chicks he received in his next flock were blind. Shawn and other growers complained that Tyson was extending the time between flocks to 20 days, the maximum allowed without paying a penalty. Several such delays could cost the farmer a whole flock per year and mean the difference between making and losing money.

In the summer of 2002, Tyson picked up Shawn's last flock and terminated his contract. The company had told him to make $10,000 in improvements to his houses. When he said he could not afford the expense, the company representative told him to borrow the money. When Shawn said he was so far in debt he could not qualify for any more loans, Tyson refused to send him more chickens. After deducting expenses from the payment for his last flock, Shawn received a check from Tyson for $33.22. Shawn's chicken houses stood empty until 2005, when he sold them and the acreage surrounding them to another grower for about one-third of what they had cost him to build.

Sam quit the broiler business too: "I had bad relations with the company. It didn't seem to me that they were doing what they had promised me they would do…. I don't know whether I assumed that the company would be grower friendly. I might have done that on my own. But they did some pretty nefarious things" (interview, August 30, 2005).

Other growers first interviewed in 1998 suffered financial setbacks and either were forced to sell or just called it quits. Of Webster County's 45 broiler complexes, 21 (140 of 225 houses) changed hands at least once in the first decade of production.

Some growers, like Shawn, sold out. Others declared bankruptcy and their houses were sold for $1.00 to the bank or to Tyson, which then ran them with hired labor. The ad Tyson ran in a local newspaper for a farm manager for one of these complexes required that applicants: "★Must be capable of bending, squatting, pulling, lifting, and prolonged walking and standing ★Must be able to work in dusty environment and inclement weather conditions ★High school diploma or equivalent preferred ★COUPLES PREFERRED." The ad also warned that: "Absences from the farm cannot be for more than two hours at a time."

Given such working conditions, coupled with financial stress, it is no wonder some growers sold out, left their houses empty, or abandoned them: "There's a gentleman up the road that instead of selling his [houses], he just moved back to Florida and just left them .... Just walked away. Had enough.... Oh, it was awful. There was dead birds, feed everywhere" (interview, August 26, 2005).

A grower who sold out after four years said: "They was just saying whatever they could to get you to grow chickens....Yeah, I think they was misleading, yep, it was all misleading. Money, payback, like the time you had and the time that you had to put into it. It wasn't right.... It just got to where I didn't like it any more. Putting up with Tyson and being there 24/7 and I couldn't go anywhere, and picking up dead chickens..." (interview, August 26, 2005).

Tyson could not stay in business if all of its growers shared these views. According to one of Tyson's best growers: "I've made more money than I was led to believe that I would make, and most of the bad press that the poultry industry got when they arrived in Kentucky, as far as I'm concerned, almost none of it has proved to be true." He likes growing chickens, but he admitted, "It probably takes more work than I thought it would. Sometimes I feel like a galley slave, but I can get up when I want to, go to bed when I want to, and I can say the hell with it for a day or so, if I want to." He has a full-time employee who helps work his chickens.

But even some successful growers became disenchanted with Tyson. In 2002, the Perdue chicken plant in Ohio County, an hour-and-half to the southeast, began expanding production. Perdue doubled its houses in three years by adding new growers and recruiting discontented ones from Tyson. At the time, Tyson's plant had excess grower capacity, and it cooperated with Perdue, offering its growers $7,000 per house to offset costs to retool to Perdue's specifications. One grower took the offer. Several others switched the next year, even though Tyson had withdrawn its incentive, because the company would not compensate them for added fuel costs during a severe winter. In all, 40 to 50 growers switched to Perdue, at a cost of $20,000 per house. Despite the initial cost to these growers, the move was worth it because as one put it, Perdue "is more grower friendly." The two companies pay about the same per pound live weight, he said, but Perdue picks up more of the costs associated with growing birds, including fuel to heat the houses and sawdust to cover the floors, and fewer birds die during the grow-out period. As a result, growers net more income per flock (Stull fieldnotes, August 18, 2005).

Tyson may have had more growers than it needed in 2002, but by 2008 it wanted 60 new houses. A tornado had destroyed six houses and another 54 houses owned by its largest grower, who lived in Alabama, stood empty and in disarray. This grower, like others, had financed construction of his houses at 110 percent of cost. But he failed to pay his loans, his taxes and utilities, and even some workers who managed his houses. In 2008, new broiler houses cost around $200,000 to build, $50,000 more than a decade earlier. In the meantime, Tyson was compressing the period between flocks, leaving its growers barely enough time to clean out their houses before another flock arrived. One Tyson grower probably spoke for many on a Saturday morning after a crew finished catching his birds. He lamented over coffee, eggs, and toast at a local café:

"I feel like I just got out of jail. I've never been in jail, but getting rid of those chickens feels like it must feel to get out of jail."

"Yeah," one of the café's regulars replied, "but you'll be back in jail next week."

"Yes, I get birds again on Friday," he said with a sigh, contemplating everything he had to do to get his houses ready for the next flock.

In April 2001, Tyson replaced its chicken catchers with the PH2000 mechanical chicken harvester at a cost of $280,000 each. *The Wall Street Journal* claimed the PH2000 could catch 150 birds a minute, compared to human catchers who "are expected to snag as many as 1,000 birds an hour" (Kilman 2003). It sounded like a big improvement.

FIGURE 3.6 Chicken catchers at work.

DEUS EX MACHINA

We stood close to the mechanical chicken harvester, which was not quite half-way down the house, keeping our distance from the forklifts as they whizzed in and out, and watched. It was hard to judge its size in the dusky darkness, but it looked to be about 20 feet long. The crew chief, Brad, brought along a flashlight and answered my questions without hesitation. A rectangular arm, which looked like a home heating-duct, swiveled from side to side "picking up" chickens. One crew member used a small black shield to push chickens gently toward the machine, while another operated the swivel, moving it from side to side as it "sucked them up." At the other end, one man stood on each side of another swivel that "shot" the birds into "holes" in the "box." The exhaust that shot the birds out looked like a big rubber hose with ribbing.

In between intake and output the birds traveled eight feet or so, maybe less. They went into the machine at ground level and came out about three-to-five feet above, depending on which hole they were shot into. The operators moved the hose back and forth across the 10 holes in each box. Each hole could hold 20 birds, but Brad preferred a limit of 15 per hole, especially during hot weather. "They don't hang dead birds at the plant," he said, and his job was to get the birds from house to plant alive and in the best possible physical shape.

The catching machine does not weigh or count the birds, so operators estimated the right number of birds as they shot them rapidly, yet apparently smoothly, into the holes. Occasionally a bird fell to the ground or onto the platform where the two hose operators stood, and they picked it up and put it in a hole. While we watched, one bird fell, apparently lifeless, to the ground. Brad picked it up gently, laid it in front of us, and turned it over. A few minutes later, it was sitting up, once again conscious. A crew member placed it in a hole and it went on its way.

The forklift operator placed the boxes lengthwise on the platform, then got off his machine and rapidly opened the doors to each hole. The platform held two boxes, perpendicular to one another in the shape of a T. Each box had 10 holes and between 15 and 20 birds were shot into each hole, so the box contained 150 to 200 birds. Each truck held 4,400 birds, assuming 20 per hole, or 22 boxes. It took five to six truckloads to empty a house, maybe even another partial load, if the house was full and the birds in the holes were on the light side.

Two of the workers on the crew I observed were Hispanics who previously had been live catchers. Brad said they would not go back to catching birds by hand, and I could see why. The process was much easier on the workers. The two operators of the discharge end of the machine worked bent over at the waist, guiding the hose, one of them moving the discharge, and the other aiming it into the holes, closing the doors and grabbing errant chickens. No doubt their backs were sore at the end of the day, but the sweepers exerted very little physical effort, or so it seemed.

Is the catching machine easier on the birds? It may well be. I was prepared to see squawking birds and broken wings, but the birds were relatively quiet, no doubt so surprised and discombobulated that they were rendered more or less speechless. I saw no evidence of major physical injury. Even the bird that was apparently knocked out by the machine recovered. I saw one or two dead birds on the opposite wall from where I stood, but they might have died of some other cause.

Although the chicken-catching machine replaced human catchers, it did not lead to fewer workers; if anything I saw more workers catching this flock. The machine required eight operators, six to work the machine and two forklift drivers, not counting the supervisor. Using a machine did not save time either. Brad said it takes three hours to catch a house at night when the birds are more docile and bunch up, and four hours during the day when the birds are harder to round up because they run to the light—about the same amount of time it takes human catchers to empty a house (Stull fieldnotes, September 9–10, 2005).

★ ★ ★

The mechanical chicken harvesters might have been easier on both workers and birds, but they did not last. By 2009, Tyson had gone back to human catchers because the cost to maintain the machines was too high. Catching crews consisted of 10 men, mainly Mexicans. According to the United Food and Commercial Workers (UFCW), the union that represents workers at the Robards plant, average wages for chicken catchers fell from $108 to $92 a day over the first decade of the twenty-first century. Chicken catchers work 12-hour shifts, yet 60 percent of the plants included in a U.S. Department of Labor survey failed to pay them overtime (UFCW n.d.). When it comes to catching chickens, men are definitely cheaper than machines.

JUSTICE DENIED

Companies and their growers are financial partners in the poultry industry. Each side puts up about half the capital necessary to support the industry, but there the equality ends. A "market" for live chickens no longer exists in the United States. Virtually everyone who grows chickens commercially raises them under contract to an integrator. While the industry depends on more than 18,000 broiler farms, the growers who run these farms are at the mercy of fewer than 50 companies, and, of these, three own more than half of all the broilers grown in the United States (Ibid.; MacDonald 2008:7). Integrators pay growers by the pound of live weight after the chickens reach the processing plant, but the growers are not present when the birds are weighed and cannot challenge head counts, weights, death loss, or the peer rankings that determine the amount of payment per pound. Growers have little recourse in disputes with integrators, and stories of abuse and intimidation are commonplace. The integrator can send you sick birds or "short" flocks; it can "short" you on feed or "short weigh" your birds when they are delivered for slaughter; it can keep your birds waiting at the processing plant scales so that they lose weight and you lose money; it can require you to make costly upgrades to your houses; it can mandate resolution of disputes through arbitration and require you to sign away your rights to sue. And if you challenge the company, it can cancel your contract.

Such was the case for Alton Terry, who in 2001 began raising chickens for a Tyson plant in Tennessee. In 2002, Terry helped organize the Tennessee Poultry Growers Association, and in 2004, he was elected chairman of its board of directors. He educated Association members on their rights under federal law and reported complaints about Tyson to federal officials. Terry feared that the plant was not weighing his birds promptly, as stipulated in his contract and as required by federal law. When he went to the Tyson plant to watch his birds being weighed, plant personnel turned him away. He complained to a federal official to no avail. After he met with Tyson's local managers to air his complaints, the company delayed placing birds on his farm for one full flock rotation, costing him $30,000. After he again met with company officials in March 2005, Tyson informed him it would no longer place birds on his farm. In January 2006, Tyson notified him that his contract would not be renewed because of his confrontational behavior and his refusal to make upgrades to his facilities, even though he had consistently placed well above average in grower rankings. Seeing no recourse, Alton Terry took Tyson Farms, Inc. to court, charging that its actions violated the 1921 Packers and Stockyards Act, enacted to protect livestock producers from discriminatory practices and ensure competitive and equitable livestock and poultry markets (U.S. Court of Appeals, 6th District 2010:2–5).

Tyson did not dispute Terry's allegations. But the outcome of *Terry v. Tyson* hinged on whether the company's treatment of Alton Terry hurt competition within the industry as a whole. The district court ruled that although Tyson had committed a number of wrongful acts, it did not violate the Packers and Stockyard Act since company treatment of Terry did not harm overall competition. Alton Terry appealed the decision all the way to the U.S. Supreme Court. In January 2011, the Supreme Court refused to hear the case, thereby upholding the lower court's decision and leaving poultry growers powerless to effectively challenge punitive practices on the part of the large integrators.

Under the current contract system, over 71 percent of all poultry growers earn below poverty-level wages (UFCW n.d.). It is a sad state of affairs, said Jean Bunting, who, with her husband William, grew broilers in Bishopville, Maryland, for half a century. "We haven't made a bit more money [growing chickens] than we did 10 or 15 years ago. I wish my mother could see what they've done to the chicken industry. They've put the farmer all the way to the bottom" (Fesperman & Shatzkin 1999:9–11).

It is indeed too bad Mrs. Bunting's mother cannot see what has happened to the chicken industry. Her mother was Mrs. Cecile Steele!

NOTES

1.   To protect them from possible company reprisals, pseudonyms are used to identify Kentucky poultry growers in this chapter.

2. Don Stull was born to a family of farmers whose roots in Webster County reach back to the early nineteenth century. Although his parents no longer live there, most of his extended family still does. From July to January 1998 and July to January 2005, he returned to Webster County to study the poultry industry and its role in the transformation of agriculture in western Kentucky. In other years, he has regularly returned for at least one month to visit family and friends and keep abreast of agricultural developments. Twelve broiler houses border his family farm. For discussion of his role as a native anthropologist and the research presented in this chapter, see Stull 2000 and 2009.

3. Tyson no longer renders dead chickens. Growers are now responsible for disposing of them, usually by composting.

4

✳

Hog Heaven: The Pork Industry

WARNING
You are entering a biologically secure facility.

Undeterred, I opened the door and led my students into a small anteroom. In front we encountered a glass door and visitors' instructions: "To enter 'Midwest State University's' Swine Facility, press bell and wait to be escorted into the building." I rang the bell, and a minute or so later, a short, rumpled, middle-aged man in blue overalls and safety glasses appeared. Frank, our guide for the day, cheerfully greeted us, led the way to the changing rooms, and then instructed us to take a thorough shower before crossing over to the "clean side."

"You'll find overalls, socks, and underwear on the other side. We'll get your rubber boots when you are dressed."

After showering and donning our new clothes, we fitted ourselves with boots at the entrance to the "clean side." The pungent odor of ammonia overwhelmed us as we entered the "clean" portion of the building. It appeared to come from beneath the metal-grated floor. Later, we learned that hog feces and urine fall through openings in the floor, before being either pumped out into a huge holding tank or collected for composting. Parts of the building were ventilated, but on this particular day, with an outside temperature in the mid-80s, we found little fresh air to be had. "Ordinarily it doesn't smell like this," Frank apologized. "You would choose the one day in the year that they came to empty the tank."

Fully assured that "pigs don't stink," we followed Frank down a long corridor to a room filled with at least 100 hogs, each in its own metal stall. The exhaust fans were going full blast, and the hogs were squealing and grunting at us, making our conversation impossible. Passing a second smaller room containing more hogs in stalls, we entered a small office, closed the door, and savored its tranquillity.

Frank reached inside a small refrigerator and grabbed a small plastic container. "This here is pig semen," he announced. "We collect our own. We inseminate the sows and expect each one to produce two litters of 10 to 12 piglets a year. We had one kid who had worked on a pig farm his whole life. He was able to get 300 milliliters of semen out of one of our boars. You just get better with practice." None of us knew whether we should be impressed—and no one asked for further details. "Everybody wants their pork chops to look the same. If they don't look the same you can't get as much money for them. Actually, you can't sell them at all. That's why when we breed our animals we try and control for leanness."

"Why the stalls?" one of us asked.

"When females are bred over and over again they become timid and are the last ones to feed. The crates allow equal-opportunity feeding. If we put you [pointing to a male student] in a room with the rest of these folks [pointing to three female students] with some pizza in it, none of you guys [pointing to the females again] would get anything to eat because he would eat it all." To ensure "equal-opportunity feeding," all the animals feed at once when an operator lowers a lever that releases feed into each animal's trough. The feed descends from a tube suspended along the ceiling and connected outside to a large grain bin.

We retraced our steps to another door that opened into the nursery. Inside were 10 sows, each confined to a metal crate with bars, which prevented the animal from turning around. They could only move to lie down on their sides and allow their piglets to suckle. In such confined quarters sows occasionally smother their offspring. Frank picked up a dead piglet, which was "striped" from a sow crushing it against the grated floor. "This happens quite often. Mama just rolled over and squashed this little guy this morning." Glancing over at the record sheet at the end of the crate, like a doctor checking a patient's medical record, Frank added, "Oh, this was the second she squashed today." (Crates are outlawed in parts of Europe because of concerns over humane treatment of animals. Recently, several states in the United States have enacted laws to phase out hog crates.)

Frank carried the piglet outside, tossed it onto a compost pile, and covered it, explaining that the piglet would decompose in about 48 hours. As if to prove his point, he picked out a small bone from the pile and easily snapped it in half. "Last week we had a 400-pound sow die that we threw on the compost pile. It should be gone within a week or two."

As Frank lectured us on how "the two best things to happen to a pig in my lifetime are grates and crates," a worker entered the nursery and picked up the latest litter, notched their ears (for identification), clipped their tales, filed their teeth, and castrated the males. Unwanted bits of pig anatomy fell through the grated floor.

"The tails are clipped because the other pigs would bite at them. This can cause infection, and if that happens you have to use antibiotics." Picking up a piglet and prying open its mouth, Frank pointed to a couple of long sharp teeth. "Do you see these little guys? Can you imagine what that feels like when he is biting down on a nipple? And [pointing to a group of piglets fighting over a nipple] do you see what they are doing? If we didn't blunt those teeth the piglets would injure each other and mama. Have you ever had bacon from a boar? You'd sure know it if you had, castrating them gives the meat a better flavor."

Our next stop was a small room off the central corridor, where Frank explained that hogs are highly vulnerable to diseases. Many operations feed them antibiotics as part of their diet. But growing concerns over human immunity to antibiotics have led the pork industry to reduce their usage. Frank added that humans sometimes transmit diseases to pigs, which explains why we had to shower and change clothes. To further assure us about minimizing the use of antibiotics, Frank opened a refrigerator door and pointed to a couple of bottles. "These are all we use."

As we proceeded down the corridor, and looked into each room, the pigs and pens got larger. As they grow operators transfer pigs to the next room, until they reach slaughter weight of about 250 pounds. A truck picks them up from the final room at the end of the corridor and takes them to a slaughterhouse.

The corridor marked the end of our tour, and we returned to the changing rooms, showered, put our own clothes back on, and returned to the "unclean side." As Frank cheerfully waived good-bye, he called out, "I've been around pigs for more than 50 years, and from a human perspective this is by far the best place I've ever been. Go out and have some pepperoni pizza—it's got pig on it." No one had pepperoni that night, but one of us did have a ham sandwich for supper (Broadway fieldnotes, April 18, 2002).

Michael Broadway

FIGURE 4.1 Hogs in a modern confinement facility.

THE ESSENCE OF PIG

Despite Frank's enthusiasm, raising pigs is not easy. In confined quarters they can easily infect one another with everything from influenza to roundworms (Skaggs 1986:148). Humans may "sweat like pigs," but pigs don't—they lack sweat glands and can die of heat prostration. As they grow, pigs become less tolerant of heat. When temperatures rise above 86°F (30°C), and pigs have no clean mud holes or shelter, they wallow in their own feces and urine to avoid heat stroke. Despite such fragilities, hogs were the major source of meat for Americans from colonial times until the 1950s, when beef overtook pork (Harris 1985).

There is no such thing as a hogboy, and no wistful ballads about rounding up piggies on the open range, but hogs have always been a more valuable source of meat than cattle. A piglet needs three to five pounds of feed to gain one pound; a calf needs 10 pounds. Four months after insemination, a sow will give birth to a litter of 10 or more piglets, and within six months they are ready for market. Beef cattle, by contrast, have a nine-month gestation period and produce a single calf, which will not reach slaughter weight for well over a year. "The whole essence of pig," according to Marvin Harris (1985:67), "is the production of meat for human nourishment and delectation."

Michael Broadway

FIGURE 4.2 Hogs being raised "the old-fashioned way"; note the shelters in the background.

THE ROAD TO PORKOPOLIS

As pioneers settled the Midwest after the American Revolution, the center of livestock production moved westward. Every farmer kept hogs, which usually ran free and scavenged for their own food. During the summer, hogs foraged on wild roots, vegetables, berries, and native grasses, and in the fall they survived on acorns and other nuts. Corn-fed hogs put on weight more rapidly, tasted better, and brought a better price at market than those fattened on nuts and roots. Farmers usually rounded up their surplus hogs in the autumn and fed them on corn for several weeks before driving them to market (Clemen 1923). Market price was based on the weight of the animal—the larger the hog the higher the price. Heavier hogs were believed to yield the highest quality pork, and the bigger and fatter the hog, the more lard it produced. Pig fat was rendered into lard, which was a major source of oil for lamps until it was replaced by kerosene in the 1870s.

Elisha Mills opened Cincinnati's first meatpacking plant in 1818, and the "Queen City of the West" dominated pork packing until the Civil War. Writing in 1845, a local journalist pontificated:

> The putting up of pork has been so important a branch of business in our city for five and twenty years, as to have constituted its largest item of manufacture and acquired for it the soubriquet of Porkopolis.... Our pork business is the largest in the world (Clemen 1923:95).

Cincinnati's location on the Ohio River gave it access to rich farming country and provided a ready means to ship pork to New Orleans and beyond. By 1844, Porkopolis had 26 packinghouses; a decade later 42.

Early winter is still known in the rural South as "hog-killing time." Winter was the farmer's ice box, and meatpacking remained a seasonal activity until the development of refrigeration after the Civil War. Pork packing usually began in November and ended when the supply of hogs ran out or it warmed up, whichever came first. Warm weather halted slaughter at the packinghouses because the meat would soon spoil. Frigid temperatures also shut down operations, since the buildings were unheated.

Workers drove hogs into a pen next to the slaughterhouse and dispatched them with a blow to the head. A dragline pulled dead or stunned animals into a "sticking room," where workers slit their throats. They hung fresh carcasses by their hind legs to drain, then dipped them into boiling water and laid them out on a table. A crew of workers, each with his own task, then set about cleaning the carcass. Some furiously pulled out handfuls of hair and bristles, while others scraped the skin with knives. An experienced crew of six could clean a carcass in 20 seconds!

Three "luggers" then carried the carcass to the next station and hung it on a hook for the "gutter" to remove its entrails and let them drop to the floor, which was covered in sawdust to absorb blood and other body fluids.

> Once cleaned and gutted, the carcass was hauled to the cooling room, which was often little more than a well-ventilated section of the warehouse into which the freezing-cold winter wind penetrated.

It remained there for twenty-four hours. When it was thoroughly chilled, a cutter severed the head with a cleaver; chopped off the feet, legs, and knee joints; split the carcass; and cut up the balance into hams, shoulders and "middles."... A four-hundred-pound hog usually was reduced to two hundred pounds of pork and forty pounds of lard. Blood-soaked sawdust, entrails, and other unwanted body parts were swept up at the end of the day and dumped into the Ohio River (Skaggs 1986:39).

Cuts of pork rubbed with salt and soaked in vats of brine or vinegar sat for several days. Meat had to be carefully cooled before being placed in the pickling mixture, otherwise the vinegar fermented and the meat could develop botulism. Meat inspection was purely voluntary and conducted by company workers.

A visitor to Cincinnati in December 1851 wrote with admiration that the city was:

crowded almost to suffocation, with droves of hogs, and draymen employed in delivering the barreled pork on board of steamers. Some 1,500 laborers are employed in the business from six to eight weeks, and in many cases it is kept in full operation both day and night, including Sundays, from the beginning to the completion of the season (Clemen 1923:97).

Pork shipped to the Caribbean and Europe accounted for 10 percent of America's foreign trade by the late 1870s. This market collapsed in 1880, when several European countries banned U.S. pork imports for fear American pork contained the parasitic nematode that causes trichinosis. The ban was not lifted until 1890 when the federal government introduced inspection for meat intended for export. It would be another decade before federal inspection was required for meat sold to Americans, however.

Chicago replaced Cincinnati as America's meatpacking capital during the Civil War. Railroads radiating from the city linked it to the emerging Corn Belt, where more and more hogs were raised. They could then be speedily shipped to the city's stockyards and slaughterhouses (Clemen 1923; Skaggs 1986). For nearly a century thereafter, Chicago remained, in Carl Sandburg's (1916) words:

Hog Butcher for the World,
Tool Maker, Stasher of Wheat,
Player with Railroads and the Nation's Freight Handler;
Stormy, husky, brawling,
City of the Big Shoulders.

HOG HEAVEN OR HELL?

The Corn Belt extends from Ohio to eastern Nebraska. Its highly productive soils, reliable rainfall, and bountiful supplies of corn made it the center of hog production in the United States from the second half of the nineteenth century until the latter part of the twentieth. Raising hogs was until recently viewed as a relatively easy way for farmers to obtain cash with minimal investment, and hogs earned the nickname of "mortgage burner" (Strange & Hassebrook 1981).

In 1976, the typical Corn Belt hog farm averaged 320 acres, met 75 percent of its own feed requirements, and produced 650 slaughter hogs. The farmer and his family provided most of the labor, collecting animal waste on site and spreading it as a fertilizer on crops and pasture (Van Arsdall & Gilliam 1979). Thirty-five years later, most of these farms have disappeared, to be replaced by large confinement operations producing hogs under contract to transnational processing firms (see Figure 1.2). And hog production has dispersed from Corn Belt states to North Carolina, Oklahoma, and Utah.

Antibiotics have reduced hog vulnerability to disease and allowed them to be raised in climate-controlled buildings with automated feeding and manure systems. Confinement facilities require substantial capital investments on the part of growers, but mechanization allows many more animals to be raised with fewer workers. Proponents of this method of pork production claim that the system is driven by consumer preference for a uniform low-cost product. Factory farms meet this demand through maintaining low labor costs, supplying hogs from the same genetic stock, and using uniform feeding practices.

Critics charge that the supposed superior feed conversion made possible by antibiotics, nutritional supplements, and climate-controlled facilities have been offset by the "stress" hogs experience in confinement, which, in turn, leads to lower feed conversion and weight gain. Newborn piglets suffer higher mortality rates when raised in large operations rather than in traditional farms, a difference attributed to the lack of attention to individual animals in hog "factories" (Strange & Hassebrook 1981). Moreover, the displacement of family hog farms by confinement operations has a disastrous impact on rural economies. Studies conducted in Missouri indicate that although a $5 million investment in contract production generates 40 to 50 new jobs, it displaces nearly three times that number of independent hog producers (Ikerd 1998). Having fewer farmers translates into fewer persons to support local businesses and a decline in tax receipts. Studies in Illinois, Iowa, Michigan, and Wisconsin have confirmed this finding (Donham et al. 2007).

The transition from family farming to corporate hog production is most evident in North Carolina. A fivefold increase in hog output between 1982 and 1997 catapulted North Carolina into second place behind Iowa. But as the number of hogs in North Carolina leapt from 2 million to 9.6 million during this period, the number of hog farms in the state plummeted from 11,400 to about 3,000 (U.S. Census Bureau 1984; USDA NASS 1999b). The 2007 Agricultural Census showed that 99.3 percent of the state's 10 million hogs were produced on just 1,600 farms (USDA 2009).

The state's rapid assent in hog production is a result of a combination of "governmental, entrepreneurial, and local market factors" (Foruseth 1997:395). As early as 1960, the North Carolina Department of Agriculture and North Carolina State University identified swine production as a desirable replacement for tobacco as a cash crop. To that end, state government provided funds for swine research, while the extension service touted the benefits of hog raising and helped farmers become established in the industry. The mild winter climate of southeastern North Carolina helps feed conversion: compared to their counterparts in the Midwest, North Carolina hog farmers save eight to 16 ounces of feed per pound of weight gain (Ibid.).

North Carolina enacted tax incentives for the pork industry and provided a friendly regulatory environment, due largely to the efforts of one state legislator, Wendell Murphy. During his 10 years in the North Carolina legislature, Murphy, a Democrat from Duplin County, cosponsored or supported a series of measures promoting the hog industry, which coincidently helped his own company become the nation's largest hog producer. He promoted the industry despite apparent conflicts of interest. In the words of the Pulitzer Prize-winning journalists who broke the story: "Members of the General Assembly are allowed to make money off the bills they introduce, the amendments they offer and the votes they cast—as long as they can say their financial interests didn't cloud their judgment" (Stith & Warrick 1995).

The legislation exempted hog farms from local zoning and minimum-wage regulations. It also banned workers from organizing unions. Murphy followed the lead of the poultry industry and contracted with local farmers to raise his hogs. North Carolina farmers were already familiar with contract poultry production, and financial and technical support from state agencies provided further incentive. In 1982, when Murphy entered the legislature, his home county of Duplin had about 142,000 hogs; a decade later it produced more than a million—most of these animals belonged to Murphy Family Farms (Stith & Warrick 1995). His company has since been bought out by Smithfield Farms. Today, the county is the nation's leading hog producer, with a population of over 2.3 million animals (North Carolina Department of Agriculture & Consumer Services 2010).

The average hog generates about 1.5 tons of solid manure and 5,270 gallons of liquid manure each year—2.5 times that of the average human (Grey 2000:170; Alberta Agriculture 2000). The industry's solution to this problem has been to pump manure slurry from underneath confinement facilities and store it in waste lagoons, which use plastic liners to prevent seepage. Water in the manure evaporates and bacterial action breaks down the remaining material to make it safe when applied to fields as fertilizer. If the concentration is higher than the nutrient absorption rates of soils and crops, the waste runs off into waterways and causes groundwater pollution.

Surplus manure in hundreds of U.S. counties has led to public efforts to curtail livestock expansion (Haley, Jones, & Southard 1998). The leaders in this fight have been environmental groups such as the Sierra Club, Waterkeeper Alliance, and the Natural Resources Defense Council. Following several lawsuits, in 2008 the U.S. Environmental Protection Agency (EPA) began requiring confined animal feeding operations (CAFOs) to submit manure management plans as part of Clean Water Act permit applications. In its press release announcing the new rule, the EPA (2008) boldly predicted that the new regulations would "prevent 56 million pounds of phosphorus, 110 million pounds of nitrogen, and 2 billion pounds of sediment from entering streams, lakes, and other waters annually."

Despite these new rules, hog barn operators continue to foul the nation's waterways. In December 2010, a group of North Carolina environmental organizations announced it would sue the McLawhorn livestock farm for persistent dumping of hog waste into a tributary of the Neuse River (Waterkeeper Alliance 2010).

Lagoons threaten groundwater, and the odor they produce affects the health of those who work and live nearby. Airborne emissions from hog lagoons include ammonia, hydrogen sulfide, hundreds of volatile organic compounds, dust, and endotoxins that cause respiratory dysfunction in workers in hog-confinement facilities. The adverse health effects of the confinement environment have been documented in more than 70 studies conducted in the United States, Canada, Europe, and Australia (Donham et al. 2007). Neighbors of large swine facilities suffer elevated rates of tension, anger, fatigue, headaches, respiratory problems, eye irritation, nausea, sore throat, runny nose, and diarrhea (Schiffman et al. 1995; Thu et al. 1997; Wing & Wolf 2000; Horton et al. 2009). Children living on farms that raise hogs are at increased risk for asthma—the bigger the hog operation, the higher the prevalence of asthma (Merchant et al. 2005).

Lana and Barry Love, Alberta farmers who successfully opposed a 24,000-feeder-hog operation near their home, speak for many who live near hog barns:

> We raised pigs a few years ago. We drive by barns currently in production in this County and let me tell you pigs stink.... Don't tell us we won't smell those barns where we live. I don't want to have to spend the rest of my life in the house because I can't stand the smell of our own backyard. This stench will be with us 24 hours a day, seven days a week all year long. (Subdivision and Development Board Appeal Hearing, Flagstaff County, Alberta, October 19, 2000.) (See Chapter 10 for a detailed discussion of this hearing.)

A detailed analysis of 2,514 swine-confinement facilities in North Carolina found they were disproportionately located in poor, nonwhite communities where residents are dependent on local wells for their household water supply. These areas also had the highest disease rates and least access to health care in the state, which raised concerns that the poor and people of color bear a disproportionate burden of pollution (Wing, Cole, & Grant 2000). Not surprisingly, a study of North Carolina middle school student exposure to air emissions from swine-confinement operations found odor problems were far more common for schools in nonwhite and low-income areas (Mirabelli et al. 2006).

In response to widespread concern about the industry's threats to groundwater and public health, North Carolina imposed a statewide moratorium on constructing any new farms with 250 hogs or more in 1997. Two years later Hurricane Floyd struck North Carolina—and the shit literally hit the fan! Flood waters overran hundreds of hog farms, inundated at least 46 waste lagoons, causing some to break and threaten drinking water and aquatic ecosystems. An estimated 120 million gallons of hog waste and innumerable drowned hogs poured into the Tar, Cape Fear, Neuse, Roanoke, and Pamlico Rivers (Food & Water Watch 2010).

The response to this environmental calamity was an agreement between state government and North Carolina's largest pork producer, Smithfield Farms, to fund research into "environmentally superior technologies" for manure disposal. In 2007, the state legislature made its moratorium on building new hog lagoons permanent. But the promised alternatives to manure lagoons have yet to materialize because the moratorium allows existing systems to continue to operate so long as they are in compliance with their initial permit (National Hog Farmer 2007). Thus, it will be some time before operators replace old lagoons, and North Carolinians will continue to suffer from health and environmental problems arising from the industry's concentration of hog farms.

Confronted by higher operational costs and growing opposition from local residents in densely settled areas of North America, the pork industry has gone in search of greener pastures.

MISS PIGGY'S NEW FRONTIERS

O, Canada

A 1998 study of hog production in North America and selected European and South American countries found the lowest costs in Canada's eastern prairie provinces of Manitoba and Saskatchewan (Martin, Kruja, & Alexiou 1998). Part of the region's comparative advantage stemmed from a 1995 decision to eliminate a federal transportation subsidy for grain farmers. The so-called Crow rate was established in 1897 to underwrite the cost to farmers of shipping their grain to Canadian ports. But in the early 1990s, a large federal budget deficit, concerns that the subsidy discouraged the establishment of regional processing facilities, and fears that it violated the North American Free Trade Agreement (NAFTA), led the Canadian government to remove it. Now that farmers must pay the full cost of shipping grain by rail, they prefer to avoid this cost and sell to local livestock producers (Ramsey & Everitt 2001).

Manitoba, with a little more than one million inhabitants who live mostly in and around its capital city of Winnipeg, was the first prairie province to see the economic potential of a livestock industry based on local feed grains. In late 1995, the province's agriculture minister proposed doubling Manitoba's pork production in five years, hoping to replace Ontario and Quebec as the capital of Canada's swine industry. He proposed replacing the province's "single desk" with an "open market" system that would allow processors to contract with individual producers to supply them with hogs. The old single-desk system had only one buyer of live hogs in the province, Manitoba Pork, which set the price for hogs and allocated them to slaughterhouses. The company guaranteed farmers the same price for the same quality of animal, regardless of how many they sold. But in an open market where processors receive individual contracts, producers who can supply large numbers of hogs have a clear advantage over smaller producers in negotiating price (Boyens 2001).

To illustrate the negative impact of contract growing on small producers, opponents of open markets cited North Carolina's experience. Between 1982 and 1997, the number of its farms with fewer than 100 hogs declined from 9,149 to 1,239, while North Carolina farms with at least 1,000 animals more than tripled (U.S. Census Bureau 1984; USDA NASS 1999a). Despite this concern, Manitoba Pork's monopoly was eliminated in 1996. Processors found it easier and cheaper to contract with large producers and so, not surprisingly, the number of hog farmers declined. But this drop is part of a much larger structural change. In 1976, the province had more than 6,000 hog producers; 35 years later fewer than 750 remain in business. Production has concentrated among 100 or so highly capitalized operations that produce feeder pigs and slaughter hogs for sale in the United States. And just like their counterparts in North Carolina, these "farms" are limited to a small geographic area—a 45-minute drive southeast of Winnipeg (Statistics Canada n.d.b)

The industry's expansion was predicated on low production costs, along with the export of feeder pigs, slaughter hogs, and pork to the United States. Thanks to improved genetics and breeding, Canadian pig production soared 79 percent from 1995 to 2008 (Canadian Pork Council 2009). The number of live hogs exported rose from about one million in 2004 to a record 10 million in 2007, while the value of pork exports went from $288 million to $1 billion (Canadian Pork Council n.d.).

All seemed right with the world until a steady rise in the value of the Canadian dollar against the U.S. dollar, from about 62 cents in 2002 to $1.10 in November 2007, sharply eroded the comparative cost advantage Canadian hog producers had enjoyed. Then, in 2008 the cost of U.S. corn, a major feed constituent, shot up due to U.S. ethanol subsidies. A year later, the United States introduced country-of-origin labeling (COOL) for meat and other food products, a move immediately challenged by Canada and Mexico at the World Trade Organization (WTO). Under COOL, pigs that begin and spend a part of their life in Canada and are then exported as live animals to the United States for finishing or slaughter must be labeled as *Product of the United States and Canada*. While labeling costs little, retailers must be able to verify the labels presented to consumers. This means segregating hogs originating in Canada, and their meat, from animals born, raised, and slaughtered in the United States. This segregation must take place all along the supply chain, which adds to production costs, and according to the Canadian government, COOL puts their hog producers at a competitive disadvantage (Sawka & Kerr 2011). In May 2011 the WTO released a preliminary report agreeing with Canada and Mexico that COOL presents an impediment to trade. The final ruling is due in September 2011, but the full ramifications of the decision will not be known for some time to come.

Michael Broadway

FIGURE 4.3 The old and the new on the prairies of Canada. Behind the bison is a hog barn belonging to Stomp Pork Farm Limited, which filed for bankruptcy in 2008. At one time Stomp Pork owned 27,000 sows, giving it the capacity to produce over half a million pigs a year.

These factors combined to put more Canadian hog farmers out of business. From 2006 to 2010, the number of producers in Manitoba fell by 41 percent; in Saskatchewan by 69 percent; and in Alberta by 50 percent. In all, 2,340 producers went belly up across the prairies in this five-year period. Despite various government programs designed to salvage the industry, the number of producers continues to fall. This Darwinian survival of the fittest model has dropped the number of Canadian hog farmers by 56,000, or 88 percent, since 1976 (Canadian Pork Council n.d.b).

Pigs Get Fat, Hogs Get Slaughtered

By 2005, Manitoba had replaced Ontario and Quebec as Canada's hog capital. The increased availability of hogs, combined with the removal of single-desk selling, enabled the province to attract a state-of-the-art pork processing plant to Brandon (2006 pop. 41,511), 120 miles west of Winnipeg. Maple Leaf Foods, a Canadian transnational company, paid the city $1.00 for 12 acres on which to build its plant. It also received $12 million (Canadian) from the city and province to construct a wastewater treatment facility. The plant opened in the fall of 1999 and became fully operational at the end of 2002. A second shift was added in 2008, enabling its 2,350 employees to slaughter more than 4.5 million hogs a year.

The provincial government was so anxious to get the Maple Leaf plant up and running that it waived Clean Environment Commission hearings on the impact of its effluent on the Assiniboine River—a violation of provincial law. Concerned citizens then organized their own hearings on the "environmental, economic, social and public health aspects surrounding industrial-scale hog production and processing" before an independent chair and six commissioners (Ramsey & Everitt 2001). For two-and-a-half days, the authors of this book and numerous others testified on the social and economic changes that accompany large meat processing facilities and the environmental impact of industrial hog production.

Within two years of the plant's opening, Maple Leaf began recruiting in Mexico. By 2010, 60 percent of the plant's labor force came from Mexico, El Salvador, Ukraine, China, Colombia, Mauritius, and other countries. Most came as temporary foreign workers, but have since applied for permanent residency and family reunification (Bucklaschuk 2008). The number of temporary foreign workers and family members living in Brandon rose from none in 2002 to more than 5,000 in 2010. As we predicted, the influx of newcomers and their families created a shortage of affordable housing, the need for English as a Second Language instruction and translation services, as well as greater pressure on the health care delivery system (Annis & Ashton 2010; Carter 2010).

With Maple Leaf's arrival, Brandon joined a growing number of similar communities—Dodge City, Garden City, and Liberal in Kansas; Lexington and Grand Island in Nebraska; Storm Lake and Columbus Junction in Iowa; Guymon in Oklahoma; Mayfield and Sebree in Kentucky; and Brooks in Alberta. Despite the great distance and divergent historical and cultural traditions that separate them, these towns face similar challenges: growth, often rapid and explosive; population mobility; dramatic increases in cultural and linguistic diversity; escalating crime, health, and social problems; strains on infrastructure and social services. These challenges stem from a common source: the meat and poultry processing industry's hunger for low-wage workers.

5

※

Is Meat Murder?

I was having lunch recently with a friend, and asked what he was going to order. Despite his wife and daughter being mainly vegetarian, my friend's a meat eater. So I was surprised when he vehemently declared that, whatever he was going to order, it wouldn't be a pig. "Why not," I asked. "Because pigs play videogames," he said. He liked the taste of pork, he explained, but he couldn't bear to order it after reading an online article about how researchers at Pennsylvania State University's College of Agricultural Sciences taught pigs to play a simple videogame that rewards the pigs with food for matching similar shapes. "I think of them using their little hoofs to move the joysticks, and I just can't do it," my friend said. "I can't eat them anymore."

Lisa Smedman (2008)

On January 30, 2008, the Humane Society of the United States (HSUS) sent a video to the *Washington Post* and then uploaded it onto its Web site. Taken with a hidden camera in the fall of 2007 at the Westland/Hallmark Meat Company slaughterhouse in Chino, California, this footage showed workers using electric prods on cows unable to stand on their own (called "downers"), ramming them with forklifts to get them to stand for inspection, and spraying high-pressure water into their nostrils (Nocera 2008).

Federal law requires humane handling and slaughtering of livestock. Cattle must be able to walk into the slaughterhouse, and U.S. Department of Agriculture (USDA) guidelines banned the slaughter of most downed cattle for human consumption because their inability to stand may be a symptom of what is commonly called mad cow disease. If, however, animals were cleared by federal inspectors and later fell down, they could be slaughtered. Responding to public outrage, the secretary of agriculture called for an investigation and the USDA suspended operations at Westland/Hallmark, while the company fired the two workers caught on film and suspended their supervisor. The district attorney later charged the workers with felony animal cruelty and misdemeanors but did not prosecute the company.

On February 17, 2008, the Food Safety and Inspection Service (FSIS) announced Hallmark/Westland was "voluntarily" recalling more than 143 million pounds of raw and frozen beef products, which it concluded were unfit for human consumption because they had not been properly inspected. This was the largest beef recall in U.S. history. Hallmark/Westland was the second largest supplier of ground beef to the National School Lunch Program, and an estimated 37 million pounds of the recalled beef had gone to schools. Because the recall involved beef that had been sold over the past two years, federal officials believed most of the recalled meat had already been eaten (Moreno 2008; Salvage 2008a). In May 2008, the USDA eliminated exceptions to its ban on the slaughter of downers (Burke 2010).

A year later, Hallmark/Westland was out of business. Looking back, one industry observer called the video and its aftermath "a watershed event that changed the discussion about animal well-being. It was the first time the activists were able to tie animal well-being to food safety" (Johnston 2009:12). It had done so with graphic images of downer cows being cruelly forced to their deaths, their flesh, possibly diseased, to be fed to unsuspecting American school children. This and subsequent videos of inhumane treatment of farmed animals have become the most effective weapon in the animal protectionists' arsenal.

Speaking at its fourth annual Taking Action for Animals Conference in July 2008, five months after the recall, Wayne Pacelle, president and CEO of the Humane Society of the United States, told 800 attendees that "We have arrived! We are in the mainstream!" (Miller 2008). So it would seem.

Founded in 1954, the Humane Society of the United States has been called the National Rifle Association of the animal rights movement—it is rich, powerful, and politically connected (Johnston 2009:17). With net assets of more than $111 million, and "backed by 11 million Americans, or one in every 28," the organization calls itself

> America's mainstream force against cruelty, exploitation and neglect, as well as the most trusted voice extolling the human-animal bond.... The HSUS promotes eating with conscience and embracing the Three Rs— reducing the consumption of meat and other animal-based foods; refining the diet by eating products only from animals who have been raised, transported, and slaughtered in a system of humane, sustainable agriculture that does not abuse animals; and replacing meat and other animal-based foods in the diet with plant-based foods. (http://www.humanesociety.org)

Its litigation department is staffed by 13 lawyers, who, at any one time, are pursuing 30–40 cases focused on four main topics: animal cruelty; hunting; fur; and farm animals (Hubbart 2009:28).

Derided as "humaniacs" by their critics, the Humane Society of United States, People for the Ethical Treatment of Animals (PETA), Mercy for Animals, and Compassion Over Killing are doing more than releasing videos to the press. They are reshaping how Americans think about nonhuman animals and the laws that govern our treatment of and relations with them.

ANIMAL LIBERATION

"[T]o discriminate against beings solely on account of their species is a form of prejudice, immoral and indefensible in the same way that discrimination on the basis of race is immoral and indefensible." Making this argument, philosopher Peter Singer (2002:243) ushered in the modern animal rights movement with the publication of *Animal Liberation* in 1975. Singer, a bioethicist who holds distinguished professorships at Princeton University and the University of Melbourne, is cofounder of the Great Ape Project, an international effort to gain basic rights to life, liberty, and protection from torture for chimpanzees, gorillas, bonobos, and orangutans. In the preface to *Animal Liberation*, Singer condemns "the tyranny of human over nonhuman animals. This tyranny has caused and today is still causing an amount of pain and suffering that can only be compared with that which resulted from the centuries of tyranny by white humans over black humans" (Ibid.:xx). Singer's goal is for humans to treat other animals as sentient beings, not as means to human ends.

As a proponent of the utilitarian school of moral philosophy, Singer maintains that "the interests of every being affected by an action are to be taken into account and given the same weight as the like interests of any other being.... black or white, masculine or feminine, human or nonhuman" (Ibid.:5). But what is a "being" and what gives one "an interest ... to be taken into account and given the same weight"? Suffering.

Singer follows the reasoning of Jeremy Bentham, the English philosopher and founder of utilitarianism, who, in the late eighteenth and early nineteenth centuries, advocated the separation of church and state, equal rights for women, decriminalization of homosexuality–and animal rights. In his *Introduction to the Principles of Morals and Legislation*, first published in 1789, Bentham established the basic creed for the modern animal rights movement: "The day may come when the rest of the animal creation may acquire those rights which never could have been witholden from them but by the hand of tyranny.... The question is not, Can they reason? nor, Can they talk? but, Can they suffer?" (quoted in Singer 2002:7)

For Bentham, Singer, and all those who have championed animal rights, "The capacity for suffering—or more strictly, for suffering and/or enjoyment or happiness—is not just another characteristic like the capacity for language or higher mathematics" (Ibid.). It is indicative of sentience—the capacity to have feelings, which include not only felt sensations, such as pain, but emotional states, such as fear and joy (DeGrazia 2002:40). And if animals feel pain, then "there can be no moral justification for regarding the pain (or pleasure) that animals feel as less important than the same amount of pain (or pleasure) felt by humans" (Singer 2002:15).

Whether all animals are sentient is a matter of debate, but there is little doubt that sentience is a characteristic of all vertebrates, and probably in some invertebrates as well (DeGrazia 2002:18–19). Regardless of where this line may be drawn, Singer (2002:8) claims that: "If a being suffers there can be no moral justification for refusal to take that suffering into consideration.... [and] the principle of equality requires that its suffering be counted equally with the like suffering ... of any other being." Thus, animal suffering must be no less important than human suffering, and human animals must give equal moral weight to the interests of nonhuman animals. To do otherwise is to be guilty of "speciesism."

"To avoid speciesism," Singer (19) says, "we must allow that beings who are similar in all relevant respects have a similar right to life—and mere membership in our biological species cannot be a morally relevant criterion for this right." Therefore, as the opening chapter in *Animal Liberation* boldly declares: "All Animals Are Equal." Or as Ingrid Newkirk, president of People for the Ethical Treatment of Animals, has famously said: "When it comes to feelings like hunger, pain, and thirst, a rat is a pig is a dog is a boy."

TWENTY-FIRST CENTURY ABOLITIONISTS

The Humane Society of the United States may be the movement's NRA, but People for the Ethical Treatment of Animals (PETA) is the most visible, most outrageous, and certainly the most feared wing of the animal rights movement. PETA came to our attention—and much of the nation's—in the summer of 1990, as we began our research on the impact of the new IBP beef plant on Lexington, Nebraska. The blazing heat that gripped south-central Nebraska got even hotter when singer k.d. lang appeared one morning on our television screen in a news story about a promotional spot for PETA's "Meat Stinks" campaign. Hugging a cow named Lulu, she declared: "We all love animals, but why do we call some of them pets and some of them dinner? If you knew how meat was made, you'd probably lose your lunch. I know; I'm from cattle country— that's why I became a vegetarian. Meat stinks, and not just for animals but for human health and the environment." The National Cattlemen's Association vehemently denied lang's allegations, and country and western radio stations across cattle country pulled her songs. The sign reading "Hometown of k.d. lang" on the outskirts of her birthplace in Alberta, Canada, was burned. The spot never actually aired on television; the extensive news coverage it received gave PETA the exposure it wanted without costing it a dime.

Founded in 1980, PETA claims two million members and supporters and bills itself as the largest animal rights organization in the world. With total revenues exceeding $34 million in 2009, and affiliates in the United Kingdom, Germany, the Netherlands, India, and Hong Kong, it may well be. PETA's brash and outlandish protests and campaigns, often featuring celebrities, have made it among the best known and most successful radical organizations in America. "We are complete media sluts," admits Ingrid Newkirk, PETA's cofounder and president. "It is our obligation. We would be worthless if we were just polite and didn't make waves" (Specter 2003:57). Polite, certainly not. Make waves; tsunamis are more like it.

In the 1980s and 1990s, Chris P. Carrot handed out buttons in Des Moines, Iowa, telling children to "Eat your veggies, not your friends," and Charlotte the

Chicken danced and waved to traffic in Wichita, Kansas. In 2010, one week after BP's Deepwater Horizon oil rig exploded in the Gulf of Mexico, causing the biggest oil spill in U.S. history, PETA flew a banner over downtown Mobile, Alabama, blaming the disaster on consumers: "Meat on your grill = Oil spill. PETA" (Riggs 2010). In between came "Holocaust on Your Plate," a traveling exhibit that juxtaposed photographs of emaciated inmates in Nazi concentration camps with chickens in cages, and "Kentucky Fried Cruelty," a campaign that organized thousands of protests at KFC restaurants. As part of this campaign, PETA also produced a video depicting broiler production and processing narrated by actress Pamela Anderson, who is also featured in PETA's "I'd Rather Go Naked than Wear Fur" campaign (Smith 2010).

Public protests and provocative banners and billboards are the most visible weapons in PETA's arsenal. But PETA also purchases shares in companies, such as Walmart, McDonald's, and Cracker Barrel, so it can submit shareholder resolutions. And it negotiates behind the scenes to convince companies and their suppliers to adopt practices it considers less cruel in the production and slaughter of farm animals. In 2007, under pressure from PETA, the Humane Society, and other organizations, CKE Restaurants, which owns the Hardee's and Carl's Jr. chains, began purchasing eggs and pork from suppliers that do not keep animals in cages or crates (Salter 2007).

In 2002, PETA began campaigning to replace the conventional method of poultry slaughter with what it considers a more humane and pain-free method: controlled-atmosphere killing. The conventional method, called electric immobilization, and still the industry norm, involves shackling live birds upside down on a moving conveyor, running them through an electrically charged water bath to immobilize them, mechanically slitting their throats, then defeathering them in tanks of scalding-hot water. Controlled-atmosphere killing removes oxygen from the birds' atmosphere while they are still in their transport crates, slowly replacing it with inert gasses. The birds should be dead before they are removed from their crates, shackled, bled, and defeathered. The USDA has approved the controlled-atmosphere method, employed with growing frequency in Europe, but American firms have been reluctant to adopt it, in part because of disagreement among researchers over the best mixtures of gas to use (Grandin & Johnson 2010:213). Some restaurant chains, such as Burger King, offer purchasing preference for birds killed by this method (PETA n.d.).

PETA directs much of its publicity toward children and youth. PETAKiDS.com targets preteens and PETA2.com appeals to adolescents and youth with age-specific Web games and contests, teen celebrity endorsements, clothing, stickers and stencils, magazines, vegetarian-starter kits, free curriculum materials and home-work packets, message boards, speakers and program leaders. As one example, in PETAKiDS.com's Super Chick Sisters game: "Princess Pamela Anderson has been captured by evil Ronald McDonald, who plans on making her a part of his unhappy meals along with the chicken tortured for McDonald's restaurants. Help free Princess Pam and save the chickens from McDonald's cruelty." The screen below the game's window directs viewers to: "Find out more about how McDonald's tortures chickens and what you can do about it."

On PETA2, the Web site for young adults, you can: "Join peta2's Street Team to Earn Free Shirts, Pins, and Other Merch for Helping Animals! It's All Free! ... Whether you're interested in taking part in **protests**, setting up an **info table** at a concert, signing **petitions**, or educating your friends **online**, we're here to support your passion to make the world a kinder place" (PETA2.com, bold signifies hyperlinks).

Or you could do what a PETA Street Team youth outreach worker did in 2005. Christopher Garnett legally changed his name to KentuckyFriedCruelty. com: "People don't believe me at first when I tell them my name, but it never fails to spark a discussion." (Associated Press 2005).

It is no wonder that those whose livelihoods derive from the use of animals, whether for food, entertainment, or clothing, call PETA a cult of hardcore wackos, but to those in the animal rights movement, they are foot soldiers in the Army of the Kind (Newkirk 2009). Although these soldiers won't win the war to abolish "animal slavery" in their lifetimes, they are certainly winning a good many battles.

"NATURE IS CRUEL, BUT WE DON'T HAVE TO BE"

According to *The PETA Practical Guide to Animal Rights* (Newkirk 2009:18–19): "People who support animal rights believe that animals are not ours to use for food, clothing, entertainment, experimentation, or any other purpose and that animals deserve consideration and what is in their best interests, ... while supporters of the animal welfare movement believe that animals can be used and even killed for purposes as long as 'humane' guidelines are followed." What Ingrid Newkirk is to animal rights, Temple Grandin is to animal welfare. Both their stories have been told on HBO: the 2007 documentary *I Am an Animal: The Story of Ingrid Newkirk and PETA* and the 2010 movie *Temple Grandin*, which cast Claire Danes in the title role, and won five Emmy Awards including Best Picture and Best Actress.

Grandin first attracted attention when Oliver Sacks featured her in the title essay of *An Anthropologist on Mars*, his 1995 collection of profiles of persons with neurological conditions. Diagnosed with autism as a child, she went on to become a professor of animal science at Colorado State University and one of the leading authorities on animal behavior in the world.

As a result of her autism, Grandin says she does not think in language, but rather in pictures, like animals. Her autism also makes her very sensitive to sensory stimuli and keenly aware of detail; characteristics she believes help her understand how animals experience their surroundings. Grandin has used her training and special insight to design equipment and procedures to dramatically improve animal handling and slaughter. Her handling techniques and equipment keep animals calm and reduce injury. Widely adopted around the world, her innovations have been so successful that half the cattle slaughtered in the United States and Canada are now handled with equipment she designed for meat plants (Saslow 2010).

A meat-eater, she maintains that "our relationship with the animals we use for food must be symbiotic.... We provide the farm animals with food and housing and in return most of [them] are used for food.... Since people are responsible for breeding and raising farm animals, they must also take the responsibility to give the animals living conditions that provide a decent life and a painless death" (Grandin & Johnson 2010:297, 300). "Most people don't realize that the slaughter plant is much gentler than nature. Animals in the wild die from starvation, predators, or exposure. If I had a choice, I would rather go through a slaughter system than have my guts ripped out by coyotes or lions while I was still conscious. Unfortunately, most people never observe the natural cycle of birth and death. They do not realize that for one living thing to survive, another living thing must die" (Grandin 2006: 234–5).

Admired by the general public for transcending her autism, Temple Grandin is revered in the meat and poultry industry and respected by many concerned with animal protection as well. Who else could be named one of the 40 most influential people in the beef industry by *Beef Magazine* and a Visionary by the People for the Ethical Treatment of Animals in the same year!

CRUEL AND UNUSUAL PUNISHMENT

Humans have always killed animals, and with domestication comes the ability to control and manipulate certain species for the purpose of killing their members. Virtually every aspect of human life is at some point linked to the killing of animals—not just for food, but also for medical research, clothing, cosmetics, pet foods, recreation, animal control, and more (Animal Studies Group 2006:3–4). What is different now than in the past is the scale: more than 11 billion animals are slaughtered each year in industrial food production in the United States alone (Pacelle 2010:38). Even so, Americans care about animal welfare, or so they say. In a 2007 national telephone survey commissioned by the American Farm Bureau, 95 percent of respondents said it is "important to them how farm animals are cared for" and 76 percent said "animal welfare was more important than low meat prices" (Bjerklie 2007).

Concerns for animal welfare focus on three broad areas: basic health; natural living; and the affective state of the animals themselves. Do farmed animals have adequate food, water, and freedom from disease? Are they raised under conditions that recognize and accommodate their "natural" behaviors and needs? Do they experience pain and suffering as a consequence of production practices? (Koeleman 2010)

Farm animal welfare is not regulated in the United States until animals go to slaughter. Instead, the federal government relies on the stewardship of farmers and ranchers and industry-developed voluntary guidelines. Each major farm animal producer group has developed its own "science-based animal welfare guidelines." Audit and certification under these guidelines are voluntary (Lobo 2009:15). For example, under the banner of "We Care," the National Pork Producers Council ratified a Statement of Ethical Principles in 2008. According to these principles, producers must: produce safe food; safeguard natural resources in all industry practices; provide a work environment that is safe and consistent with the industry's other ethical principles; contribute to a better quality of life in communities; protect and promote animal well-being; and ensure practices to protect public health (Salvage 2008b). Laudable principles, all, but are members of the National Pork Producers Council living up to them? PETA and the Humane Society don't think so. And what exactly does it mean to protect and promote animal well-being, anyway? Especially when you are in the business of raising animals for food.

Ideas about animal-human relations, and thus what constitutes humane treatment of animals, are not universal. They are culturally embedded in occupations, localities, ethnicities, and religions. Judaic and Islamic religious precepts require that animals be well treated in life and death. Slaughter is a grave responsibility, an act of purification, a recognition of lives that are divinely given. *Shechita* and *halal* are religious proscriptions on methods of animal slaughter that help define Jewish and Muslim identities, as does *jhatka* for Sikhs. These methods of religious slaughter, which require slitting the animal's throat while it is conscious, have often been opposed by animal rights and welfare advocates, who have in turn been accused of anti-Semitism and racism. In contrast, secular methods of slaughter in the United States, Canada, and other Western countries, mandate that animals be rendered unconscious before they are killed (Burt 2006).

Slaughter of red meat animals in the United States is regulated by the Humane Methods of Slaughter Act of 1958, which states: "the slaughtering of livestock and the handling of livestock in connection with slaughter shall be carried out only by humane methods." Animals are supposed to be rendered insensible to pain "by a single blow or gunshot or an electrical, chemical or other means that is rapid and effective" (Jones 2008:29). A specific exemption is provided for ritual slaughter, and poultry are not covered by this Act. As amended in 1978, humane handling practices require access to water and feed, and limit the use of electric prods to move animals. The Act gives federal food safety inspectors the authority to withhold inspection, and thus stop production, if they observe cruel handling or improper slaughter practices. It also places equivalent regulations on the slaughter of imported meat (Ibid.:30).

Regulations are one thing; compliance with them is another. In the 1990s, an investigator for the Humane Farming Association uncovered widespread violations of the Humane Methods of Slaughter Act (Eisnitz 1997). And McDonald's sued two London Greenpeace activists for libel after they distributed a pamphlet called "What's wrong with McDonald's?" which claimed, among other things, that the corporation is responsible for torturing and murdering animals. The trial, which became known as the McLibel trial, ran for more than two years— the longest in British history. McDonald's stated that all the claims in the pamphlet were false. In the United States, the plaintiff must show that the accusations are libelous. In contrast, English law requires defendants to prove that they did not libel the complaining party. The Greenpeace activists, Dave Morris, a former postman, and Helen Steel, a gardener, had to prove the claims made in the pamphlet were true.

Denied legal aid, Morris and Steel defended themselves against McDonald's, which spent several million pounds on legal fees. The case drew widespread attention, none favorable to McDonald's. In June 1997, the judge handed down a 1,000-page decision that found Morris and Steel liable on several points—but not all. The judge ruled their allegations that McDonald's was to blame for starvation in the Third World, destruction of rainforests, and lying about their use of recycled paper were unjustified. But he did find that McDonald's exploited children with misleading advertising, paid low wages, and discouraged unions. It was also "culpably responsible for cruel practices in the rearing and slaughter of some of the animals which are used to produce [its] food" (quoted in Jones 2008:23). The judge awarded McDonald's 60,000 pounds in damages, but Morris and Steel could not, and would not, pay the fine. McDonald's did not pursue the settlement because it already had enough bad publicity. In 2005, the European Court of Human Rights ordered the United Kingdom to pay Steel and Morris 57,000 pounds ($103,000) for failure to provide a fair trial and protect their freedom of expression (see the film *McLibel* and http://www.mcspotlight.org).

As the Humane Farming Association's investigation of slaughterhouses and the McLibel case were beginning to raise public consciousness to issues of humane treatment and slaughter of farm animals, Temple Grandin was educating members of the meat and poultry industry on their need to improve the handling and slaughter of animals. In a 1996 audit of 24 federally inspected slaughterhouses in 10 states conducted for the USDA, she found that only 30 percent met requirements for adequately stunning cattle before slaughter (Jones 2008:23).

"CONFINED IS NOT KIND"

Even more disturbing to many than how farmed animals die is how they live. The Farm Animal Welfare Council (2003:2) has concluded that killing "may only be the final stressor in a sequence of equally or more stressful events" in the lives of industrially farmed animals. Practices prevalent in the meat and poultry industry foster what are called production diseases, which have become endemic: chickens bred for large breasts that suffer from leg problems; dairy cows bred for milk production that suffer from inflammation of the udder; animals kept in close confinement that develop obsessive, repetitive movements called stereotipies (Thompson 2008:307).

Animal protectionists are pushing the industry to abolish several longstanding practices they consider unnatural and the cause of great pain and suffering: close confinement of dairy calves in veal production; gestation and farrowing crates for hogs; beak trimming, forced molting, and confinement of laying hens to battery cages in egg production (Marcus 2005). In opposing these practices, they are finding common cause with environmental, citizen, and consumer groups who oppose farm animal confinement in general.

Veal calves were the first farm animal to attract the attention of the modern animal rights movement. As a byproduct of the dairy industry, the primary value

Michael Broadway

F I G U R E 5.1 Farrowing or gestation crates do not allow sows to turn around in their stall and are designed so piglets can suckle relatively easily. They are banned in the United Kingdom.

of male calves born to dairy cows is in the production of veal. Tethered or confined to stalls or hutches to restrict movement, fed a diet deficient in iron, and slaughtered at anywhere from a few days to 25 weeks of age, these calves produce a tender, pink flesh that commands a premium price in the market.

The vast majority of hogs that go to market in North America are raised indoors. Within these large "barns," breeding sows are confined to barren concrete stalls called gestation crates—they can stand up and lie down, but they cannot turn around. Not only do these crates severely restrict their mobility; they also maximize the number of animals per building and allow workers to better monitor each animal. Sows give birth in farrowing crates that have recessed pockets, called creep boxes, where piglets lie while nursing to prevent them from being crushed (Marcus 2005:28–30, 37–38; Grandin & Johnson 2010:176, 183).

The poultry industry recognizes two kinds of chickens: broilers raised for their meat, and layers raised for the eggs they produce. Although animal activists object to the living conditions imposed on both types of birds, they have concentrated their campaigns on three interrelated practices in egg production: close confinement in battery cages; forced molting; and beak trimming. Virtually all eggs produced in the United States—97 percent—come from hens that live in battery cages. According to guidelines established by the United Egg Producers, these stacked, interconnected wire cages must give each bird a minimum floor space of 67 square inches—roughly two-thirds the size of this book when it is open and lying flat. Not all growers follow these guidelines (Marsh 2010:WK3).

Maximizing the number of birds and minimizing the space they occupy is one way to cut costs and increase profits. Another is to extend their productive lives. Commercial laying hens' egg production peaks at about seven months of age, falling off gradually thereafter. For backyard chickens, molting naturally occurs in the fall. Old feathers fall out, new ones grow in, and hens stop laying eggs for a few weeks as their reproductive tracts rejuvenate. Commercial laying hens raised indoors in controlled environments do not naturally molt, but after about a year of continuous laying the number and quality of eggs they produce decline. Forced molting extracts a second or third year of egg laying. Molting, brought on by shorter days and stress, can be artificially induced by cutting the hours of light in houses each day and withholding food and water (Marcus 2005:21–22; Grandin & Johnson 2010:216).

The kinds of chickens used in egg production in the United States are aggressive when kept in close confinement, and pecking, feather pulling, and cannibalism can become serious problems. To reduce injury, the ends of chicks' beaks are trimmed or seared, in a process critics call "debeaking" or "beak searing." This process blunts chickens' beaks and reduces the damage birds can inflict on one another. It also makes it more difficult for them to eat and can, if done improperly, cause severe pain (Marcus 2005:16–17).

HAPPIER MEALS

Animal rights and animal welfare have become global issues, and corporations and governments are responding to calls for more humane treatment of farmed animals. Europe has been leading the way. In 1976, the 47 member states of the Council of Europe adopted the European Convention for the Protection of Animals Kept for Farming Purposes, which required that all farm animals be given care "appropriate to their physiological and ethological needs" (Matheny & Leahy 2007:339). In the 1997 Treaty of Amsterdam, the European Union (EU), now comprised of 27 countries, defined animals as sentient beings whose welfare should be given full regard. The EU has set minimum standards for farm animal husbandry, which include phasing out veal cages, swine gestation crates, and battery cages for laying hens (Block 2008). EU member states are free to adopt more stringent regulations, and some have done so. For example, Sweden requires stunning poultry before slaughter. It has also eliminated veal crates, sow gestation crates, battery cages, and beak trimming, and it has established strict limits on the number and density of animals in confinement (Matheny & Leahy 2007:341).

European food retailers have gone even further: Dutch branches of Aldi and Lidl supermarkets and Burger King and McDonald's have stopped selling pork from castrated pigs (Wilcox 2008). The Royal Society for the Prevention of Cruelty to Animals (RSPCA) now recognizes supermarkets in the United Kingdom for promoting animal welfare through its People's Choice Award, which allows shoppers to vote for the supermarket chain that has made the biggest strides in improving animal welfare. The 2009 winner was The Co-operative, which sells only free-range eggs and egg ingredients and meat and poultry certified under the RSPCA's Freedom Food animal welfare standards (Royal Society for the Prevention of Cruelty to Animals 2009).

Standards of farm animal welfare in the United States lag far behind those in Europe, but pressure has steadily mounted on the industry to improve its record on farm animal welfare and humane slaughter. In 1999, McDonald's began third-party audits of the slaughter practices of its meat suppliers and announced it would stop buying from those who repeatedly violated humane slaughter standards. Burger King followed in 2001. In the same year, restaurant and food industry trade associations accepted humane handling and slaughter standards set by the American Meat Institute and the National Chicken Council, but these standards are a far cry from what animal rights and welfare groups want. And it is these groups that are swaying the jury in the court of public opinion.

Although the federal government has resisted regulating farm animal welfare, several states have enacted laws to phase out hog gestation crates (Oregon and Florida), veal and hog crates (Arizona, California, Colorado, Maine), and give laying hens more space (California, Michigan, Ohio) (Marsh 2010). California has also banned importation of eggs from other states that have been produced in crowded cages.

Under pressure from consumer and animal advocacy groups, the American Veal Association has said it will phase out close confinement of calves (Eckholm 2010). In July 2011, the Humane Society of the United States and the United Egg Producers agreed to jointly petition Congress to enact a single national standard to expand space and improve environments for laying hens, ultimately moving from conventional cage housing to "enriched" colony housing (Smith 2011).

Although state governments are beginning to regulate production of farmed animals, the real push for reform is coming from food retailers who can put direct pressure on their suppliers. Burger King, Denny's, Carl's Jr., Golden Corral, Hardee's, Quiznos, and Subway now serve cage-free eggs. Walmart's and Costco's private labels use only cage-free eggs, and Helmann's mayonnaise is converting the 350 million eggs it uses annually to cage-free (Humane Society of the United States 2010). Burger King, Wolfgang Puck, and Carl's Jr. are committing to purchase portions of their pork from crate-free suppliers, with the goal to eventually rely exclusively on such sources. Smithfield Foods, the world's largest pork producer, promises to phase out gestation crates over ten years, and Canada's Maple Leaf Foods says it will do the same (Johnston 2008:17–18).

Fast-food chains are mandating improved standards for the care and slaughter of the animals they purchase. McDonald's has required producers that provide its eggs to ban forced molting by feed withdrawal and increase the space allocated to laying hens to 72 square inches per bird. It has ordered its beef suppliers to reduce use of electric cattle prods, and in slaughterhouses, it insists on the use of knock boxes designed by Temple Grandin, which make livestock more comfortable and calm when they are stunned. McDonald's mandates unannounced random third-party audits to ensure compliance, and producers who fail audits risk cancellation of their contracts. Its competitors are doing the same (Matheny & Leahy 2007:356).

For Chipotle Mexican Grill, "fresh is not enough anymore." Chipotle serves: "Food With Integrity … our commitment to finding the very best ingredients raised with respect for the animals, the environment and the farmers." Chipotle literally crows on its Web homepage that its meat comes from "naturally raised animals [that] are raised in a humane way, fed a vegetarian diet, never given hormones and allowed to display their natural tendencies" (http://www.chipotle.com/en-US/fwi/animals). Local restaurants are going the chains one better. At an upscale restaurant in Lawrence, Kansas, the menu proudly tells the diner that "We've been to many of the farms, we've been to the slaughterhouses, we know many of the people who raise the food we serve you here." It is not enough to describe each main course, diners learn where the meat they are about to eat was raised and that their steaks were "processed at a facility designed by Dr. Temple Grandin."

SO, IS MEAT MURDER?

Eating is about more than hunger and nutrition. As the writer and farmer Wendell Berry famously said, it is an agricultural act—one that has social, political, environmental, and moral implications and consequences. To eat or not to eat meat is now more than a personal decision, or a religious tenet. Animal rights activists, such as Farm Sanctuary cofounder Gene Baur, may "dream of a vegan world," but according to *Vegetarian Times*, only 3.2 percent of Americans, or 7.3 million people, follow a vegetarian-based diet, and only 0.5 percent, 1 million people, are vegans, who use or consume no animal products whatsoever (Animal Agriculture Alliance 2010; Carlisle 2010).

The connection between human evolution and the interaction with and exploitation of other animals is clear. These interactions have in many ways been reciprocal, and it is not an exaggeration to say that humans and our close animal companions have domesticated one another. From the human perspective, domesticated animals serve as living tools that provide us with valuable renewable resources (Shipman 2010:519, 525). Humans have always killed other animals for food, and until recently animal slaughter was a familiar act. Despite steadily increasing levels of meat consumption in developed and developing countries, the vast majority of meat eaters are protected from, and ignorant of, this necessary act. By the time meat reaches the eater, its animal origins, and the processes by which it became meat, have disappeared. Even so, a growing number of people are also deeply concerned with the welfare of farmed animals.

In *The River Cottage Meat Book*, homage to and guidepost for "moral meat," Hugh Fearnley-Whittingstall (2007:23) says that "it is not only the death of our farm animals over which we have such complete control. It is also their birth, and their life. We breed them and we feed them; and after we kill them." "Of all the animals whose lives we affect," he continues, "none are more deeply dependent on us—for their success as species and for their individual health and well-being–than the animals we raise to kill for meat.... This dependency would not be suspended if we all became vegetarians.... The nature of our relationship would change, but the relationship would not end. We would remain their custodians, with full moral responsibility for their welfare" (Ibid.:16–17).

"So what happens to these animals in a vegetarian Utopia?" Fearnley-Whittingstall asks. And "Who says it's wrong [to kill animals]? What makes it wrong? ... That animals kill other animals for food is a fact of nature. That all animals will eventually die is another.... Humans and the animals they raise do not operate outside this natural sphere" (Ibid.:17–18). But all eaters of meat, not just farmers, ranchers, and slaughterhouse workers, must take responsibility for the deaths of the animals from whom that meat is made. After all, he reminds us, "if you buy something, you support the system that produces it" (Ibid.:25).

Fearnley-Whittingstall is what Peter Singer and Jim Mason call a "conscientious omnivore." Even Singer and Mason cannot find fault with "the view that it is ethical to eat animals who have lived good lives and would [otherwise] not have existed at all" (as quoted in Haspel 2006).

But how do we know if the pig that gave us our pork chops or the steer that surrendered our steaks lived a good life? The meat and poultry industry, state and national governments, and animal rights and welfare organizations differ, often dramatically, in their definitions of humane care, handling, and slaughter (Kopperud 2009:13). Short of raising and slaughtering their own meat and poultry, how are shoppers to know if they are eating conscientiously? In the United Kingdom, they can look for the Royal Society for the Prevention of Cruelty to Animals' Freedom Food stamp of approval. In the United States, shoppers may find labels from several organizations that certify that meat or poultry came from animals raised under humane conditions: the Animal Welfare Institute's "Animal Welfare Approved"; the American Humane Association's "Free Farm Certified"; Humane Farm Animal Care's "Certified Humane Raised and Handled." Whole Foods grocery chain has developed its own "Animal Compassionate" designation for natural meat and cage-free poultry (Storck 2007). And we can look for other grocers and restaurants to do the same as they vie for the conscientious omnivores' food dollars.

In the end, each of us is left to answer for ourselves: Is meat murder? Not quite—or not yet—it would seem, depending on your predilection. But pressures to alter practices common today in industrial meat production will continue. And even conscientious omnivores should beware. In 2010, Swiss voters cast their ballots on whether the state should be required to represent the interests of pets and farmed animals in court–they said no. But a dead fish has been represented in Swiss court in a suit against the fisherman who caught it. Lucky for the fisherman and meat eaters everywhere, the dead fish lost its case (Anderson 2010).

6

✳

The Human Price of Our Meat

THE JUNGLE

Most people think little about where the meat on their dinner table comes from and even less about the industry that puts it there. For those who do, awareness of meatpacking usually begins—and too often ends—with *The Jungle*, Upton Sinclair's landmark novel about the squalid conditions in which immigrants lived and worked in Chicago's packinghouses at the beginning of the twentieth century. Thanks to countless high school literature teachers, *The Jungle* has become, and no doubt will remain, the icon for every writer who wants to evoke the ills of this bloodiest of businesses.

Labor historians are fond of pointing out that the February 1906 publication of *The Jungle*, with its revelations of wretched working conditions, filthy packinghouses, and tainted meat, prompted enactment of the Meat Inspection Act and the Pure Food and Drug Act, both signed into law by President Theodore Roosevelt on the same day, June 30, 1906 (Barrett 1987:1; DeGruson 1988:xvi; Skaggs 1986). They are equally fond of quoting Sinclair's (1962:126) famous lament: "I aimed at the public's heart and by accident I hit it in the stomach."

In the summer of 1980, a young man pulled his truck up to the library at Pittsburg State University in southeast Kansas. He went inside and fetched Gene DeGruson, the university's curator of rare books, to come take a look at the rotting, mildewed papers in the bed of his pickup. The young man had been hired to clean out the cellar of a farmhouse in nearby Girard. When he noticed Upton Sinclair's name on several letters, he decided to see if the library wanted the papers before he took them to the dump.

> Too fragile to handle, the papers were covered with brightly colored mold, dyed purple by typewriter ribbon and red and green by inks used to write and print the documents. The fetid mass eventually proved to

Michael Broadway

F I G U R E 6.1 Don Stull and Michael Broadway stand under the arch that once served as the entrance to Chicago's Union Stock Yards. The authors journeyed to see what remained of the Yards in August 2002, as they were completing the first edition of this book. The photo was taken by a friendly passerby.

be over a thousand business records, inner office memos, and correspondence of the *Appeal to Reason,* once the nation's leading Socialist newspaper. (DeGruson 1988:xiii)

In September 1904, *Appeal to Reason* editors selected 26-year-old Upton Sinclair to investigate the working conditions in Chicago's packinghouses. With $500 and a plot outline from the paper's editors, Sinclair traveled to Chicago in October (Ibid.:xiv–xv). For seven weeks, he conducted what anthropologists call participant observation among packinghouse workers and their families: "Dressed in overalls and carrying a metal lunch pail, Sinclair haunted the killing floors and canning rooms, the saloons and tenements of Packingtown" (Barrett 1987:1).

Appeal to Reason financed Sinclair's research in exchange for the rights to publish his work as a serial. The first installment appeared in February 1905, and by October of that year the newspaper had published 28 installments before discontinuing the final chapters because of disagreements with Sinclair and a disappointing response from subscribers. However, in January 1906, Sinclair signed a contract with Doubleday, Page & Company, which published *The Jungle* the following month.

> Despite his protestations that he wished the novel published as he had written it, revision was drastic. It reduced the work from thirty-six chapters and a conclusion to thirty-one chapters and a conclusion. The greatest number of deletions was passages pertaining to Socialism, followed closely by paragraphs dealing with what Sinclair termed the Press Trust, prostitution, and derogatory comments about "big business," especially those concerning the self-made man or "captain of industry." Paragraphs were added to emphasize the malpractices of the meatpacking industry.... Carefully eliminated were ... statements containing Socialist sentiment.... The most curious deletions are those of passages which made the immigrant workers more empathetic or less alien to the reader. (DeGruson 1988:xxiv–xxv)

For all its sanitizing, *The Jungle* was an instant best-seller and remains today a powerful indictment of the evils of capitalism, industrialization, corporate greed, and exploitation of working men and women.[1] While his novel failed to inspire labor reforms, as Sinclair had hoped, it did reveal in stark detail the dire circumstances under which working men and women toiled and lived at the turn of the twentieth century. It remains the benchmark against which the meat and poultry industry is measured.

Despite the intervening century, with its dizzying array of technological advances and dramatic social reforms, meat and poultry processing early in the twenty-first century is regrettably reminiscent of what Sinclair described early in the twentieth. In the 1890s, Swift and Armour vertically integrated meatpacking, from ownership of animals and other raw materials through production to distribution of meat products; three-quarters of a century later Tyson and Perdue accomplished this feat in the poultry industry (Barrett 1987:15). The Big Five of the Beef Trust are gone, only to be replaced by a new Big Four—JBS-USA, Tyson Foods, Cargill Meat Solutions, and National Beef Packing Company.

Profit margins were no higher in the nineteenth century than in the twenty-first, and the packers still make much of their profit from the sale of byproducts. Hoof, horn, blood, bone, gland, and hair are still ingredients for glue and soap, tallow and leather goods, but to that list we can now add deodorants and detergents, shampoo and shaving cream, marshmallows and mayonnaise, cigarette papers and matches, asphalt and antifreeze, Sheetrock and wallpaper, and a host of pharmaceuticals, including insulin, amino acids, blood plasma, cortisone, estrogen, and vitamin B-12 (Kansas Beef Council n.d.; Zane 1996).

The industry's processing plants abandoned Chicago and other major cities, which in Sinclair's day teemed with immigrants desperate for work, for small towns in the Midwest and South. But immigrants and refugees still flock to packinghouse gates; only now they speak Spanish, Burmese, Somali, or K'iche Mayan instead of German, Polish, Czech, or Lithuanian.

Multistoried plants that slaughtered cattle, sheep, and hogs have been torn down, along with the stockyards that once supplied them, to be replaced by single-story plants that kill and process one species only. No matter, they are still factories that mass produce meat. This should come as no surprise. It was, after all, from the Chicago packinghouses that Henry Ford got the idea for the automotive assembly line. They were the first American workplaces to fragment tasks, deskill work, and mechanically regulate output with a continuous-flow production process (Horowitz 1997:17).

Although Sinclair would certainly recognize much of what goes on in a modern beef plant, he would also marvel at the dramatic modernization of the disassembly line. Steers still enter the killfloor through the knock box, where they are rendered unconscious before slaughter. But in the 1950s, the knocking hammer gave way to the cylindrical captive-bolt stun gun, which propels a steel bolt into the skull upon impact with the animal's forehead.

No longer is the animal laid out on the floor as workers scurry around the carcass performing their assigned jobs, then hoisting it onto an overhead trolley and moving it down the line for another work crew to lower, do its duties, raise, and send on its way. The Can-Pak system, invented in Canada in the early 1950s, allowed "on-the-rail dressing." Standing underneath the knocker, the shackler wraps a hook and chain around the animal's left hind pastern (ankle), and as the stunned animal falls forward and down, it hangs upside down by one leg. It then moves continuously along an overhead rail past stationary workers who stick,

Michael Broadway

FIGURE 6.2 An abandoned packinghouse in Chicago's stockyard district, 2002.

bleed, skin, gut, saw, and split the steer into a carcass, from stations positioned to maximize their specific task (MacLachlan 2001:172; Stull 1994).

Moving platforms, mechanical hide pullers, hydraulic skinners and hock cutters, electric band saws and skinning knives have combined with on-the-rail dressing to produce a higher quality carcass and make work on the killfloor less difficult and dangerous. They have also decreased by almost half "carcass throughput," the elapsed time from when the steer is knocked until its carcass, now gutted, skinned, and split into "swinging sides" enters the "hot box," where it cools for about 24 hours before entering the "cooler," there to be assigned a yield and quality grade by USDA meat inspectors.[2]

From the cooler, the carcass goes to fabrication, or processing, where workers wielding razor-sharp knives break it down into ribs, loins, and rounds; they then shrink-wrap these "subprimal cuts" and box them for shipment to supermarkets. At one of the world's largest beef plants outside Garden City, Kansas, the trip from the knock box to the hot box takes a mere 42 minutes. And only two or three days pass from the time a steer rolls up to the plant's holding pens in a bull wagon until it leaves in a box in the back of a refrigerated semi-trailer (Stull 1994:62). (See Figure 6.3.)

By mechanically moving the carcass along a "chain" where stationary workers disassemble it, the time lost and the dangers associated with walking around carcasses on bloody floors has diminished. In mechanizing and modernizing the process, the work was also simplified—or deskilled—and worker productivity has substantially increased. In 1952, one man-hour of labor produced 51 pounds of meat; 25 years later that same hour accounted for 155 pounds (Horowitz 1997:253). As worker productivity rose, so did company profits. On-the-rail dressing reduced labor costs and boxed beef saved on transportation costs, since unusable bones and scraps were eliminated at the plant and could be converted into salable byproducts. Along with reorganization of work on the kill and fabrication floors came relocation of the plants where this work is done. As the old Big Five closed their plants in the stockyard districts of Chicago, Kansas City, and Omaha, a new Big Four were building plants and giving birth to new Packingtowns in remote places like Garden City, Kansas; Guymon, Oklahoma; and Brooks, Alberta, Canada. While the packers were abandoning the cities they had called home for a century, they were also crushing the unions and driving down the wages and benefits for which workers had struggled so long.

"ON TO ORGANIZE"

Horrendous working conditions and low wages made meatpacking workers ripe for union organizing. Chicago cattle butchers organized the first meatpacking union in 1878. For the remainder of the nineteenth century and into the early twentieth, meatpacking was the most strike-prone of all American industries (Barrett 1987:119). Campaigning for the eight-hour work day, the Knights of Labor, which represented the majority of organized workers in the United States

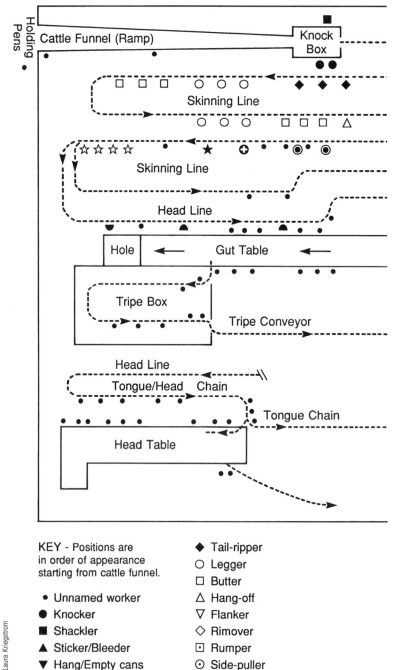

FIGURE 6.3 Killfloor of IBP's plant in Finney County, Kansas, summer 1989.

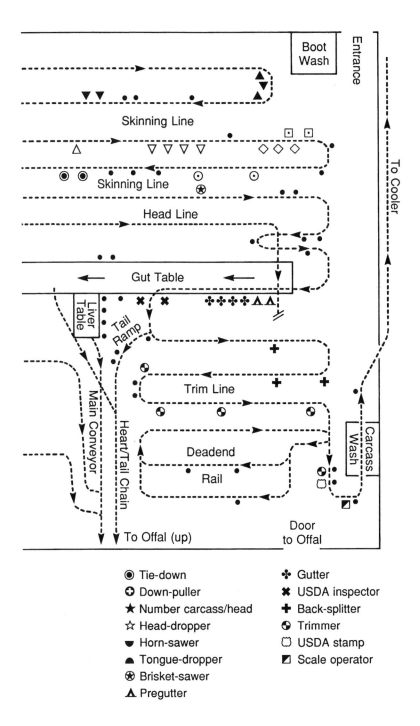

Boot Wash

Entrance

Skinning Line

Skinning Line

Head Line

To Cooler

Gut Table

Liver Table

Tail Ramp

Main Conveyor

Heart/Tail Chain

Trim Line

Deadend Rail

Carcass Wash

To Offal (up)

Door to Offal

◉ Tie-down   ✚ Gutter
⊕ Down-puller   ✖ USDA inspector
★ Number carcass/head   ✚ Back-splitter
☆ Head-dropper   ◐ Trimmer
▼ Horn-sawer   ◌ USDA stamp
▲ Tongue-dropper   ◨ Scale operator
⊛ Brisket-sawer
△ Pregutter

in the 1880s, focused its organizing campaign on meatpacking. It won the eight-hour day in 1886, and then promptly lost it that same spring in the public back-lash against organized labor in the aftermath of Chicago's Haymarket Riot, which resulted in several deaths after anarchists allegedly threw a bomb at police as they dispersed a rally (Skaggs 1986:111; Barrett 1987:121–125).

Effective unionization in meatpacking began with the founding of the Amalgamated Meat Cutters and Butcher Workmen of North America in 1897. By 1904, it was able to mobilize 50,000 workers in a nationwide strike for higher wages. With an ample supply of meat in their coolers and an economic recession fueling unemployment, the packers broke the strike, and union membership plummeted. It was Upton Sinclair's account of this strike in *The Jungle* that immortalized the struggle of working men and women for fair wages and decent working conditions. The company forced striking workers back to work on its terms and at lower wages than before the strike, but working conditions and wages soon began to improve, and the ranks of the union rose once again (Skaggs 1986:113–118).

Extreme division of labor on the disassembly lines and deskilling provided employment opportunities for women, who occupied meatpacking's bottom pay scale. Their share of the workforce rose from under 2 percent of those employed in Chicago's packinghouses in 1890 to almost 13 percent in 1920 (Barrett 1987:52). Despite the growing presence of women in the packing-houses, it was nationality, race, and language that marked plant floors. Bohemians and Slovaks, Germans, Lithuanians, Poles, and native-born whites each made up at least 10 percent of Chicago's packinghouse employees in 1909 (Ibid.:39).

The structure of the meatpacking industry and its production methods, the diverse composition of its workforce, and the militancy of union stalwarts made packinghouses ripe for unionizing. In the bitter strikes that often followed, southern blacks and other "new" groups entered meatpacking as strikebreakers (Horowitz 1997:3–5). Management and unions competed for the newcomers' loyalty, but common grievances and ethnically mixed work crews helped organizers transcend gender, ethnic, and national divides to build strong unions.[3]

The Packers and Stockyards Act of 1921 forestalled vertical integration by forbidding packer ownership of stockyards and apportionment of supplies of live-stock between companies. The National Labor Relations (Wagner) Act of 1935 established the National Labor Relations Board (NLRB), guaranteed workers the legal right to organize and bargain collectively, and outlawed unfair labor practices, such as blacklisting. Divided between the Amalgamated Meat Cutters and Butcher Workmen of North America, who favored negotiating with the packers, and the Packing House Workers Organizing Council (PWOC), who would rather strike, meatpacking workers struggled for the eight-hour work day, the 40-hour work week, and time-and-a-half overtime pay. By the close of World War II in 1945, collective bargaining had been accepted in the industry, and some companies had signed "master contracts" that covered workers in all their plants (Skaggs 1986:159–165). However, the Labor Management Relations (Taft-Hartley) Act of 1947 greatly restricted union ability to challenge management. Its provisions empowered the president to suspend strikes for 80 days in the interest of national health and safety; required unions to bargain with management; outlawed sympathy strikes and secondary boycotts; and, to gain access to the NLRB, it required union officials to sign affidavits that they were not members of the Communist Party (Skaggs 1986:199–200; Horowitz 1997:181). The Taft-Hartley Act banned closed shops, which require employers to hire only union members and make union membership a condition for employment. Union shops are permitted, however, except in right-to-work states, which outlaw agreements between employers and labor unions making union membership a prerequisite for employment.

Union power peaked in the decade following World War II, as successful strikes and joint efforts by United Packinghouse Workers of America (UPWA) and Amalgamated Meat Cutters led to master contracts with Armour and Swift that granted wage increases and better working conditions. As it gained concessions from management, the UPWA also fought for civil rights, opposing discrimination in hiring, as well as in housing, retail businesses, entertainment, and public facilities (Horowitz 1997: Chapter 9).

Organizing efforts in the poultry industry lagged behind those in meatpacking: it is a newer industry; its plants were located in the rural South, long known for anti-union sentiment; and it drew heavily on African American women to work its lines. In June 1953, poultry workers in the East Texas town of Center asked the Amalgamated Meat Cutters to help them organize. At the time, poultry workers were paid the minimum wage of 75 cents an hour; they worked 10 or 11 hours a day in filthy conditions without overtime pay, and their employers denied them grievance procedures, seniority, and paid holidays. Center's two poultry plants—one staffed by black workers, the other by whites—voted to join the union. When the companies refused to negotiate in good faith, the Amalgamated Meat Cutters organized a national boycott of plant products, and the workers staged wildcat strikes.

At the time, less than a quarter of the poultry sold in the United States was federally inspected, and neither of the Center plants employed inspectors. With the support of its 500 locals and the endorsement of the AFL-CIO, the Amalgamated Meat Cutters organized a national campaign to mandate federal inspection of poultry. Subsequent congressional hearings revealed that one-third of known cases of food poisoning could be traced to poultry. Despite opposition from the poultry industry and the U.S. Department of Agriculture, which oversees meat inspection, a poultry inspection bill eventually passed Congress. In August 1957, President Dwight Eisenhower signed the Poultry Products Inspection Act, which requires compulsory inspection of all poultry that crosses state lines or is sold overseas.

And what of the striking workers? Eastex, the plant that employed only black workers, settled after 11 months, agreeing to wage increases, time-and-a-half overtime pay, three paid holidays and vacations, a grievance procedure, and reinstatement of strikers. Eastex subsequently sold out to Holly Farms, which later sold out to Tyson. In 1958, three years after the Eastex strike ended, Amalgamated called off the strike against Denison, the all-white plant.

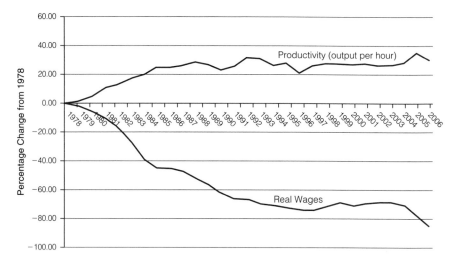

FIGURE 6.4 Changes in beef and pork production wages versus productivity since 1978.
SOURCE: U.S. Department of Labor, Bureau of Labor Statistics, various years.

By then Amalgamated's boycott had cost the company most of its markets, and it eventually went bankrupt (Green & McClellan 1985).

Union efforts won significant benefits for meatpacking workers. In 1960, for example, meatpacking wages were 15 percent above the average wage for manufacturing workers in the United States (Broadway 1995:25). However, union victories were elusive and short lived. In that same year, financed by a $300,000 loan from the Small Business Administration, Iowa Beef Packers opened its first plant. It was the opening shot in what came to be called the IBP Revolution, which would rapidly restructure meatpacking—and, as many have argued, make jungles once again of its killfloors and fabrication lines (Stull 1994; Horowitz 1997; Nunes 1999; Warren 2007).

The transformation was sudden and complete. In the wake of mechanization and plant closings, 46,000 meatpacking workers lost their jobs between 1960 and 1990, even as jobs in poultry processing more than doubled. The United Pack-inghouse Workers of America and the Amalgamated Meat Cutters and Butcher Workmen merged in 1968, then merged again with the Retail Clerks International Union in 1979 to form the United Food and Commercial Workers (UFCW), which represents meat, poultry, and grocery workers today. By the mid-1980s, master contracts were a thing of the past, and by 1990 wages in meatpacking had fallen to 20 percent below the average wage in manufacturing (Broadway 1995:24; Horowitz 1997:246). Wages have continued to fall, even as worker productivity has risen (see Figure 6.4).

Meatpacking unions did not give up without a fight. Strikes closed IBP's beef plant in Dakota City, Nebraska, four times between 1969 and 1984 (Skaggs 1986:204). In August 1985, UFCW Local P-9 went out on strike against Hor-mel's pork plant in Austin, Minnesota, over company demands for wage and benefit concessions. By the time it ended in defeat the following June, the Hormel strike had captured national attention (Hage & Klauda 1989; Green 1990). In December of that same year, IBP locked workers out of its Dakota City plant after they rejected demands for pay cuts and concessions. Giving in to IBP's demands the following July, the UFCW accepted a two-tiered wage scale that paid new workers 60 cents less per hour than continuing workers and assured substantial savings—and a significant competitive edge—for IBP (Horowitz 1997:273–274).

"IT DON'T PAY GREAT"

Industry critics say the meat and poultry industry has returned to the days of *The Jungle*. Industry spokespersons scoff at what they claim are simplistic comparisons and point to "remarkable progress" in ergonomics and injury reduction, food quality and safety (Nunes 1999). No one can deny many of its transformations—most evident in poultry processing, which has led the way in mechanization and further processing of its basic product. The shorter interval between generations and the controlled environment for raising chickens enable the poultry industry to select for specific genetic traits and improve upon them (Nunes 1995:38). These factors, and chickens' small and uniform size, have allowed poultry processors to replace many workers with machines. But, as Horowitz and Miller (1999:3) observed, chickens are not pretzels, and "despite the best efforts of the companies, the chicken remains an irregular natural product."

> In the "modern" processing plant, mechanical devices are extensively applied in a wide variety of cutting operations once performed by workers with knives. Separating a carcass into quarters, for example, is accomplished by machines which perform the necessary cutting operations.... But the chicken still needs to be inserted into the machines and positioned properly for the cuts to be applied in the right place.... Labor may have been deskilled, and the number of knife workers reduced, but the need for labor remains in the many positioning and transitional stages of the dismembering and cutting operations, as well as hand and eye tasks such as inspecting and separating kidneys and hearts. The increasingly important deboning operations remain the province of relatively skilled workers equipped with sharp shears and knives, rather than machines. (Ibid.)

Machines may now work alongside men and women on meat and poultry lines, but jobs on the line remain tedious, monotonous, and risky. And workers who fill them rarely earn a "living wage," one sufficient to feed, clothe, and shelter themselves and their families. The Bureau of Labor Statistics reported that in May 2010, wages for line workers in meat and poultry plants averaged $11.27 an hour, or $23,440 a year. Hourly wages for line workers in the beef plants in southwest Kansas averaged $12.53; $12.41 for pork plant workers in northeast Iowa; and $10.34 in the chicken plants in northeast Arkansas.

Adam Reynolds

F I G U R E 6.5 Tools of the trade—then and now.

Depending on their jobs, line workers may be paid for "skill premiums" that boost their hourly wages. But even with such premiums, wages in meat and poultry processing now average less than half of the average hourly rate of $23.33 for manufacturing (Bureau of Labor Statistics n.d.a).

As a line worker at a Tyson chicken plant put it, "It don't pay great, but it's, well, down here it's one of the better paying jobs for a family." Work on a meat or poultry line does indeed offer some of the better paying jobs in rural areas. But such wages mean that the income of line workers in these plants often falls below or only slightly above poverty thresholds required for one or more federal assistance programs. In 2010, for example, a family of four earning $22,350 met the federal poverty guidelines; and school children living in a household earning $29,055 or less were eligible for the federal free lunch program. Not only do many meat and poultry workers and their family members qualify for federal and state assistance programs, but they also draw upon local charities and food banks to supplement their income. Thus, the industry offsets its costs of production and adds to the hidden cost of our "cheap food."

MEATPACKING HAS ALWAYS BEEN DANGEROUS

Work on the killfloor and processing line has always been dangerous. In 1917, eleven years after *The Jungle* was published, and long before the federal government required companies to report worker injuries or illnesses, the welfare director of Chicago's Armour plant reported that 50 percent of the company's 22,381

T A B L E 6.1   Occupational Injury and Illness Rates for Production Workers, 1975–2009 (selected years)

	Meatpacking	Poultry Processing	Manufacturing
1975	31.2	22.8	13.0
1980	33.5	22.1	12.2
1985	30.4	18.3	10.4
1990	42.4	26.9	13.2
1995	36.6	18.3	11.6
2000	24.7	14.2	9.0
2005	12.6	6.7	6.3
2009	9.3	5.5	4.3

SOURCE: U.S. Department of Labor, Bureau of Labor Statistics, various years, *Occupational Injuries and Illness in the United States by Industry*, Washington, DC: U.S. Government Printing Office.

workers became ill at work or were injured over the course of the year. Historian James Barrett (1987:69–71) attributes the high injury rate to sharp knives, damp and cold working conditions, and the speed of the work.

By the time we began studying meatpacking in the mid-1980s, workers were bedecked from their hardhats and earplugs to their steel-toed and rubber-soled boots in an amazing array of gear intended to protect them from injury. Even so, from the mid-1970s until the end of the twentieth century, it had the highest injury and illness rate of any industry in the United States—about three times greater than the overall manufacturing average (Stull & Broadway 2010:81) (See Table 6.1.).

The most significant illnesses and injuries in modern meatpacking plants are associated with musculoskeletal disorders, arising from repetitive motions, most notably, carpal tunnel syndrome: "a condition in which the nerve passing through the wrist to the hand is pinched and compressed because of fast repeated forceful motions" (Personick & Taylor-Shirley 1989:5). It "can frequently lead to severe nerve damage, and the crippling of the hand or wrist, making it impossible for workers to grip or pick up everyday objects" (Brooks 1988:13).

In 1990, Secretary of Labor Elizabeth Dole initiated a study of repetitive motion injuries. Ten years later, President Bill Clinton concluded this process by issuing a set of ergonomic standards designed to reduce on-the-job repetitive motion injuries (U.S. Department of Labor, OSHA Office of Communications 2001). Within days of taking office in 2001, President George W. Bush repealed these standards, saying his administration would pursue a "comprehensive approach" to ergonomic injuries. This "comprehensive approach" consisted of voluntary guidelines for specific industries and laxer injury reporting requirements. In 2002, OSHA issued a new work accident report form that eliminated the column for musculoskeletal disorders. A year later it decided employers do not have to record when workers report ergonomic injuries (Center for American Progress; OMB Watch 2004). As of 2011, there is still no requirement for businesses to report such injuries. The effect has been dramatic.

Between 2000 and 2009 meatpacking's occupational injury and illness rate dropped from 24.7 per 100 full-time workers to 9.3 (Bureau of Labor Statistics n.d.b). The rate for poultry workers dipped from 14.2 per 100 to 5.5, only slightly higher than the rate of 4.3 for manufacturing in general. Rates for repeated trauma went from 8.1/100 workers in 2000 to who knows what in 2009, when the government no longer collected the data! Injury and illness rates for meat and poultry workers have declined steadily since peaking in the mid-1990s, but this dramatic drop is clearly a function of changes in reporting procedures, aided by Bureau of Labor Statistics sleight of hand that fails to classify plant cleanup crews as meatpacking workers because they work on contract. (See Horowitz [2008:22–24] for a detailed discussion of the 2002 changes in recording criteria and the damage they have done to our understanding of injury and illness in meat and poultry plants.)

ON THE LINE

In 2005, the Government Accountability Office (GAO) concluded that: "Because of the many hazards in meat and poultry plants and the type of work performed, the dramatic decline in the industry's injury and illness rates has raised a question about the validity of the data on which these rates are based" (GAO 2005:4). According to the Occupational Safety and Health Administration, underreporting of illnesses and injuries is still a problem in the industry. Some plants award crews or supervisors money or prizes for low or no accidents, which only serves to encourage underreporting (Ibid.:28–30). Regardless of whether plants offer rewards, line supervisors and company nurses and doctors do all they can to hold down reported injuries. Take the case of two western Kentucky poultry plant workers we shall call Betty and Peggy. They worked as "presenters and trimmers" on either side of the same Department of Agriculture inspector on a poultry line. As Betty described her job,

> The presenting is when you open up the bottom half of the chicken to present the guts for the USDA inspector. We reach in and we pull the guts out of them. The inspector looks at the guts, like the kidneys and things like that, to see if the chicken has a disease. And they call the birds according to what they see down into the cavity of the chicken.... And the trim person on the other side [of the inspector] makes the necessary marks or handles the chicken according to what the USDA says that is wrong with the bird.... You make different marks on, like, the chicken's back, the legs, ya know, for the people down at the end of the line to know what parts of the chicken to take off. (Stull interview, November 7, 1998)

One Sunday in October 1998, Betty and Peggy, who lived 30 miles apart, each came down with severe nausea, cramping, and diarrhea. Peggy was "up all night long, hurtin'."

> I stayed on the toilet all night. I tried to call into work. I couldn't get no answer. I tried every number that I had to get ahold of someone.

I couldn't get no answer. So when I went into work that morning and I went straight to that nurse's station, and I told 'em what was wrong with me. She gave me two pills to take for diarrhea, plus a tube of medicine for throwing up. I told her, "I'm not throwing up. I got blood in my stools. And I know that's not normal."

And she said that everyone is coming down with a virus. So she gave me these two pills to take.

"You don't think I need to see a doctor?" I said, "That's what I came in here for."

She said, "Well, everyone is coming down with the virus. If you feel you need to go to the doctor after work, you can."

So I had to go back out on that line and work in that chicken! (Stull interview, November, 9 1998)

Peggy, Betty, and four others on their line came down with what they were told was *E. coli*. By the time they were interviewed, three weeks later, Peggy's and Betty's gall bladders had been removed because of complications from their illnesses.

I kept bleeding on that line all that day. The girls had to keep takin' my place. I had blood [running down] my leg, so that's when I come home and I had to go to the hospital. I was done dehydrated. The doctors don't understand why in the world they let me touch that meat down there, knowin' that I had diarrhea and had blood. And I told them, "I guess they didn't believe me." I didn't know what else to say. And I've been off ever since that day. And they [the company] refused to pay any kind of medical bills to me or anything.

I asked them if I could sign up for workmen's comp, and they refused to take [my application]. But the fourth day, some woman, she heard me in there talking, and I guess she realized that I'd done been down there four different times that week, and she told me she would fill one out on me. And she did. And a man come in there and looked at me real funny and said, "What's wrong with you?" I said, "I'm sick." And he said, "Well, just what's wrong with you? What do you want workmen's comp for?" I said, "I'm planning on, I think I'll be off for a while. I'm fixin' to have surgery." He said, "You don't get workmen's comp for having surgery. What's wrong with you?" And I showed him them papers and he looked at them. He said, "Don't you know that after you change a baby you're supposed to wash your hands?" I said, "Don't start with me, 'cause I haven't changed a diaper in 17 years." And he dropped his head and he walked out that door. Now, he's the plant manager!

They was really rude to me. I guess when you get sick they're done with ya. (Stull interview, November 7, 1998)

Despite lamentations about how much they spend training their line workers, plant managers and floor supervisors have little use for injured workers or those who can't "pull their count"—keep up with the rapid pace of the line: 200 or more chickens a minute; 1,000 hogs an hour; 380 cattle an hour.

The Holmes Foods chicken plant in Nixon, Texas, for example, claims it picks and eviscerates 265 birds a minute. According to its plant manager, "we are a speedboat of efficiency, moving and changing with the winds of uncertainty as needed to protect our customers and our industry partners" (www.holmesfoods.com). But who protects the safety of those who work in this and the industry's other "speedboats of efficiency"?

The USDA assesses permissible line speeds to ensure food safety—as long as USDA inspectors have time to examine the product for possible contamination, the speed is acceptable. OSHA is responsible for worker safety, but it sets no standards for acceptable line speeds (Human Rights Watch 2004:37).

Peggy and Betty showed up every morning at 6:30 and went directly to their lockers. Peggy remembers:

> I would get my old stuff out, put my rubber boots on, and then you go form a line where they hand out your supplies and there's somebody right there that'll hand you a red smock or white smock depending on the department that you're in, and then you step to the window and she hands you your plastic—the blue gloves, the plastic apron, a pair of ear plugs, and a hair net. Or a cutting glove; you need to show a cuttin' glove to get a cuttin' glove.
>
> It took 30 to 45 minutes a day just gettin' ready to, ya know, the process of getting ready and finishin' work. You can't walk outta there with blood up to your elbows, I'm not driving home like that.
> *And you don't get paid for that?*
> No.[4]

Work started promptly at 7:00 A.M. They were given a break from 9:30 to 10:00, then another, for lunch, from 12:30 to 1:00.

> I don't know anyone who can eat in 30 minutes, I mean, I can't do that. I know that me and Betty worked on the same line and when the last chicken was gone we would step down off our stand and go to a wash area on the wall. We would soap our hands, our (rubber) gloves, and down the front of our aprons and throw water on ourselves to get it off. And we hang up our smocks, then we would go back to the same sink and wash our arms 'cause you're bloody up to your elbows, with chicken blood. You wash your arms down and dry 'em. And then we always went to the bathroom and I redone it again before I went to the bathroom and after I finished using the bathroom. Then by the time you get up there it's 20 minutes till, 15 minutes till 1:00, you didn't have time to go and get you enough food to eat.
> *What about bathroom breaks?*
> There is no bathroom breaks. You do not leave that line. They will relieve you to go to the bathroom, but you get in trouble for it. They say you don't, but you do. The day I was sick and needed to leave the

line, like in a hurry, I waited 10 or 15 minutes before I was allowed to leave the line, before somebody come to do my job so I could leave, because you do those chickens or USDA shuts the line down. (Stull interview, November 9, 1998)

After lunch, the line ran without a scheduled break until quitting time at 3:30 P.M., but sometimes the day shift ran on till 4:30 or 5:00. "It just varied. When you run outta chickens you were through. We've been ready to leave the line and, 'Oops, we found another semi-and-a-half of chickens in the back.' I'm like, 'How do you lose a semi-and-a-half full of chickens?'" (Peggy, November 9, 1998).

Peggy and Betty were one of four teams of USDA helpers, their official job title. They sat through a week of orientation, mainly watching films. After that, "you go out on the line and you learn, ya know, you're standing there with somebody, helpin' somebody. But after orientation, you work maybe a week with somebody or until you feel comfortable that you can do it by yourself."

Betty and Peggy were the first people to touch the birds after the live hangers, who pull them out of the metal cages in which they travel from the broiler house. In the words of anthropologist Steve Striffler (2002:306), who worked in a Tyson chicken plant in Arkansas, live hangers "grab the flailing chickens, hooking them upside down by their feet to an overhead rail system that transports the birds throughout the plant." The birds were stunned, killed, beheaded, plucked, and partially eviscerated—all by machines—before they came to Peggy and Betty (Griffith 1995:135).

Meat&Poultry magazine

FIGURE 6.6 USDA inspector examining chicken entrails for disease.

Peggy presented and Betty trimmed 35 birds a minute—every hour and a half they switched positions to give their arms a rest from the constant motion. Peggy remembered, "Oh, your hands hurt and between your shoulder blades hurt, but they say after you're there over time that goes away. Well, I wasn't there that long. I was there for the month and your hands do cramp." This was her third stint at the plant. The other two times she quit within two months because she did not like her hours on third shift, 11:30 P.M. to 8:30 A.M. Betty, who had worked at the plant for two years, complained of knots in her hands and carpal tunnel syndrome, but she never went to the doctor because she was afraid of surgery.

Betty and Peggy are representative of both the "old" and the "new" line workers in meat and poultry processing. They were born and raised within a few miles of the plant where they worked when they became ill. Betty had worked in tobacco and other seasonal agricultural jobs for $6.00 an hour and no benefits before the plant opened. She still did in her spare time. Peggy had been a country club chef and cake decorator for a local grocery store, but she never received enough hours to qualify as a full-time employee and thus receive health insurance and benefits. The chicken plant offered full-time work on a regular schedule and insurance.

"A LOT OF PEOPLE LEAVE"

Peggy and Betty are the kind of workers meat and poultry companies promise to hire when they tout the industry's economic benefits to government officials, economic development officers, and chambers of commerce. But there are never enough local Bettys and Peggys to bring a new plant to full operating capacity, much less to keep it running, not in an industry where workers continuously come and go. Betty and Peggy did not know the rate of turnover in their plant; they just knew "a lot of people leave."

Industry spokespersons do all they can to avoid revealing turnover rates, but everyone agrees that employee turnover is higher than virtually any other industry (Kay 1997:31). For the beef plants in Kansas and Nebraska, annual rates averaged 72 to 96 percent for established plants and 250 percent or more for new plants in the 1980s and 1990s (Wood 1988; Gouveia & Stull 1995:98–99). Mark Grey (1999:18–19) reported annual turnover of 120 percent at the "Hog Pride" pork plant in 1997. "On a typical day, nearly 25% of workers had been on the job for less than one month, and 60% had been employed less than one year!" After implementing a "quick-start" program designed to reduce turnover by raising wages and allowing workers to rapidly qualify for the highest pay rates for their job, annual turnover at this plant fell to 80 percent. Still, a third of the workers quit in the first 30 days, before they could qualify for the program, and half were gone in 75 days.

As unemployment rose in the wake of the recession that began in 2007, employee turnover in the beef plants of southwest Kansas reportedly fell (Stull fieldnotes, February 14, 2011). But even when the workforce is at capacity and turnover is down, plant managers still wish for "low" annual turnover rates of 36 to 50 percent; they don't even talk in terms of annual rates of turnover. They speak, instead, of monthly rates—after all, 5 percent turnover per month sounds so much better than 60 percent per year. Besides, monthly rates more accurately reflect the constant movement of many workers in and out of their jobs.

It doesn't much matter whether you present chicken innards all day long to a USDA inspector in between machines that transform a chicken into a breaded chicken breast, halve hog carcasses with a hydraulic splitting saw, or use a knife to "drop" cattle tongues and then hang them on hooks that pass endlessly by overhead—the work will wear you down, and sooner or later you'll get fired, get hurt, or quit.

> Marcial gave his two weeks notice and worked his last day at IBP on August 6, eight years and one day after he started. When he began working on the IBP killfloor, he was Number 500 on the seniority list, and when he quit he was Number 75. The woman who administered his exit interview asked why he was quitting, and he replied, "The lines go too fast, the supervisors are too mean, they push their workers too hard, and I don't like anything about working there." Startled at his candor, she looked blankly at him as he laughed. She left the space on the form for why he quit blank.
>
> Marcial took more than his two weeks vacation pay with him when he walked off the killfloor for the last time; he also took stiff wrist joints from his years chiseling meat off cow heads. His wife Mary says he "sounds like Rice Krispies" when he gets up in the morning. Marcial asked the company nurse about his joints, and she told him it was nothing to worry about, a bone specialist had told her it was just "carbon of the bones." Marcial was not surprised the nurse told him not to worry—that's her job—but "popping/cracking noises from wrists or elbows" was number 9 of the 16 cumulative trauma symptoms listed in IBP's publication on this subject (IBP 1989:13).
>
> Marcial said the killfloor had changed immensely since he helped map it in the summer of 1989 (Stull 1994).[5] Some jobs had been eliminated, and new machines were making others easier. But the new machines were not without their price. A knocker had been killed recently by the new air gun that replaced the old captive-bolt stun gun. Even Marcial's job used a new machine. Once he got the hang of it, the machine made his job much easier, compared to using a simple sharpening steel to chisel meat off cow heads. But it took him about two weeks to get the hang of it, and during that time his wrists hurt badly.
>
> Marcial was glad IBP was promoting more Mexicans to supervisory positions, but when asked if the company was becoming more concerned with worker safety, he replied, "No, they just want to go faster." (Stull fieldnotes, July 25, 1993)

"Getting it out the door" has always been the order of the day in meat and poultry processing, and plant managers endlessly strive to cut costs and boost worker output. But meat and poultry workers like Betty, Peggy, and Marcial are "not the hopeless, animal-like creatures described in Sinclair's novel" (Barrett 1987:9); they are active human agents in a continuing contest with management over control of their work and their workplace. Deskilled, degraded, and stuck in dead-end jobs, packinghouse line workers are hard working, proud, and determined to do the best they can amidst inhumane circumstances. They resist exploitation and oppressive working conditions in varied ways—some large, some small; some evident, some veiled; some individual, some collective.

NOTES

1. Thanks to the late Gene DeGruson (1987), Sinclair's original version of *The Jungle*, as it first appeared in *Appeal to Reason*, is once again available.

2. Since 1926, beef carcasses have been graded according to yield and quality. Yield grade measures "cutability"—the percentage of the carcass that can be transformed into boneless, closely trimmed retail cuts of meat. Carcasses are assigned a numerical yield grade (YG) from 1.0 (54.6 percent) to 5.9 (43.3 percent) (Boggs & Merkel 1984:106). Quality grade (QG) is judged by the age of the animal, as determined by physiological indicators of maturity, and degree of marbling, the white flecks of intramuscular fat. Color, texture, and firmness of lean meat in the ribeye of the twelfth rib are the indicators used to assign one of eight quality grades. Quality grade determines the value of the carcass—and the cost of the retail cuts that come from it. Choice and Select are the only quality grades regularly designated for retail sale. USDA graders have only about seven seconds to assign—by sight—both a YG and a QG to each carcass (Seibert 1989).

3. It is not our intent to trace the rise and fall of meatpacking unions. Roger Horowitz (1997) has already done a masterful job of that in *"Negro and White Unite and Fight!": A Social History of Industrial Unionism in Meatpacking, 1930–90*.

4. Whether line workers should be paid for the time it takes to put on (don) and take off (doff) clothing and protective gear required in their job has long been a source of contention between management and labor in the meat and poultry industry. See Chapter 11 for more detail.

5. Marcial Cervantes was employed at IBP when he and Don Stull mapped the kill-floor represented in Figure 6.3, and in earlier publications he was known as "Enrique" to protect him from possible reprisals. When he quit IBP, he granted permission to use his real name, and we are pleased to now acknowledge his valuable contribution to our research.

7

✳

On the Floor at Running Iron Beef

THE WALKOUT

On August 27, 1992, the Running Iron Beef plant in Valley View[1] announced that hours for second-shift fabrication would be changed from 1:15–9:45 P.M. to 3:15–11:45 P.M. The next day 38 workers called in sick, and management fired 22 of them. This action triggered a wildcat strike in which some 200 second-shift fabrication workers walked off the job. This walkout caught management and union officials by surprise. Running Iron Beef was an industry leader in wages and benefits, yet striking workers complained of unfair treatment, racism, poor working conditions, an unsafe workplace, and low morale.

The walkout was settled a week later, when company officials agreed to rehire the fired workers after they served a month's suspension. Management agreed to make changes in the operations of its second-shift fabrication lines, adequately staff crews, work to improve communication between line workers and management, and not punish returning strikers. The company and the union formed a joint cultural diversity committee to address issues raised by the striking workers, most of whom were Mexican immigrants. Corporate executives were concerned with their "inability to recognize cultural differences and then manage them," and they wanted a researcher to identify issues of current concern to management and labor, recommend changes, and work with them to implement improvements. A year after the strike, the company's labor relations officer met with Don Stull and invited him to propose such a study. The following is an account of his research.

ANTHROPOLOGISTS IN THE JUNGLE

I asked Ken Erickson, an anthropologist and a former member of the Garden City research team who speaks Spanish and Vietnamese, and Miguel Giner, an industrial psychologist and Mexican immigrant, to work with me on the project. The company accepted our proposal, and we began research in February 1994 with a visit to Running Iron Beef's Valley View plant. Other commitments prevented continuous fieldwork, so we conducted research on and off for eight months. We came and went in tandem to maximize our presence on site, logging a total of 75 days in the field.

The executives who hired us initially expected survey research that used a standardized questionnaire, which they viewed as "proper scientific research," but we chose participant observation as our primary method. It began with a tour of the plant one Saturday in February. By August, we could give tours ourselves—and did on one occasion. In between we went through new-hire training, talked with and interviewed managers, office staff, union representatives and stewards, and line workers. Our workdays began at 7:00 A.M. with the "morning management meeting," and often did not end until well after mid-night when the second shift shut down.

We interviewed a sample of management and union officials, line supervisors and line workers, men and women, English and non-English speakers, Anglos, Hispanics, and Asians. Interviews were problem focused and questions were open ended. We took notes during or immediately after interviews. In a few cases, we tape recorded interviews and later transcribed them.

We selected respondents by purposive, or structural, sampling, interviewing knowledgeable individuals and those who held key positions, such as union business representative, plant manager, or trainer. We took care to replicate social and cultural diversity in the workplace.

We considered using formal focus groups but decided against it, fearing participants would be reluctant to "tell it like it is" unless we held numerous meetings to establish rapport. Also, pulling people off the line could cause conflict between participants and fellow workers, and it would slow production. Holding sessions before or after shifts would require overtime payments and still might cause conflict.

Instead, we took advantage of naturally occurring focus groups. We attended workshops on workers' compensation held for managers by officials from the company's home office. I spent one Sunday afternoon at the union hall talking with union stewards and their families as they fried steaks and drank beer. The plant manager came late in the day, and a lively interchange took place with several workers on the plant's problems and what to do about them. On another occasion, I hosted a get-together of supervisors and foremen at a local bar to talk about their concerns. We frequently visited the home of the union's local business manager, a Mexican immigrant who had worked on the line and was respected, if not always liked, by management, union leadership, and line workers. We spent many an afternoon at the union hall, listening to workers who came to the business manager with their problems.

Our presence and the methods we employed showed the company was concerned with improving working conditions. This was a very important message to send to men and women who are rarely afforded the courtesy of someone in an important position sitting down with them, asking their opinions, and hearing them out. As one shop steward put it at the steak fry, "Look, he's writing this down. He's listening to us."

MANAGING RUNNING IRON BEEF

For 16 hours a day, six days a week, thousands of animals snake along the disassembly line at Running Iron Beef, being killed, their carcasses bled, skinned, gutted, sawed, boned, cut, trimmed, shrink-wrapped, boxed, and loaded into tractor-trailers for transport to markets across the nation and around the world.

Out on the floor, a rigid hierarchy enforces managerial authority. Job type—and status—are marked by the color of the hardhats everyone must wear: blue for managers, yellow for line supervisors, red for trainers, gray for maintenance workers, gold for union stewards, baby blue for trainees, and white for hourly line workers.[2]

Meat&Poultry magazine

FIGURE 7.1 Skinning a beef carcass.

For whitehats and their supervisors, the work is hard. One Mexican immigrant who worked at another plant called it *"esclavitud"*—slavery. As a line supervisor said: "They make you hump for your seven or eight dollars. The first 90 days it's tough till you get in shape…. It's no place to be if you don't like to work."

Management controls employees in several ways: mandatory urinalysis during job application; a probation period for new hires; the ever-present threat of write-ups by line supervisors; who gets promoted and who gets fired; the very speed of the chain itself.

A newly hired hourly employee is on probation for 90 days. After successfully completing the probationary period, the worker gains seniority and may bid on any posted job within the same department: Slaughter; Fabrication, often called Fab; Hides; Offal; Loadout. The qualified bidder with the highest seniority wins the job.

Whether workers are on probation or have won seniority, they are subject to strict rules and rigid sanctions. Probationary employees may face discharge without notice or recourse. Employees are written up for being late or absent without an excuse, excessive excused absences, failure to report on-the-job injuries, overstaying lunch or relief breaks, deliberate discourtesy, horseplay, and substandard job performance. Workers with four such infractions within a calendar year are discharged. More serious offenses bring even quicker termination—malicious mischief that causes property damage or injury, gambling, alcohol or drug use, theft, and abusive or threatening language. Fighting, even in the parking lot, results in immediate discharge—with so many knives so close at hand, it must be so.

RUNNING IRON BEEF'S WORKFORCE

Running Iron Beef is owned by one of the world's largest food processing firms. When we studied it in 1994, it employed more than 2,000 workers and had a slaughter capacity of some 5,000 head of cattle a day.

According to plant records, the workforce was two-thirds Hispanic (68 percent), one-fifth white (19 percent), one-tenth Asian (8 percent). Other ethnic groups were only a small fraction (5 percent) of the workforce. But overall figures are misleading: 76 percent of the plant's officials and managers were white males, and 7 percent were white females; 11 percent were Hispanic men, and 2 percent Hispanic women. Most personnel classified as professionals, technicians, and sales workers were also white men. White women made up 83 percent of the office and clerical staff. The majority of those classified as (unskilled) laborers were Hispanic men (61 percent), followed by Hispanic females (13 percent), then white males (12 percent).

Managers at Running Iron Beef averaged 20 years with the company, ranging from two months to more than 40 years. Hourly workers averaged only three-and-a-half years with the company. Fifty-five percent of the hourly workers had been with the company less than two years and averaged a little more than one year of service; the other 45 percent averaged more than six years, including some who had been at the plant since it opened more than a decade earlier.

Non-Hispanics appeared disproportionately among those with more than two years of service. They were more likely to work on first (day) shift and hold positions that demanded less stamina and physical exertion. Hispanic hourly workers were apt to be short-term employees and work in more physically demanding jobs subject to higher rates of injury and turnover. They also lacked suitable job alternatives and were likely to leave the plant for varying intervals of rest and rehabilitation, only to return later. Of hourly employees who had been hired during the previous two years, one in five was a rehire.

Managers must supervise not one but two workforces. One force has much in common with the managers: they are native-born and mainly Anglo American, with many years of experience in the industry. The other workforce—the majority of hourly workers—is decidedly different; they are likely to be new to the industry and may well be new immigrants, with little or no command of English and a poor understanding of the culture and expectations of native-born Americans. It was this cultural divide that Running Iron's executives found so vexing, and it was to our team that they turned for help.

LABOR ISSUES

The problems that daily beset Running Iron's multicultural and multilingual workers were revealed by what happened after the death of Agustin's grandmother.

> Agustin's grandmother died in Mexico last week. His mother panics in times of crisis and has convulsions, so Agustin needed to get to the airport in a hurry to catch a plane to Mexico for the funeral. He had to get permission to leave and then drive 200 miles to make his flight. He couldn't find his regular foreman, and when he did find someone—a trainer—to ask for a leave, that person sent him to Personnel. They told him he had to go back to his foreman to get final approval. Agustin couldn't wait any longer; he told someone he'd be back on Tuesday and left.
>
> When he came back to work on Tuesday, as he said he would, he was fired because he left without permission. Agustin understood that sometimes Mexicans say they have a family emergency in Mexico and then take off for a month or so, but he said he would be back on Tuesday, and he was. His bosses told him he had to have documentation of his grandmother's death, which he took to mean a death certificate, but in small-town Mexico, you have to send to the capital for a death certificate, and that may take a month or more. They generally do not place announcements in the paper or provide programs at the funeral: "They just bury people," said Jose, the union local's business manager and an immigrant from Mexico. Although someone in authority might have told an Anglo that something simple like an

announcement was enough, no one told Agustin, and he did not know to ask. The union steward ran into him as he was coming off shift and said he would try to help.

Agustin kept asking, "Why are you doing this?" This impressed the Anglo steward, who kept telling Agustin that this is what stewards are supposed to do. So the steward came to the union office to get Jose to intercede on Agustin's behalf. He made it clear that Agustin was a good worker; he came to work and did his job. Jose did not see it as a problem; he would talk to Personnel and get them to let Agustin come back to work pending receipt of a death certificate. Then if one was not forthcoming, he could always be terminated. (Union steward, Stull fieldnotes, June 7, 1994:14–25)

Agustin's dilemma was emblematic of some of the most serious problems at Running Iron Beef:

1. *"Passing the buck."* No one in authority wants to make the final decision because then he can be held accountable. Any of several people could have given Agustin permission to go to the funeral, but if something went wrong they would get yelled at. As Ray, who was among those listening to the story, said, "The motto of most supervisors is, 'Not heard, not seen, not in trouble.'"

2. *Mistrust of Mexicans.* A widespread belief held among non-Hispanics is that you can get any kind of verification you want in Mexico. Racism also played a part in this case, according to the steward. He felt that if it had been him, or another Anglo, he would have had no problem getting time off for the funeral.

3. *Cultural and linguistic problems.* Agustin does not speak English and does not know the American system. Distressed over his grandmother's death and in a hurry to catch his plane, he did not ask what he needed to do to verify the funeral. Even in calmer circumstances, he might not have understood proper procedures, but no one volunteered to help him or explain things until he got back and had the good fortune to run into the helpful steward.

4. *Relations between supervisors and employees.* The consensus among longtime line workers is that if you let yourself get pushed around, you will get pushed around. Employees who stand up for themselves may make their supervisors angry, but after a time they will be treated with respect.

5. *Longevity.* The longer you have worked at the plant the more likely supervisors are to cut you some slack. Seniority is the formal aspect of this factor; longevity is the informal aspect—the former is codified, the latter is not. Both are important.

This incident illustrated widespread problems at the plant. It also showed that employees sometimes try to understand, learn from, and help each another. The Anglo union steward came to the Mexican union business manager, Jose, who understood both the workings of the plant and the cultural practices in rural Mexico, to ask him to intercede for Agustin. Cultural brokers such as Jose facilitate cross-cultural communication and are indispensable in the everyday workings of the plant.

CORPORATE AND WORK CULTURES
AT RUNNING IRON BEEF

Running Iron Beef strives to instill the values of quality, safety, and productivity in its employees, and documents these values, along with other aspects of its corporate culture in mission statements, training manuals, and on signs posted throughout the plant. Running Iron's corporate culture is management-centric. Top and middle managers espouse corporate norms and behaviors, using them to define corporate reality and dominate employees (Alvesson 1995:44,90). Running Iron transmits its values and corporate culture to new employees using its Employee Handbook in training and orientation. Interaction with supervisors and fellow employees and continuing education, such as workshops, are the mechanisms for reinforcing or modifying corporate culture. But in the plant itself, corporate culture must make room for what is often called work culture, which is tied closely to circumstances employees share in the workplace and on the job (Ibid.:32).

One or more work cultures exist in any corporation and take shape wherever employees share common tasks over time. Work cultures may be dominated by a particular occupation (accounting), or they may be grounded in the collective experience of men and women who work day in and day out at a certain job or in a particular location (Slaughter, Fabrication). The work cultures out on the plant floor are intertwined with the national cultures of a multicultural and multilingual workforce, and these may run counter to the goals of Running Iron's corporate culture.

Every culture has a limited number of themes that control or stimulate behavior. Whether these themes are declared or implied, tacitly approved or openly promoted, they find their expression in behavior. The importance of a theme is related to its frequency, the breadth of its distribution, the intensity of reactions to its violation, and the factors that limit its frequency, force, and variety (Opler 1945).

The dominant themes of Running Iron's corporate culture manifest themselves in the answers managers give when asked about corporate goals, policies, and procedures. These themes permeate the company's publications, manuals, organizational charts, plant maps, slogans, and advertising materials. They reveal themselves in the structure of corporate and plant computer databases and in stories recounted by employees. Because Running Iron is a large organization, no single individual knows all aspects of its corporate culture. And in some situations, the same individual may say different things about the corporate culture. In this way, Running Iron is truly a society in miniature, with specialists who control various aspects of corporate activities and knowledge, and with ideal cultural patterns that may bend according to local needs.

Most managers would agree that safety, quality, productivity, and loyalty are key themes at Running Iron. They permeate its official documents and behavior and represent the company's core values.

Safety

"Safety First" appears on bulletin boards and walls throughout the plant. Celebrations and rituals highlight safety; it appears prominently in corporate and plant competitions, awards, training meetings, and paperwork. Supervisors who ignore requirements to turn in their records of safety meetings face rebuke on bulletin boards and in company memoranda. Plant managers may summon injured employees to explain how they were hurt and suggest ways to prevent such occurrences.

Quality

According to the company's human relations manual, every task "we don't do right the first time, we must redo ... at a cost." The word "quality" appears on the company's logo and throughout its publications—even on its promotional coffee mugs. Company trainers and training materials say product quality is essential to profitability, which in turn means continued employment for workers and managers alike.

Productivity

Running Iron Beef measures productivity in "product" output and values it as monetary return per head (of cattle slaughtered and processed). The company's goal is to keep labor costs per head to a minimum, as well as lost time due to injuries and down time due to equipment failures. New project proposals require formal documentation to justify initial and long-term costs to the corporation. Each morning's management meeting includes output reports from the previous day and goals for the day ahead.

Loyalty

Employees must work for Running Iron Beef for six months before they are eligible for benefits. Although it does not appear in company symbols or publications, loyal service to the corporation reaps rewards. Seniority determines the right to claim a job, so senior employees can acquire the least demanding jobs. The corporate magazine recognizes employees when they reach service milestones, such as five or ten years on the job. Reassignment rather than termination is the likely punishment if a senior employee fails to fulfill job expectations. Quit twice, and you will not be rehired.

Top management strives for safety, quality, productivity, and loyalty through efforts to reduce workers' compensation costs; identify and eliminate factors contributing to high risk for injury or illness in certain jobs; reduce turnover and unplanned absenteeism; and maintain a high level of production. They see many factors standing in the way of these goals: language and cultural difference; poor communication, including uneven and inadequate interpretation and translation; the union; failure of employees to "buy into the quality process"; inadequate or irrelevant training; "Corporate's" lack of awareness and unresponsiveness to individual plant needs and concerns; and the constant pressure to "get the product out the back door."

These same themes underlie the everyday culture of work on the floor and the workers who perform it. How line workers interpret these themes and put them into practice is not always in concert with managers. Discrepancies between what workers perceive as corporate ideals and the reality of daily management practices can create serious conflict, especially where management and labor do not share the same language or the same expectations.

Real Work Culture: Safety

Safety is always written first on "to-do" lists maintenance supervisors use to guide their daily work in Slaughter. But as they come and go from their offices, they discuss work priorities, allocation of time and effort, and strategies to solve current problems. They do not talk about safety, except to jokingly say, "Safety second!"

Line workers bitterly complain that management is unresponsive to requests to fix broken equipment and unsafe work areas. "Nothing gets fixed until someone gets hurt" is an oft-repeated refrain. Workers say many people in positions of authority "pass the buck" to avoid making decisions for which they will then be held accountable. That "they only fix it after someone gets hurt" is borne out by management's regular discussion of problems after, rather than before, they result in injuries.

Safety, quality, and productivity are three principal goals of Running Iron Beef, "but sometimes safety and product quality take a back seat to production," as one longtime worker put it. In some circles, people say "if you get injured at Running Iron, you're gonna get fired" (Workshop leader, Stull fieldnotes, March 23, 1994:3).

"In the first 45 days they can fire you for any reason, and the union can't do anything," said one goldhat (union steward).

Trainers are not supposed to be in the line, but they get put in the line if they're short-crewed. Put them in the line and injuries go up because foremen push new hires [to work fast] like everybody else.

The company tells us to tell them if things are wrong. You tell them and you tell them and you tell them, and nothing happens. Pretty soon, you just don't give a shit.

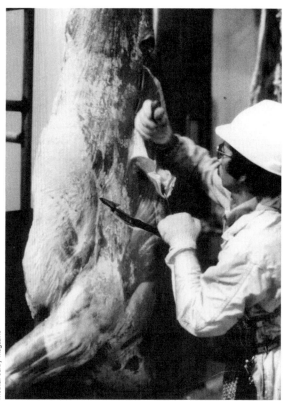

Meat&Poultry magazine

FIGURE 7.2 Despite many technological advances, the knife and the meat hook remain the basic tools in modern meatpacking plants. Note the worker's chain mail apron.

And if you report something to the USDA [federal meat inspectors who work on the plant floor], the company gets mad. (Stull fieldnotes, June 12, 1994:4)

Policies and recommendations on safety are often in apparent conflict with the needs of line supervisors and general foremen to keep production rates up. Superintendents and supervisors "don't want to see the chain shut down," and they may ignore calls for changes. Workers often say "not enough attention is paid to safety until someone is hurt." And they point to examples: a worker in Fab got his finger chopped off in a machine. The guard on this machine had been missing for four weeks, but nobody had reported it (Stull fieldnotes, July 18, 1994:12).

Managers often view injured workers as malingerers who want to work the system to their advantage. The case of Eusebio, who had a shoulder strain, came up at upper management's morning meeting. He hired a lawyer to help him get a job change. According to the bluehat (manager) reporting on this case, "It doesn't matter what he does, he hurts. When he drives to work it hurts. He has the perfect lawyer answers to everything. 'Yes, I'll do whatever you want, but it hurts.'" These comments reflect a prevalent view among managers that malingerers hire lawyers who encourage them to claim to be hurt so they may split the injury settlement. Although this suspicion may be true in some cases, their general attitude allows them to avoid facing the fact that injuries ruin the health of many workers (Stull fieldnotes, June 9, 1994:1).

This attitude is common among managers who remember the old days when you "worked through" pain and injury. Old-timers often swap "war stories" and show each other their scars. They reminisce of the days when supervisors patched up injured workers with Superglue and electric tape, and then sent them back to the line with the admonition to "work through it." Such stories are a matter of industry pride, and though the tellers make the point that things have changed, they seem almost nostalgic for the days when it was a rough and ready business (Stull fieldnotes, August 8, 1994:6). Their nostalgia for the old days is no doubt influenced by their current responsibility for daily production quotas.

Real Work Culture: Quality

> People who work at Running Iron but have worked somewhere else say Running Iron treats its workers better than other packers but works them harder and expects them to do a better job in terms of product quality. The expectation is that treating workers better and stressing product quality will equate to loyalty to the company, but that's not always the case. (Manager, Stull fieldnotes, June 6, 1994:4)

When asked what he would do to bring workers' compensation costs down, if money were no object, this same manager said he would slow down the line and maintain adequate crews (Stull fieldnotes, June 6, 1994:3).[3] But money is always an object, and turnover and injury remain the most enduring dilemmas facing the meatpacking industry.

Hourly employees take pride in their work and consider themselves to be professionals. Like upper and middle management, they too are concerned with safety, product quality, and productivity. They respect experience and actively seek advice from old-timers. Those who have close relationships with supervisors feel intense loyalty to the job and to the boss. Some workers will even transfer to work under a supervisor they respect and trust. Most, if not all, workers see Running Iron's interests as their own and recognize that if the plant does not make money, they are out of a job. Yet the comprehensive ideal of quality—doing the job right, following measurable specifications, and maintaining good relationships on the floor—is not always evident in the day-to-day reality in the plant. On a daily basis, "hitting the numbers" matters more than product quality—or safety (Stull fieldnotes, July 20, 1994:6).

Equity and Quality

Fairness, or equity, is a recurrent theme in worker complaints. They often accuse supervisors of setting bad examples by enforcing rules they themselves do not follow: "If we can't do it, then neither should they." If quality is a corporate value, workers argue, supervisors and workers should be held to the same standards. This is not always the case.

An Anglo yellowhat (supervisor) in his 40s came into the Fab foreman's office about 7:15 A.M. and reported that someone on the floor was not wearing a company-issue hairnet. The worker, a Latina, was wearing a hairnet, but it was not one of the company's white ones. He told her she had to wear one of company issue, and she became upset. An Anglo female union steward (goldhat), who was in the office at the time, remarked that a hairnet is a hairnet: What does it matter what kind it is? The yellowhat replied that the "regs" require a company-issued one. The goldhat asked to see the regs, politely but firmly, and with a clear tinge of hostility. The yellowhat left and returned to read the regulation to the steward. The regulation explicitly requires company issue. The union steward responded that this regulation had never been posted and was news to her. The yellowhat replied that it had been company policy since 1988 or 1989. The situation worsened when a Chicana yellowhat walked in the room sporting a brown nonissue hairnet.

This incident set off a minor crisis, as several women with nonissue hairnets got upset because they now had to change their net. They claimed that their own, which they must pay for out of pocket, worked just as well as the free company-issue hairnets. The Chicana yellowhat voiced the objections of many women. She had long, "heavy" hair, and she claimed her net had bigger, stronger netting, and was better.

Another union steward in the room remained seated at the long counter with the computers, egging the female goldhat on. "Tell [the yellowhat] to fuck himself," he said while the yellowhat was gone to get the regs. He viewed the yellowhat as essentially a light-duty person who had nothing better to do than go around the floor once or twice a month and hassle people about chewing gum, their hairnets, and the like. Jose, the union business manager, had arrived by this time. He remained calm: If the policy says company issue, then so be it. But the female goldhat was not satisfied; she asked for a copy of the regs and said she would bring it up at the next union meeting.

This incident reveals how little things become big things, and how the union and line management figuratively and sometimes literally "bump chests." Management wants everyone to wear the white, company-issued nets because (1) they are visible from a distance and (2) they know they are of sufficient quality. Some workers do not like company nets for essentially the same reasons. It seemed to be primarily women who were bucking the system on this matter. Young women often do their best to look good on the floor by wearing makeup, matching attire, attractive headscarves. By using their own brown or black hairnets they can cover up the fact that they are wearing a hairnet, which they regard as unbecoming. Those with long hair think the stronger nets they purchase work better than company issue. They want to go beyond "sufficient" to achieve "quality," yet managers reprimand them for adhering to one of Running Iron's basic principles.

The female goldhat did not help matters either. She sees herself as the defender of "the people" and is anti-management, and probably anti-company. She had been hurt on the job, and her case was in a protracted settlement phase; she believed the company tried to deliberately screw her. The male goldhat egged her on when the yellowhat was out of the room, but kept quiet when he came back in. The union business manager, on the other hand, tried to be a mediator and realized little was to be done, and probably little reason to fight this fight. Nevertheless, the Chicana yellowhat and others ended up being hassled because this became a big issue, and now they became resentful, probably on several counts. They resented: (1) the worker for getting caught; (2) the yellowhat for being "an asshole"; and (3) the company for a dumb and inflexible policy. They viewed this incident as just another example of management wanting to make its work easier at the expense of workers. (Stull fieldnotes, June 7, 1994:1–2)

Line workers say management is hypocritical—saying one thing in private and another in public—and inconsistent.

One foreman will tell you this, one that, but they all have the same authority, so you can get written up even if you are following orders, merely by one foreman chewing your ass for doing what another told you to do. They try to buffalo everybody out there, and if you stand up to them they try to get rid of you. (Recently fired worker, Stull fieldnotes, June 12, 1994:3)

Management talks a good line about quality, but reality on the floor leads workers to distrust what they have heard. In the work culture of Running Iron, quality is not second—it is a distant fourth.

Real Work Culture: Productivity

Workers and management alike value efficient, timely production. Workers complain when the line runs fast, but seasoned workers also brag about their ability to "pull count" (to keep up, to pull their weight). Workers must learn their jobs quickly, and be able to do them right, to make it on the line. They must "hang with it"—otherwise, they will soon quit or be fired. Meatpacking is a tough business; as the safety director at another plant put it, "We don't change their diapers for 'em."

It is the line supervisors, the yellowhats, who must keep the lines running smoothly and efficiently. From the plant manager to hourly workers and everyone in between, line supervisors are seen as key to good working conditions—or bad. Responding to management's demands, they push productivity into first place among all values in the real work culture of the floor.

Like most industry managers, Running Iron supervisors come up through the ranks. Experience helps them earn the respect of those who work under them because workers do not respect those who have not "earned their spurs" and look down on those who fail to pull count on their own lines. Yet this promotional system ensures new supervisors learn to manage people from how their supervisors treated them, rather than what they were taught in formal managerial training. Supervisors catch all the flak when things go wrong, and then all the fancy training goes out the window. "As they say in this business, 'Shit flows downhill.' If things are going well, the supervisor job is a breeze, but as a company gets larger and more complex, it gets harder to manage" (Plant manager, Stull fieldnotes, June 6, 1994:5).

Lead people (assistants to the line supervisors) are often promoted to supervisory positions, and that is good, according to the plant's management, but "we do nothing to prepare them." Some supervisors are good ("new school"), some are bad ("old school"). The bad ones cling to the "Big Stick" approach—"Do the job my way or there's the door" (Yellowhat, Stull fieldnotes, March 16, 1994:8). The Fabrication floor supervisor told of one line supervisor who stood out on the floor, wadded up a written request for time off two weeks hence, and then loudly declared, "No fucking way," would he give the person time off. This yellowhat was later fired.

Supervisors and foremen who come up through the ranks often lack "people skills." College trainees, on the other hand, often lack sufficient experience and empathy with line workers. As a result, both kinds of supervisors frequently resort to the Big Stick with their people, especially when things go wrong: "Two days out on the floor with those hardheads and everything they learned in training goes out the window" (Floor supervisor, Stull fieldnotes, March 23, 1994:4–5). The Big Stick still rules.

Hourlies say, "We're not encouraged to do a good job, just get the product out the door."

> The same old pressures remain.... The company is too protective of management. Fred and others at the top get told about problems and agree something needs to get done, but nothing does. Their excuse is "I forgot"—and they probably did. They shouldn't be burdened with the petty stuff, but those under them don't do their jobs. Porfirio, a whitehat, says "they only listen when you've got them by the balls. They don't give a shit about the people." Management is buddy-buddy with one another: "Kiss their ass and you get a good job; otherwise, forget it." Management continues to put productivity above all else. They turn up the chain speed, people can't do their job right and this causes "leakers" [poor seals on cuts of meat]; they then have to be rebagged. Increased speed doesn't therefore translate into more product—or better product. In the long run it reduces both productivity and quality, and, of course, it reduces safety. (Stull fieldnotes, June 7, 1994:17)

Line workers often believe managers do not value their expertise and fail to listen, even when hourlies have good ideas, because "we're just peons." Over and over workers asked for respect. They want to be treated like professionals, "which we are," said one longtime meatpacker.

Communication and Trust: Productivity

Workers want to have input into and be informed of decisions that affect their jobs and work space. They want supervisors, maintenance workers, and engineers to ask their opinions on how to improve things. Paradoxically, they may be reluctant to express their views if asked: their view is that seeking their opinion is often a mere formality designed to rubber stamp plans already formalized. Workers are not used to being consulted and may be reluctant to express themselves on issues of productivity, quality, or safety. They do not always feel commitment to the company or ownership and just want to put in their hours and go home. The deafening noise on the floor and the relentless chain speed make it difficult to discuss issues fully, and meeting space is limited. Line supervisors rarely hold meetings with their crews, and when they do, the discussion usually focuses on what the crew is doing wrong. "Regular" meetings on safety and quality, held sporadically as time permits, are hurried and often concerned with other matters, usually production.

Related to accountability and productivity is trust: hourlies do not trust managers to treat them fairly and with respect; managers expect hourlies to manipulate the system and abuse it. Anglos are especially skeptical of the motives of Mexicans who ask for leaves or report illness or injury. In such an environment, it is unlikely that good communication will take place, with or without command of a common language.

Real Work Culture: Loyalty

The value placed on longevity at Running Iron Beef has interesting corollaries. It means many people in management have worked their way up; they almost all know what it is like to "hang with it and pull their count." But because of the sharp distinctions between workers and management, exacerbated by language and cultural differences, the way Running Iron rewards and recognizes seniority masks problems. Supervisors conduct their business in separate spaces and become isolated from workers. When workers and managers share the same language and culture, separation is less of a problem, but being out of touch with workers who have different backgrounds raises the specter of serious misunderstandings.

Upper management shares a restroom with USDA inspectors. In Fab, management, safety, and maintenance crews use a restroom upstairs. Downstairs, supervisors have their own locker rooms and separate toilets. These facilities are clean and tidy. The downstairs restrooms provided for hourly workers are dirty and unpleasant, with toilet paper littering the floors around the stalls. The sad state of the hourly workers' restrooms is inescapable evidence that managers never go there.

The messy condition of the workers' restrooms is not simply a matter of careless littering. The mess stems in part from differences in the national cultures of Mexico and the United States. In Mexico, septic systems rather than centralized wastewater processing are the norm. Most of these systems cannot tolerate

Adam Reynolds

F I G U R E 7.3 A company translator interviews non-English-speaking job applicants.

waste paper, and nearly all private bathrooms in Mexico contain a lined trash receptacle next to the stool. Absent such trash receptacles, some Mexican workers continue to place paper on the floor next to the stool for later pick up and disposal. A sign in the Fab restroom showed that Running Iron was aware of the problem. The sign, in Spanish, asked people to please dispose of toilet paper in the stools. Worker training did not include any mention of the problem, however, and the sign was barely visible above the stalls.

CULTURAL AND LANGUAGE DIFFERENCES

Cultural differences between managers and line workers are exacerbated by language differences. "Interpretation is a problem on the line. You need something done, you need it done now. It is not a problem in the office; you can always get someone. But on the line, yes, it is a problem" (Fab supervisor, Stull fieldnotes, July 21, 1994:5).

"I have three Vietnamese who speak no English," one Anglo yellowhat who speaks only English told us. "One job has a Spanish and a Vietnamese who argue all the time. Neither of them speaks English." When he communicates with them, he must rely on double translation.

Despite interpretation and translation difficulties, we found managers and hourlies were continually bridging language and cultural barriers in innovative ways. In the process, they built trust and reconciled differences between the ideal and real cultures in the plant. When we asked supervisors and workers what made a good supervisor, they responded that respect and trust were more important than bilingualism. Line workers and supervisors agreed that lacking a shared national language was a barrier to effective work, but it was not an insurmountable one. In addressing immediate problems to be solved, even where languages differed, managers and workers were at their very best.

Randy, a maintenance man who speaks only enough Spanish to greet or cuss out a friend, provided an example of an effective response to language barriers:

> As he walked past the tripe room, a Vietnamese worker caught
> Randy's eye and signaled "broken" by pretending to break a twig and
> make a face…. Randy did a quick right face and stepped over to a
> conveyor that usually carries tripe. There stood a Mexican whitehat,
> and Randy greeted him in perfect colloquial Spanish, "Eh, Fernando,
> ¿que pasó hombre, como 'sta?" He went straight to work [fixing the
> conveyor that] was off the tracks. (Erickson fieldnotes, August 8,
> 1994:13)

Our research demonstrates that the knowledge and experience of hourly workers is critical to productivity, quality, and safety. Take, for example, the squeegee operator whose job is to mop up blood and grease from the killfloor. This is arguably the simplest job on the floor, the one that requires the least amount of skill, but squeegee operators must know their tools and how to effectively use them. Without the right kind of squeegee, the operator will be unable to do this job properly, and if it is not done right others will slip and fall, perhaps seriously injuring themselves.

Supervisors must appreciate the specialized knowledge of their crew members if the workplace is to function smoothly and efficiently. Unfortunately, line supervisors often lack adequate knowledge of the craft skills needed to perform the jobs they supervise. Equally troublesome is an absence of shared knowledge about the craft of supervision itself. As a result, new supervisors are often improperly socialized, which in turn prevents them from effectively training new hires on their crews. For example, knife sharpening is a crucial skill on the floor, and very difficult to master—dull knives contribute to cumulative trauma disorder and fatigue. A good supervisor, said one Mexican whitehat, is one who knows how "to speak to the people and help them, and sharpening is the most important." A Spanish speaker praised an English-speaking supervisor: "He comes to see what I need, to see if my knife is sharpened" (Giner fieldnotes, August 8, 1994:3). Despite the critical importance of knife care, supervisors had different techniques for the care and use of knives and the steel used to keep them sharp. One worker simply said, "I've seen a lot … of supervisors that can't keep a knife sharp." This translates into inconsistency in how line supervisors train their new hires in the most important "trick of the trade."

Line supervisors hold the key to productivity, quality, safety, and loyalty out on the floor through their actions and their example. They can inspire their crews to work hard and well, or they can contribute to low morale, elevated turnover, and increased injury. While line workers and managers agree that line supervisors are vital to good working conditions—or bad—no consensus emerged from our interviews about what makes a good supervisor, or what makes good supervision at Running Iron Beef.

OUR FINAL REPORT AND ITS IMPACT

Eight months after our first tour of Running Iron Beef's Valley View plant, we submitted our final report. It concluded that the company's ideals of safety, productivity, quality, and loyalty were widely shared by its multicultural and multilingual workforce. Unfortunately, managers and workers often differed in how they interpreted these ideals and put them into practice on the plant floor, resulting in conflict.

Running Iron Beef had two workforces, not one, and managers and line workers were mirror opposites in language and culture. Despite constant and often intimate daily contact, relations between ethnic groups were often framed by stereotypes. For example, most Asian and Mexican hourly workers had a basic formal education. Some were even professionals, such as engineers and teachers, who because of poor English language skills or visa status, had limited employment opportunities in the United States. Management treated them all as if they were uneducated, however.

F I G U R E   7.4 Confusing signs can be found in any language in a meatpacking plant. Michael Broadway photographed this sign at IBP's Dakota City, Nebraska, beef plant.

Translation of English to Spanish presented an urgent problem at Running Iron Beef. While many documents exist in translation, from the Employee Handbook to informal signs and postings, most were done by Mexican Americans whose literacy in Spanish was inadequate. Badly translated signs are not just annoying to Spanish-speaking employees, they compromise company efforts to get workers to "buy into the quality process." A glaring example was the Employee Handbook, which opened with the word "Welcome." In the Spanish version the word for "welcome," *bienvenidos*, was misspelled as "Bienveido"! Handwritten notes and announcements prepared by line workers were at times more professional and more motivational than those prepared by the company.

Despite many good efforts, safety did not appear to be a primary concern out on the Slaughter and Fabrication floors. Orientation and training sent clear messages to workers that discouraged them from reporting safety violations and problems. In the end, productivity—"hitting the numbers"—was the ultimate, and only true, goal at Running Iron Beef. Nothing was allowed to stand in the way of "getting the product out the door."

Our report did more than point out these problems, of which company executives were well aware long before we came on the scene. We presented a series of recommendations on how to improve relations between plant managers and their multicultural workers, address recurrent complaints by hourly workers, and improve training for supervisors and new hires.

In February 1995, a year after we began our study, we met with the executives who had commissioned it at corporate headquarters. At that meeting, they asked us to propose ways to resolve major problems identified in our report. Three months later we submitted a proposal for a pilot training program for Running Iron Beef supervisors. We never heard from Running Iron Beef again.

The working conditions that led to the wildcat strike at Running Iron Beef in 1992 are common throughout the meat and poultry industry. Managers will tell you that they care about their workers and that they spend huge sums on training, but they will also tell you that rates of employee turnover and occupational injury and illness found unacceptable in other workplaces are the price of doing business in the meat and poultry industry. Despite what managers say, solutions to the problems that continue to plague Running Iron Beef—and the rest of the industry—are no mystery. Pay a fair wage. Provide better and longer periods of training for supervisors and line workers. Adequately assign staff to work crews. Vary job tasks to relieve muscle strain. Provide longer recovery periods for injured workers. Most importantly, slow down the chain!

The executives who hired us to help them "recognize cultural differences and then manage them" knew what we would find. They had heard recommendations like the ones in our report many times over. But as Andy Adams (1903:52) said of his days driving cattle up the Western Trail in the 1880s, "Men were cheap, but cattle cost money." The men who sit in the corporate boardrooms that control today's meat industry, and those who do their bidding in the massive factories that turn animals into meat, know the truth of those words. And so, as long as men are cheaper than cattle, little will change.[4]

NOTES

1. We have changed the name of the company, its employees, and the town.

2. Although the color of the hardhat worn by the floor supervisor, the general foreman, line supervisors, maintenance workers, or quality control officers varies from company to company, hourly line workers are always whitehats.

3. Meat and poultry lines are "short crewed" when members are absent or positions are unfilled; lines are "undercrewed" when they are not adequately staffed to begin with. Reasonable expectations (RE) for crew staffing and line speed are set according to studies conducted by company industrial engineers. The key to setting RE is "100 percent effort." The "100 percent rate" is supposed to be the normal pace for workers, and company engineers say if workers maintain 100 percent they will never be injured. But 100 percent differs, depending on whether company or union engineers set the rate. For companies, 100 percent means getting your job done before the next piece of meat gets to you. For union engineers, 100 percent is what the average person working at a comfortable pace can do without risk of injury.

   A recurrent problem is workload balance. Different workers on the same line have different levels of training and ability; consequently, studies designed to set RE find that some workers perform at 100 percent, others at 80 percent, and still others at 110 percent. Engineers make adjustments to achieve workload balance all along the line by adding and removing workers until they achieve optimum speed. Once RE is set and workers are able to keep up with it, a new RE becomes the standard, and the chain speed becomes progressively faster. Line workers complain that companies use studies of RE to reduce the number of discrete jobs on the line and thereby impose more work on each worker.

   Productivity and worker safety are in conflict, and supervisors are primarily concerned with production. Workers complain that when company industrial engineers do line speed studies, managers slow down the chain and do not send "hard meat" (frozen meat), which is harder to work with, down the line. Once studies are over, things go back to normal (Stull fieldnotes, October 28, 2009).

4. On January 5, 2011, Don Stull received the following e-mail:

   I am an attorney who represents a meat processing company that employs a large number of Somali refugees. Many of the refugees, along with the Equal Employment Opportunity Commission, have sued our client in Colorado and Nebraska for alleged religious discrimination. One of the major claims is that the company failed to make reasonable accommodation for the Somalis' religious practices, by allegedly failing to provide breaks for Muslim prayers. Prayer breaks pose a particular challenge for the company as well as the non-Muslim employees, as the breaks interfere with the continuous production line process, meaning more work for the others to perform. The company denies the legal claims. In fact, when the company attempted to accommodate the Somali employees' requests for breaks for prayer, the non-Muslim employees (mostly Hispanic) walked out on strike. When the company later tried to implement a compromise break time, both the Muslim and non-Muslim employees engaged in unauthorized work stoppages.

   We wish to have the benefit of an expert witness to assist us on the subject of conflicts between Somali refugees in the U.S. and Hispanics, African-Americans and persons of other ethnic and racial backgrounds (but principally Hispanics). We also wish to have expert testimony contrasting the cultures of the Somali refugees and Hispanics in the U.S. Have you studied the relations between the Somali refugees

and Hispanics, African-Americans and persons of other ethnic and racial backgrounds? Or the different cultures of those groups? If not, perhaps you could refer
me to an anthropologist or sociologist who has studied these subjects.

Later that day, Stull responded:

I followed the news stories about the incidents you mention with considerable
interest. I have studied the meat and poultry industry for 25 years, focusing specifically on its impact on communities, workers, and producers. In that capacity, I have
studied ethnic relations in packinghouse towns and management-labor relations in
a large ethnically mixed packinghouse in the aftermath of an unauthorized work
stoppage. So, I understand the issues you summarize quite well. Having said that,
I do not have specific research experience with Somali refugees or other Muslim
refugees (Burmese) who are now working in packinghouses, although they are a
growing presence in several communities and plants where I have done research.

Off hand, I don't know any social scientist with the expertise on "Somali
refugees and Hispanics, African-Americans and persons of other ethnic and racial
backgrounds" that you seek. I will, however, make some discrete inquiries and let
you know what I find out. In the meantime, I would be happy to be of assistance in
any way I can. Feel free to e-mail or call me. Best of luck to you and the company
you represent in resolving these matters,

The attorney did not reply.

8

✳

Garden City, Kansas:
Harvest of Change

BEEFPACKING'S GOLDEN TRIANGLE

In January 1952, Earl C. Brookover, Sr., opened the first commercial feedyard in southwest Kansas. In December 1980, IBP opened what was then the world's largest beefpacking plant 10 miles west of Garden City, near the hamlet of Holcomb. In the time between these signature events, southwest Kansas emerged as beefpacking's "Golden Triangle," and Garden City became the "trophy buckle on the beef belt."

Innovations in irrigation technology and the development of hybrid corn and grain sorghum (milo) as cheap sources of cattle feed in the late 1950s helped catapult southwest Kansas to preeminence in commercial cattle feeding. By 1980, Kansas was feeding more than three million cattle a year, and two million of these cattle were being fed within a 150-mile radius of Garden City (Krause 1991:5; Austin 1988:10A).

An abundance of fed cattle and water from the Ogallala Aquifer attracted beef processors who were abandoning their aging plants in large midwestern cities and moving closer to their source of animals to reduce costs. In 1964, a cattlemen's cooperative opened Producer Packing Company in Garden City, and in 1969 National Beef built a plant in Liberal, 65 miles to the south on the Oklahoma line. In 1980, Excel Corporation opened a plant in Dodge City, 50 miles east of Garden City. In 1983, Val-Agri purchased the idled Producer Packing plant on the eastern edge of Garden City and quickly doubled its capacity. (Val-Agri later sold this plant to ConAgra.) The industry's expansion in southwest Kansas was complete in 1992, when Farmland Industries purchased National Beef's Liberal plant and the old HyPlains Dressed Beef plant in Dodge City and doubled its slaughter capacity. By the 1990s, southwest Kansas contained the largest concentration of

130

FIGURE 8.1 Brookover Feed Yards, Garden City, Kansas.

beef plants in North America. The five plants in the Golden Triangle had a combined slaughter capacity of 23,500 head a day and employed more than 10,000 workers (Dhuyvetter, Graff, & Kuhl 1998).

THE FASTEST GROWING TOWN IN KANSAS

When IBP opened its Finney County plant in 1980, and Val-Agri began operations in 1983, area unemployment hovered around 3 percent. With virtual full employment, it was apparent that most of the 4,000 workers needed to run these facilities would have to come from elsewhere. Fortunately for the packing plants, the early 1980s were a time of increased immigration and refugee flows to the United States. Southeast Asian "boat people" were being resettled across the country, and many of them lacked the English-language abilities necessary to compete for skilled jobs. Meatpacking offered entry-level employment and a chance for a new life in the United States, much as it did the immigrants Upton Sinclair described in *The Jungle*.

Fueled by new jobs in beefpacking, Garden City grew from around 18,000 people to more than 24,000 between 1980 and 1990. Most of this increase occurred in the first half of the decade, as Garden City became a modern-day boomtown and the fastest growing city in the state. Not only was Garden City's population exploding, it was also becoming more diverse. Of these 6,000

FIGURE 8.2   IBP's Finney County plant. Its cattle pens are in the foreground.

newcomers, approximately one-third were Mexicans, who came north to escape economic hardship and runaway inflation in their homeland. Another one-third were refugees from Vietnam and elsewhere in Southeast Asia. Many initially settled and found employment in Wichita, sponsored by officers at McConnell Air Force Base. When Wichita's light aircraft industry laid off workers during the recession of the early 1980s, some sought work in Garden City. At the same time the federal government was under pressure to push refugees off welfare.

While Southeast Asians were new to southwest Kansas, immigrants were not. Those who first settled Garden City a century earlier included Protestants, Catholics, and Jews from northern and eastern Europe, as well as midwestern farmers and Texas cowboys. By the turn of the twentieth century, Mexicans were immigrating to southwest Kansas to work on the Santa Fe Railroad. Soon they were joined by Japanese and Russian Mennonites, who labored alongside them in the emerging sugar beet industry. The end, no less than the beginning, of the twentieth century witnessed rapid growth and ethnic transformation in Garden City, but this time Garden City's latest immigrants included social scientists.

THE CHANGING RELATIONS PROJECT

The 1965 amendments to the Immigration and Nationality Act removed discriminatory immigration quotas favoring northern and western Europeans and altered immigrant flows to the United States. The developing world has since become the primary source for U.S. immigrants and in the process changed the composition of American communities. Immigration, both authorized and unauthorized, accounted for up to one-third of the nation's population increase in the 1980s, and the 1990 census recorded the presence of nearly 20 million foreign-born residents in the United States (Bach 1993:1; Stull 1990:303–304).

Responding to the reemergence of immigration as an important national concern, the Ford Foundation commissioned a project called "Changing Relations: Newcomers and Established Residents in U.S. Communities" to investigate how new immigrants and established residents were adjusting to one another. After a national competition, the Changing Relations Project Board selected interdisciplinary teams to conduct ethnographic research for two years in five metropolitan areas: Philadelphia, Miami, Chicago, Houston, and Monterey Park, California. The sixth site—Garden City, Kansas—was chosen to represent the small towns of America's heartland (see Lamphere 1992).

Alejandro Portes and József Böröcz (1989) say the modes of incorporation of new immigrants into host societies are largely determined by (1) conditions of exit, (2) class origins, and (3) the contexts of their reception in host communities and societies.

The circumstances that inspire emigrants to leave their homes for a distant land—and their economic and educational backgrounds—are beyond the control of the receiving community, but the reception a community offers to newcomers is not. According to Portes and Böröcz (Ibid.:620), the context of reception for new immigrants is determined by governmental policy, labor market demand, the presence or absence of preexisting ethnic enclaves, and public opinion.

Work in meatpacking and related jobs fueled Garden City's growth and rapidly changing ethnic composition. Hispanics first became a significant presence in Garden City at the beginning of the twentieth century, but by 1980 the descendants of those earlier immigrants had become Mexican Americans and were culturally differentiated from newly arriving Latino immigrants. Fewer than 100 Southeast Asians called Garden City home in 1980, and most residents of Garden City were ill prepared for the sudden arrival of hundreds of Vietnamese refugees.

Federal immigration law and its enforcement, the labor needs of meatpacking plants headquartered in distant cities, and the ethnic makeup of the community were beyond the influence of the average Garden Citian in 1980. But the fourth factor that contributes to the context of reception—public opinion—was not.

Clergy, educators, social service providers, city government and law enforcement officials, and local journalists have struggled to provide a positive context of reception for Garden City's newcomers, whatever their backgrounds. It has not been easy. Sustained growth combined with high population mobility and dramatically increasing ethnic and linguistic diversity created housing shortages, soaring school enrollments, rising crime and social problems, insufficient medical services, and an overburdened road system. But Garden City has not shied from these challenges.

We submitted our final report to the Ford Foundation—and to the people of Garden City—in February 1990 (Stull et al. 1990). Our research, and that of colleagues on the Changing Relations Project team, produced an extensive literature about how one town grappled with rural industrialization, rapid population growth, and an almost continuous flow of immigrants and refugees. It has drawn the attention of other social scientists, historians, journalists, filmmakers, and photographers.

In the decade following the Changing Relations Project, we studied the impact of meat and poultry processing on a half-dozen communities across North America. In the course of our studies, we developed a good idea of what happens to communities when a packinghouse comes to town (Broadway 1990, 2007; Broadway & Stull 1991; Gouveia & Stull 1995; Stull & Broadway 1990; Stull, Broadway, & Erickson 1992). But what about the long haul? Would the transformations we documented in Garden City and later in other towns continue unabated? To find out, we have returned again and again to "the Garden," where it all began—for us, at least. When it opened the world's largest beef plant 10 miles west of Garden City, IBP launched a protracted boom, fueled by migrants from around the United States and immigrants and refugees from across the globe who came to work on its killfloor and processing line. Almost exactly two decades after IBP opened its doors, on Christmas night 2000, Garden City's ConAgra plant burned. Eleven years later, it remains an abandoned shell.

This chapter reviews Garden City's social and economic "ups and downs" over the past 30 years and how it has dealt with them.

WILL IT EVER SETTLE DOWN?

Garden City and surrounding Finney County roiled with change in the 1980s. As the two beef plants that bookended Garden City, one 10 miles to the west and the other on its eastern edge, came on line, population skyrocketed. Even before the plants opened, housing had become a major problem. In June 1980, as construction of the IBP plant was in full swing, Garden City's need for housing became so critical that city officials held a press conference to ask home owners to make sleeping quarters available to the many workers unable to find accommodations (Reeve 1996:219). In fall 1981, a year after its plant opened, IBP surveyed more than 600 employees and found that 5 percent were living in motels or cars, while 33 percent felt they were paying excessive rent. IBP used this survey to convince local officials to rezone land on the eastern edge of town for a mobile home park. East Garden Village grew to more than 500 units, housing nearly a tenth of the town's population. After Val-Agri opened, just up the road from East Garden Village, many of its employees moved there.

By 2000, these two packinghouses had a combined workforce of 5,300, of which 90 percent were hourly employees. The need to fill so many jobs, coupled with employee turnover exceeding 100 percent in 1990 (Cultural Relations Board, 2001:14), forced IBP and ConAgra to recruit far and wide.

Led by the creation of thousands of beefpacking jobs, the economy expanded. New restaurants, retail outlets, and motels opened. However, many of these newly created positions relied upon part-time employees and paid poorly. Garden City's school enrollment rose dramatically. Voters responded by approving bond issues to build three new elementary schools and expand existing facilities. The town's rapid growth in the 1980s was based upon a low-wage economy, and this coupled with increasing ethnic and linguistic diversity strained the abilities of social, health, and law enforcement providers to meet rapidly rising community needs. A soaring population, and a highly mobile one, contributed to rising property and violent crimes, most due to domestic violence.

Although growth slowed late in the decade, Finney County was still the fastest growing county in Kansas in the 1980s (39%) and its rate of growth (22%) was surpassed by only one other county in the 1990s, a sprawling well-to-do residential area of Kansas City.

WHAT GOES UP MUST COME DOWN

The apex of Garden City's growth coincided with the 2000 federal census. Nine months later, a fire on Christmas night closed the county's second largest employer, ConAgra, putting 2,300 out of work. With the fire "Garden City lost its swagger," as a former mayor put it. ConAgra announced it would decide whether to rebuild the plant by April 1, 2001. In March of that year, state, local, and city officials offered the company a $2.5 million incentive package to reopen the plant. It included worker training, road and physical plant improvements, and odor abatement, which had been a recurrent issue. ConAgra said it would respond by May, but after repeatedly extending that deadline, it fell silent. The city sent a delegation to ConAgra's Greeley, Colorado, headquarters, but: "They didn't meet with us; they sent someone out [to the waiting room] to say they would not be meeting with our delegation. I don't see how a company can do that to a community. They cut us off at the legs" (Authors' fieldnotes, October 11–16, 2004).

ConAgra sold its Red Meats Division in 2002 to investors who operated under the name Swift & Co. In 2007, the Brazilian firm JBS S.A. bought Swift and now operates under the name JBS USA. Hopes that the Garden City plant will reopen or be sold surface from time to time, but nothing has materialized.

Single ConAgra employees departed soon after the fire, but workers with families did not immediately leave, choosing instead to finish out the school year and hope the plant would reopen. When it didn't, some packed up and moved to other packinghouse towns, only to return when these communities did not measure up to Garden City. Some former ConAgra workers found different jobs in town, others commuted to packinghouse jobs in Dodge City, Liberal, and Guymon, Oklahoma, 100 miles to the south. But when the price of gasoline soared during the buildup to the 2003 Iraq War, commuting became too expensive, and more and more former ConAgra employees moved away (Broadway & Stull 2006:62).

Table 8.1 shows the dramatic growth in Garden City and Finney County during the boom from 1980 to 2000. It also shows the devastating impact of the bust that followed. Although employment and population are again on the

T A B L E 8.1   Population Changes, Finney County and Garden City, Kansas, 1980–2010

		1980	1990	2000	2010
Population	Finney County	23,825	33,070	40,253	36,776
	Garden City	18,256	24,097	28,451	26,658
% Foreign Born	Finney County	3.2	9.9	22.7	20.4
	Garden City	3.3	9.8	22.8	21.3

SOURCE: U.S. Census.

rise, population is still well below the historic highs achieved before the fire. These trends are even more evident in Table 8.2, which presents enrollment figures for Garden City's public schools. Garden City's schools lost only 63 students in the first year after the fire. But enrollment dropped steadily through the 2008–09 school year, before finally beginning to rise in 2010–11. Garden City had indeed lost its swagger.

Rapid growth and more recent decline is only part of Garden City's story. More dramatic are the increase in its immigrant population and the resultant alterations in its ethnic composition. In 1980, just over 3 percent of Garden City's population was foreign born. By 2010, one in five Garden City residents was an immigrant. Hispanics increased from 16 percent of the county population in 1980 to 47 percent in 2010. Non-Hispanic whites, on the other hand, declined from 82 percent in 1980 to 30 percent in 2010. Yet, these broad census categories mask the human tapestry that Garden City has become. The Hispanics enumerated in 1980 were Mexican Americans, with a deep history in the town (Ávila (1997). The label "Hispanic" now encompasses not only these established residents, but new immigrants from Mexico, El Salvador, Guatemala, and Cuba. At the same time, non-Hispanic whites have become more diverse as Low-German-speaking Mennonites entered southwest Kansas from Chihuahua in northern Mexico. Fleeing drought and runaway inflation, they found work on area farms and feedyards. By 2010, between 3,000 and 4,000 of them had settled in central and western Kansas, and some had bought their own farms.

T A B L E 8.2   Ethnic Composition of Garden City Public Schools (USD 457) (selected years)

School Year	Enrollment	% White	% Black	% Hispanic	% Other
2000–01	7,864	38.0	1.5	57.0	3.5
2001–02	7,801	36.0	1.5	59.0	3.5
2004–05	7,572	31.0	1.0	60.0	8.0
2008–09	7,286	26.0	1.0	62.5	10.5
2010–11	7,557	25.0	1.0	67.0	7.0

Other category includes: American Indian or Alaska Native, Asian, and Multiethnic.

SOURCE: Kansas Department of Education.

One-third of the newcomers during Garden City's economic boom in the early 1980s were Vietnamese and other Southeast Asian refugees. Their numbers dwindled as this immigrant stream slowed to a trickle and earlier settlers moved to climates more akin to their homeland; took jobs or started businesses elsewhere with money saved from working in the beef plants; or followed their children when they left for college. Of those Vietnamese who remain, some still work at Tyson (formerly IBP), but a growing number are entering white-collar jobs (tax preparers), skilled trades (plumbing), and small businesses (dry cleaning, retail stores, small markets, and restaurants). Only a few of those who have gone away to college have returned.

As the Southeast Asian labor supply shrank, the packers turned to another ready source of workers—Latinos. By the late 1980s, IBP and ConAgra recruiters were traveling to Texas and New Mexico in search of workers. During the 1990s Mexican immigration to Garden City surged. Companies had always recruited in border cities by advertising on radio stations reaching into Mexico. Beginning in the mid-1990s, IBP, with the blessing of the Immigration and Nat-uralization Service, established a labor office in Mexico City, offering to pay recruits' bus fares to the United States (Cohen 1998). As a result, between 1990 and 2000 the Hispanic share of IBP's workforce rose from 58 to 77 percent; at ConAgra it jumped from 56 to 88 percent (Cultural Relations Board 2001).

The results of this migration are evident in Garden City's landscape. Among the employers listed by the Garden City Chamber of Commerce in 1994, not a single one was identifiably minority owned, although many counted significant numbers of minorities and immigrants among their employees. Ten years later, the chamber of commerce listed 100 businesses owned by Hispanics and 16 owned by Asians. A Spanish-language radio station, KSSA, was serving the region.

Today, Latino businesses line major thoroughfares on the east and west sides of town, while downtown with its banks, jewelers, clothing stores, soda shop, Internet café, and upscale Mexican restaurant caters primarily to the shrinking Anglo population. Most Latino and other immigrant businesses are small—restaurants, groceries, clothing stores, bakeries, auto repair shops, car dealerships, bars, and liquor stores—but they constitute a robust sector of Garden City's economy, and an expanding one. For example, a Mexican businessman who opened a grocery in 1983 has added a bus line that employs 80 drivers and regularly runs from Garden City to El Paso, Texas, then on to Juarez, Mexico, and beyond. It travels north as well, to major U.S. cities, such as Denver and Los Angeles (Stull & Broadway 2008:127).

In recent years, Tyson has begun to recruit refugees once again, and Garden City's newest immigrants have come from the Horn of Africa and Southeast Asia. Somalis began arriving in 2006. More followed in 2008 after Tyson closed its beef slaughter operation in Emporia, Kansas. Since then, other Somalis have arrived from Minneapolis, which is home to the largest Somali community in the United States. An estimated 300 Somalis now live in town, along with 100 or so Ethiopians and Oromos (a Cushitic-speaking people from northeast Africa). The first Burmese arrived in Garden City in December 2007, recruited by Tyson, and others followed to find work on its floor. Current estimates of the

FIGURE 8.3 One of Garden City's newest Muslim immigrants.

Burmese population in Garden City range from 150 to 700. Businesses catering to these new arrivals are only now beginning to appear.

Education and Schools

Garden City's schools dramatically reflect this demographic transition. Hispanics now make up more than two-thirds of the school district's pupils, while the portion of non-Hispanic whites has declined to a quarter. Young Burmese women in *hijabs* (head coverings worn by Muslim women) sit in the cafeteria and English as a Second Language (ESL) classrooms alongside Somalis, Guatemalans, and Mexicans. More than a dozen languages are spoken in the Garden City schools, and 23 percent of the district's students are enrolled in ESL courses.

The changing demographic profile of Garden City's school children reflects the future of the community, and to their credit, the district's school board, administration, and faculty have embraced this increasing diversity. In 2003, James Mireles became principal of Garden City High School, the first Hispanic to be named to such a post in Kansas. Mireles has made an effort to recruit Latino teachers and staff, but the proportion is still under 10 percent. Teachers from Spain, India, and the Philippines also serve as role models for minority and immigrant students in the high school.

In 2004, one of his major concerns was "the loss of color" as students advanced through the grades and more and more minority and immigrant students dropped out. When we visited Mireles in the winter of 2011, he showed us the class picture for the year before he was named principal, and then flipped through each class picture thereafter. He pointed out how the faces changed from primarily white to a much richer ethnic palette. His point was that more and more Latino and other minority students are now graduating from high school. At the time Mireles took over as principal, students in the honors classes were virtually all Anglo Americans, but seven years later honors students have become a mosaic of colors and nationalities (Authors' fieldnotes, October 11–16, 2004; January 25–29, 2011).

The high school has an Asian club and Latin Lingo, a modern dance group that focuses on contemporary dances such as salsa rather than traditional *ballet folklorico*, which performs regional folkdances of Mexico. In 2004, the high school held its first Latino dance, which drew 250 attendees of whom 60 percent were ESL students. Many of them had never been to a school dance before.

Perhaps, most symbolic of the changes has been the rise of soccer as a school sport. When we began our research in Garden City, immigrant students in general, and ESL students in particular, had few opportunities to participate in extracurricular activities. Prompted by a recommendation from the Changing Relations Project team, the district established a high school soccer club and funded a coaching position (Stull et al. 1990:113). The man who took that position and still holds it, Juan Padilla, a high school guidance counselor and an immigrant who grew up in Michoacan, Mexico, convinced the administration to make soccer an official team sport in 1996. In 2003, Garden City High School's boys' varsity soccer team advanced to the state semifinals, before losing to Wichita Heights High School. The team roster consisted of eleven sons of Mexican immigrants, five of Salvadoran immigrants, one of Vietnamese refugees, and one of Anglo Americans. Sam Quinones (2007) masterfully tells the story of their magical season, and what it meant for these boys and their school, in a collection of essays on Mexican immigration titled *Antonio's Gun and Delfino's Dream*.

The elevation of boys' and girls' soccer to team sports, as well as an active intramural sports program, has been instrumental in increasing involvement of students from immigrant families with the schools. A cross-section of the student body now participates in athletics, encouraged by the high school's athletic director, Martin Segovia, a native Mexican American who graduated from Garden City High School.

Garden City's Boom, Bust, and Recovery?

Garden City's boom came in the 1980s, when the number of employed persons shot up by more than 50 percent (see Table 8.3). Job numbers increased by 23 percent in the 1990s, but employment fell after the ConAgra fire, as did payrolls and the number of business establishments. These numbers are climbing once again, but they have yet to recover to 2000 levels. One of the most visible gains is an ethanol plant, which opened in 2007. The plant's operator credits it with creating 32 jobs and an additional 50 spin-off jobs (Farley 2009). In 2008, voters approved a $97.5 million bond issue to build a new high school; 210 people worked at the site in summer 2010 (Ahmad 2010). The new high school will have a field reserved for soccer when its doors open in the fall of 2012.

TABLE 8.3   **Finney County's Changing Economic Profile (selected years)**

Year	Total Employment	# of Establishments*	Total Annual Payroll ($000)*
1980	13,117	744	90,610
1990	19,938	914	218,353
2000	24,592	1020	384,011
2002	22,162	1024	352,331
2005	21,311	971	389,139
2008	22,914	986	446,648

*Excludes self-employed, agricultural employees, and most government employees.
SOURCE: The University of Kansas Institute for Policy and Social Research n.d. *Kansas County Profiles: Finney County.*

With jobs in meatpacking have come new jobs in the service sector, though many pay poorly and are only part-time (see Table 8.4). As a result, the average wage in Finney County fell from 92 percent of the Kansas average in 1980 to 84 percent in 2000, and there it remains. Per capita income has also fallen relative to the state and, more significantly, relative to rural Kansas. Sadly, in 2009 Finney County had the dubious distinction of the lowest per capita income in the state (see Table 8.5).

Crime and Law Enforcement

Crime increased in Garden City throughout the 1980s. Crime reports rose and fell and rose again during the 1990s. By 2002, the number of reported crimes

TABLE 8.4   **Finney County's Average Wage Per Job**

Year	Wage $	% of Kansas Average Wage	% of Non-Metro Kansas Average Wage
1980	11,756	92	105
1990	17,324	87	105
2000	24,664	84	107
2008	33,071	84	107

SOURCE: The University of Kansas Institute for Policy and Social Research n.d. *Kansas County Profiles: Finney County.*

TABLE 8.5   **Finney County's Per Capita Income**

Year	Income $	% of Kansas Per Capita Income	% of Non-Metro Kansas Per Capita Income
1980	9,340	100	100
1990	15,431	86	96
2000	21,215	75	90
2009	26,529	68	78

SOURCE: The University of Kansas Institute for Policy and Social Research n.d. *Kansas County Profiles: Finney County.*

TABLE 8.6   Finney County Crime Index,* 1990–2009 (selected years)

Year	Reported Crimes
1990	2,522
1994	3,324
1998	2,469
2002	2,585
2006	1,797
2009	1,425

*Crime Index crimes include: murder, rape, robbery, aggravated assault, burglary, theft, motor vehicle theft, and arson.
SOURCE: The University of Kansas Institute for Policy and Social Research n.d. *Kansas County Profiles: Finney County.*

had settled back to 1990 levels, despite a 22.5 percent population increase during that decade. Since then, "Crime is down, down, down," according to James Hawkins, Garden City's chief of police. This trend suggests that Stan Albrecht (1982) was right when he hypothesized that social disruption in rural boomtowns is temporary and declines as newcomers develop neighborhood, friendship, and community ties.

Population loss in the years following the ConAgra fire may help explain some of this fall in crime. Other factors may also be at work. The increasing proportion of non-English speakers may chose not to report crimes because of immigration status, language, or cultural barriers. While unauthorized immigrants may be reluctant to report crimes, Garden City's newest immigrants, Somali and Burmese refugees, show no such hesitation, according to Chief Hawkins.

The decline in crime in Garden City over the past decade may also be related to the size of the police force. Staffing in the 1990s did not keep pace with the rising population, and turnover in sworn officers was a problem. But the department has been fully staffed since 2008, and turnover is now much lower. "Officers are sticking around now," according to Chief Hawkins. He credits higher retention to his policy of recruiting officers from the surrounding region, who are more likely to remain. Efforts to recruit minorities are also paying off: of the department's 58 officers, eight are Hispanic, though not all are bilingual. A Spanish-speaking dispatcher is now on duty at all times, and the chief believes that Spanish-speaking dispatchers are key to successful policing.

When local translators of less common languages—Somali, Russian, Mayan, Low German—are not available, the police department uses AT&T's Language Line. Burmese immigrants may speak one of three languages, and finding translators has been challenging. The local Burmese tend to know and protect each other. Some are reluctant to cooperate with police because they feel it will violate social trust if their translation causes embarrassment to their countrymen or gets them into trouble. On one occasion, the department had to go to Denver to find a Burmese translator because no one in Garden City wanted to take sides in the case.

For Garden City, property crimes, especially burglary, are the main concern. Gangs were just making their appearance during our initial research in the late 1980s, and over the next decade they became a serious problem. By 2004, Garden City had 13 active gangs, totaling about 400 members, ranging in age from early teens to mid-twenties. Gangs were ethnically based rather than territorial, and most members were Hispanics. Gang identity and membership sometimes crossed over between Garden City and Dodge City, but they were not connected to gangs in large urban areas. Graffiti, much of it gang related, had become a common sight. In recent years, however, problems with gangs and graffiti have subsided. One reason for the decline in graffiti is the Neighborhood Improvement Program (NIP), which began as an anti-graffiti effort. The officer assigned to this program coordinates community efforts to clean up trash and paint over graffiti. NIP volunteers collected and disposed of 300 tons of trash in 2010.

Garden City's chief of police speaks several languages. He has a monthly call-in show on Garden City's Spanish-language radio station, and many calls concern immigration. The police department's progressive policies are a reflection of its leadership. These policies have found favor among Garden Citians, many of whom have made a sincere effort to embrace its growing ethnic diversity. Illustrating the Garden City attitude, Chief Hawkins told us that: "When the Somalis came, nobody said, 'Aw, shit, here comes another group.' It was just par for the course" (Authors' fieldnotes, January 25–29, 2011).

Housing

Housing is perhaps the single greatest concern in rapidly growing rural communities. Thirty years after city officials pleaded with established residents to open up their homes to newcomers who could not find a place to stay, affordable housing remains a critical issue. Most newcomers cannot afford single-family homes, and very few rental units are available because building slowed in the years following the ConAgra fire. Many immigrants have little choice but to live with friends and relatives in crowded conditions. Some landlords base rent on the number of people living in the apartment, not its size or quality. In any given month, approximately 300 housing units are occupied but not hooked up to any utilities. According to Garden City's planner, "These people are not squatters; they simply cannot afford to pay for the utilities" (Authors' fieldnotes, January 25–29, 2011).

The police chief told us housing codes, largely lacking in the 1980s, are improving, and the city now has a housing inspection office. Substandard housing is much less common in the city than in years past, and it is doing a better job of getting rid of houses that should not be standing. The county, on the other hand, still has plenty of ugly mobile homes, but it is moving toward getting some of them cleaned up (Authors' fieldnotes, January 25–29, 2011).

Social and Health Services

Welfare reform cut the number of food stamp recipients in Finney County in half—from a January 1993 high of 2,722 to a low of 1,263 in January 2000. Thereafter, the number of food stamp recipients in Finney County soared to over 4,100 in 2010. Rising demand for food stamps is a national phenomenon, but the county's 226 percent increase far surpasses the statewide increase of 130 percent during the same period.

The number of children in the county who receive free or reduced-price lunches also rose from what was an all-time high of 50 percent in fall 2000 to an alarming 70 percent during the 2010–2011 school year. Given income levels, it is not surprising that the proportion of students in Garden City public schools who receive free or reduced-price lunches has risen so sharply (see Table 8.7).

Church volunteers founded Garden City's Emmaus House[1] in 1979 to provide temporary shelter and hot meals for indigents, drawn by the construction of IBP and a regional power plant. During the 1980s, the number of persons sheltered and fed by Emmaus House increased by 250 percent. The number of food boxes it distributed and the number of people it served rose by 70 percent in the 1990s.

The loss of jobs associated with the ConAgra fire dramatically affected Emmaus House. The number of food boxes it dispersed doubled from 2000 to 2001, while meals provided on-site tripled. Although demand for these services dropped in 2002 and 2003, the number of meals served soared by nearly 400 percent during the decade, and the number of food boxes increased by a third. More and more people in Garden City are dependent upon charity for food; many of them work for Tyson. Tyson sometimes gives surplus meat to Emmaus House, but never money, even though Emmaus does much to subsidize company employees, providing temporary housing until they are settled and food to supplement their incomes.

With its paid staff of six people, three of whom get health insurance, it costs $18,000 a month to operate Emmaus House. In the fall of 2010, at a time when

TABLE 8.7   USD 457 Income Data, 2000–2010 (selected years)

School Year	Number of Students with Free or Reduced Lunches	% of Students with Free or Reduced Lunches
2000–2001	3,917	50
2002–2003	4,087	53
2004–2005	4,378	58
2006–2007	4,479	60
2008–2009	4,714	65
2010–2011	5,317	70

SOURCE: Kansas Department of Education.

Michael Broadway

FIGURE 8.4 A guest relaxes on the lawn of Emmaus House, Garden City, Kansas.

the need for its services had never been greater, donations dried up. Emmaus House's director pleaded with the Garden City Council to pay its $15,000 a year utility bill (Ahmad 2010). She also asked for donations in the newspaper, radio, and television. The council rejected the proposal, but several businesses, trusts, and individuals made substantial contributions. As a result, Emmaus continues to fulfill its mission.

Access to health care is a serious problem, thanks to an economy based on low paying jobs that provide few benefits. In the early 1990s, Finney County placed in the bottom 10 percent of Kansas counties on the Primary Care Status Index, which includes percent of births lacking early prenatal care, children lacking adequate immunization, and births to mothers without a high school education. The county's poor performance stems from inadequate "access to and

TABLE 8.8 Emmaus House Services (selected years)

Year	Food Boxes Distributed	Total Meals Provided
2000	10,818	114,339
2001	21,184	384,537
2002	14,058	241,651
2009	14,304	327,129
2010	14,402	435,536

SOURCE: Emmaus House, Garden City, Kansas.

availability of health resources for low-income minority households" (Hackenberg & Kukulka, 1995:195). Twenty years later, a nationwide survey of health behaviors also placed Finney County in the bottom 10 percent of Kansas counties: reported rates of adult obesity, adult smoking, binge drinking, and teen pregnancy far exceeded statewide averages (University of Wisconsin Health Institute n.d.).

United Methodist Western Kansas Mexican-American Ministries Care Centers and Health Clinics, or Mexican-American Ministries (MAM) for short, is the region's primary health care provider for persons without medical insurance. (St. Catherine's Hospital in Garden City also provides care for persons without health insurance through its emergency room—it must, by law.) Founded in 1987, Mexican-American Ministries recorded 6,000 primary care medical visits in 1990; by 1995 the number had increased to 17,652, and by 2000 it had reached 22,207—an increase of 270 percent for the decade. It serves persons regardless of ethnic, religious, or language background, and provides all services in both Spanish and English. Translation is also available in Low German, Burmese, and Somali. Two-thirds of its clients need language translation. By 2010, the number of clinic visits reached 24,783, an increase of almost 12 percent over the previous decade. Even this staggering figure does not reflect true demand. According to MAM's director, Garden City's clinic must turn away 15 to 20 people a day because of insufficient staff (Authors' fieldnotes, January 25–29, 2011).

GARDEN CITY'S GREAT BIG MEAT ADVENTURE: 30 YEARS AND COUNTING

When the lines started up at IBP's Finney County plant in December 1980, Garden City became one of the first towns to be transformed by the restructuring and relocation of the meat and poultry industry. Three decades later, Garden City has proved to be a bellwether for food processing communities throughout North America. Garden City has taught us most of what we know about what to expect when the packers come to town. It has also shown us what happens when they pack up and leave. Closely monitored by scholars, journalists, and other communities, it serves as an exemplar for modern boomtowns created by rural industrialization.

Boomtowns have always been a part of the western landscape. Rapid growth, high wages, and increases in social disorders characterized the energy boomtowns that sprang up in the intermountain West in the 1970s. Beefpacking has created a different type of boomtown on the High Plains. With their high turnover, minimal benefits, dangerous working conditions, and low wages, these plants have created few jobs for local people. Instead, the packers target immigrants and refugees. In packinghouse towns, wage levels fall and communities face rising tides of impoverished residents. These "booms" produce dramatic surges in demand for social, educational, and health services, while taxpayers and voluntary organizations bear the financial costs associated with these developments. And permanent residents bear the social costs.

As Garden City has so painfully learned, sooner or later booms go bust. The costs of Garden City's boom and its bust alike were created and externalized by the meatpacking industry, which enjoys billions in sales and hundreds of millions in profits. In the globalized economy, these companies have few loyalties to their workers and little concern for the towns where they work and live. ConAgra executives' refusal even to meet with Garden City's delegation is only one example of the industry's callous disregard for the welfare of its employees and the communities where it operates. Perhaps a more telling, if less costly, example comes from Tyson. When asked to help fund the first piece of public art in Garden City—a statue depicting young children of various ethnicities to be erected near a major thoroughfare—Tyson refused to contribute, despite repeated written requests (Broadway & Stull 2006:64).

The twentieth century ended in Garden City with the ConAgra fire, and with it two decades of boom. Garden City has spent the twenty-first century trying to climb back to where it had been before the fire. The Tyson plant remains a magnet for those with little command of English who are not afraid of hard work. And these latest newcomers—Burmese, Somalis, Ethiopians—provide new challenges for a community with a long history of accommodating immigrants.

Garden City may have lost some of its swagger, but it retains its multicultural vibrancy. Its expanding immigrant communities have enriched the economy and society of southwest Kansas. Entering Garden City from the east along U.S. Highway 50, a visitor is immediately aware of its diverse population.

F I G U R E 8.5 Children playing on a street in East Garden Village, Garden City, Kansas.

On the edge of town are Latino dance halls and retail stores; nearer town, and adjacent to East Garden Village, two mini-malls house Asian markets and a billiard hall, Mexican bakeries, and a Latino-owned liquor store. U.S. Highway 50 becomes Fulton Street in town, and the stores and restaurants that line this major thoroughfare further testify to Garden City's cosmopolitan quality. Sharing a parking lot and a sign are Iglesia de Dios Pentecostal Church, Bad Boyz Boxing Club, and Lam Gia Thai Restaurant. Across the way are El Remedio Market, Pho Hoa Vietnamese restaurant, and the Grain Bin.

We were reminded how much Garden City keeps changing on a January evening in 2011. After six hours on the road, we drove into town after dark and headed straight for the Grain Bin, a landmark watering hole where a stiff drink and a good steak could always be found. As we pushed open the door, bleary-eyed from the long drive, we were taken aback by its new decor—sombreros and serapes (ponchos). We had just entered Mio, Garden City's newest Mexican restaurant.

Thumbing through the Yellow Pages confirms this windshield ethnography—of the 68 restaurants listed, 22 are chain franchises, 23 are Latin American, and five are Asian. Glancing at the names on virtually any page of the telephone book shows the many people that call Garden City home—Murillo, Murphy, Nanthavongdouangsy, Nguyen, Nichols, Nunez.

Garden City is not a multicultural Heaven on Earth. Conflicts and resentments between ethnic groups, and between new immigrants and established residents, are evident. For example, Anglo Americans tend to lump Mexican Americans and immigrants from Mexico and elsewhere in Latin America into a single category—Hispanic—despite important cultural and linguistic differences between them.

Michael Broadway

FIGURE 8.6 Mio recently opened on the site of the Grain Bin, once one of Garden City's finest restaurants.

When our team first studied Garden City, Arthur Campa (1990) saw little interaction, and at times open hostility, between established Mexican Americans and new immigrant Latinos. After Tomás Jiménez (2010) interviewed 60 Garden City Mexican Americans in 2001 and 2002, he concluded that Mexican Americans have been socioeconomically, residentially, and culturally assimilated in Garden City. Many have intermarried with Anglo Americans and they play an increasingly central role in the city's civic life. Although Mexican Americans feel a certain kindred to Latino immigrants, many also feel a distinct discomfort in their presence, or as he put it, common ethnicity is a tie that both binds and divides Latinos in Garden City.

Change is never easy, as Garden Citians will attest. Although some resent their presence, Garden City's newcomers nevertheless reaffirm America's faith in the immigrant dream—they seek a new life in a new land where their children can pursue their own dreams. Immigrants come to work, and many stay to become citizens and raise the next generation of Americans. As Juana "Janie" Perkins said while being sworn in as Garden City's first new-immigrant, Latina mayor on April 14, 2005: "I am living proof that [the American Dream] is not only possible, but alive and well…. I feel like Laura Ingalls[2] of the 21st century. Forty-two years ago, I was born in a small village with no electricity, plumbing or a place to get primary education…. I want to thank my parents for having the courage to seek a better life for their children" (Tietgen 2005:A1). Later that year, the governor appointed Perkins to the Kansas Board of Regents, which oversees higher education in the state.

In 1980, four out of five Garden Citians were Anglo American. Who would have predicted then that three decades later Garden City would be a majority-minority community—the first in the state? Who would have anticipated that within three decades 70 percent of school children would be so-called minorities, or that high school administrators would one day brag that the children of immigrant and refugee meatpacking workers star on varsity athletic teams and excel in honors classes? Or that Anglo professionals would one day lunch next to refugees and new immigrants on *pho* (Vietnamese noodle soup) or *papusas* (Salvadoran thick corn tortillas stuffed with cheese, meat, or beans)? Or that a direct bus service would connect Garden City, Kansas, to Chihuahua City, Mexico?

The past three decades have taught Garden Citians that in a globalized economy, multinational corporations have few loyalties to the communities in which they operate. Their experience offers a cautionary tale to other towns, their elected officials, and economic boosters, about the "benefits" of the meat and poultry industry, and the price packinghouses extract from communities. But Garden Citians have also learned to compensate for their economic and social handicaps and embrace the steady stream of newcomers, their strong work ethic, and the rich heritages they bring with them. This willingness to accept and offer a helping hand to all who come has become the hallmark of Garden City and the foundation for a resilient community. The lessons it holds are what keep drawing us back.

NOTES

1. According to the Gospel of Luke, Jesus first revealed himself after his resurrection to two of his disciples when they shared a meal with a "stranger" they met walking from Jerusalem to the town of Emmaus. Sponsored by an ecumenical coalition of local churches, Emmaus House served as a model for shelters citizens established in the packinghouse towns of Lexington, Nebraska, and Guymon, Oklahoma.

2. Laura Ingalls wrote the popular book *Little House on the Prairie*, which became a long-running television series, about her childhood on the Kansas frontier in the 1860s.

9

✳

Don't Shoot the Messenger: Technical Assistance to Packinghouse Towns

The Garden City Changing Relations Project final report concluded with 15 recommendations to the people of Garden City—four concerned education, and the remainder dealt with community issues such as housing, health care, day care, and social services (Stull et al. 1990). In collaboration with the school district, we organized the Multicultural Action Committee, an advisory board representing public school teachers, city government, Garden City's three main ethnic groups, and service organizations. We worked with this committee to fine-tune our recommendations and present them to appropriate institutions and agencies.

Our report was soon put to local use: social service agencies used our findings to obtain external funds; the school district revised policies and procedures on curriculum, bilingual and English as a Second Language (ESL) instruction, extracurricular activities, community outreach, personnel training, evaluation, and retention with our recommendations in hand; the city commission established a cultural relations board with wide community and ethnic representation; and local law enforcement sought minority personnel. Garden City Community College, in cooperation with the Kansas State University Extension, inaugurated a Five-State Multicultural Conference to showcase the community's cultural diversity and share lessons learned with regional educators and service providers.

As we carried out our research in Garden City, we wondered whether what we were finding there was also happening in other packinghouse towns. We soon had the chance to find out. Late in 1988, IBP announced plans for a new beef plant in Lexington, Nebraska, about 250 miles northeast of Garden City. It was to be the first beef plant built in the United States since the one near Garden City opened in 1980. Lexington established a Community Impact Study Team, which visited packing towns and sponsored public forums. A study team representative visited us in Garden City in January 1989. The following April we addressed a public forum in Lexington. We followed up with a report on changes Lexington might expect, provided materials from our Garden City research, and fostered interchanges between public and private agencies in both communities.

The study team included leaders in business, government, social services, health care, education, media, and the church. In December 1989, it completed its data-gathering mission, disbanded, and issued an exit report; by then the community was mobilizing to meet anticipated needs. Efforts influenced by our input included organization of a countywide ministerial association, which contributed to several community preparedness activities, and an interagency council intended to develop and implement an integrated strategy to deal with growth. When the Lexington study team disbanded, we began to identify and work with key agencies and individuals.

Of the original Garden City team, we were the only ones to take up work in Lexington. Lourdes Gouveia, a bilingual Latina sociologist from the University of Nebraska at Omaha joined us. In the summer of 1990, we collected baseline data on welfare caseloads, school enrollments, crime, and characteristics of newcomers. We conducted participant observation and interviews with civic and religious leaders, service providers, IBP officials, cattle producers and feeders, proprietors of local businesses, and "everyday citizens." We arranged for ongoing collection of data from the school district, Nebraska Department of Social Services, Lexington Housing Authority, Nebraska Job Services, City of Lexington, and the police and sheriff's departments. Our status as outside experts, and our early and ongoing presence, fostered a working relationship with the city manager and others who were guiding community responses to the changes taking place in Lexington.

The nonprofit Community Services Center sponsored public forums and community leadership workshops. Following our advice, and working with the ministerial association, it purchased a building and opened a shelter for low-income newcomers in January 1991. Known as Haven House, and patterned after Garden City's Emmaus House, it provided short-term housing, meals, and social service referrals for newcomers. The Salvation Army selected Haven House as a national pilot project, and for the first time funded and staffed a food program in a facility it neither owned nor operated.

We conducted intermittent fieldwork in Lexington through 1992 and monitored developments for several years thereafter. We reported on our research in the press, public forums, publications, and a 1996 report to the community (Broadway 1991; Broadway, Stull, & Podraza 1994; Gouveia & Stull 1995, 1997; Hackenberg et al. 1993).

THE PLIANCY FACTOR

Members of our team have taken what we learned first in Garden City and then in Lexington to other communities and have worked with them to try to modify and mitigate the negative consequences that attend the meat and poultry industry. In doing so, we have sought to apply what Allan Holmberg (1958:14) called the pliancy factor: "When a generalization on behavior is communicated to people who are also its subjects, it may alter the knowledge and preferences of these people and also their behavior."

Three factors limit the pliancy of communities that host meatpacking plants: the nature of the industry, the timing of interventions, and the approach to development taken by the community.

Elsewhere we have stated that "communities … cannot alter the nature of meatpacking, its relative low pay, hazardous work conditions or recruiting practices" (Broadway 2000:41). That packing plants bring to their new homes significant levels of growth, turnover, and social problems is not only predictable, it is apparently inevitable. At least it has been in North America.

Companies do not usually announce plans for a new plant until a final decision has been reached, and they play competing towns against one another. If plans become public too soon, opposition often surfaces, especially now that our research and that of others offers clear evidence of packing plants' consequences for host communities. How then are small communities best able to respond to the challenges posed by meat and poultry processing plants?

COMMUNITY DEVELOPMENT MODELS

Many communities, rural and urban alike, pursue economic development without considering larger issues of community development. They equate development with jobs and see economic development as the sole means for community maintenance and improvement. But unless economic development results in an improved quality of life, it can actually be detrimental to community development. Jobs, like lunches, are rarely free. Certainly not in an age when corporations expect public subsidies and tax holidays; when companies threaten to leave host communities for "greener pastures" unless taxpayers dig ever deeper into their pockets. And low-wage jobs and the transient work forces they often create, coupled with corporate welfare, can harm the quality of life in a community.

Most members of host communities have little, if any, say in whether a processing plant comes to town. But the chorus of "jobs, jobs, jobs," sung in unison by the packers' front men and local boosters gives way to the "slaughterhouse blues" once people realize these new jobs will bring significant social and economic costs—and that most will be filled by immigrant workers.

At this point, those in leadership positions and citizens start to look beyond the narrow confines of economic development schemes to broader issues of community development. For community development to occur, problems must be identified, competing courses of action considered, resources recognized and mobilized, and strategies implemented. Though communities and their goals differ widely, Flora et al. (1992:251ff) identify three general models of community development: self-help, technical assistance, and conflict.

The self-help model emphasizes process—community members working together to arrive at group decisions and then taking actions to implement them. Broad-based participation in the decision-making process and subsequent actions are necessary for this model to succeed. Interest and motivation on the part of a wide spectrum of community members are essential, and decision making must be participatory and democratic. Unless the process itself is institutionalized, the effort will fail, since community involvement is a primary goal of this approach.

In contrast to the self-help model, technical assistance is task oriented. Local people are consumers of development, not its architects. Definitions of community needs are couched in technical terms that call for expert advice. The goal of development is the achievement of predetermined outcomes, and the degree of efficiency in reaching those outcomes is the measure of success. Cost-benefit analysis is the common language of this approach. State and local governments emphasize recruitment of new employers as the primary vehicle for development. Throughout rural North America, especially where jobs and population are in decline, rural communities target industries that add value to local commodities. Meatpacking is a prime example of this strategy: value is added to grains produced by local growers by feeding them to cattle or hogs raised or finished in the area, and value is added to livestock by slaughtering and processing animals locally.

The conflict model is like the self-help approach in bringing people together to discuss community issues, develop local leadership, and devise and implement strategies to achieve agreed-upon goals. It differs from self-help by seeking to redistribute power and in the strategies used to achieve this general goal, which often involve confrontation, protest, and litigation. This is usually the only model available to citizen groups who oppose government-sponsored development schemes. Citizens groups fighting proposed packinghouses and concentrated animal feeding operations often employ this model.

In testing the pliancy factor through research and technical assistance to packinghouse communities in the United States and Canada, our goal has been to develop what Fred Gearing (1979) called "alongside-of relations" among social scientists, community members, and the institutions they represent. Sometimes we have achieved this goal; sometimes not.

HOPE FOR THE BEST AND PREPARE
FOR THE WORST

The trade-off between economic development and its accompanying social costs is clearly evident in the efforts of the western Canadian province of Alberta to attract investment in its beef industry. To entice potential investors, the province's economic development publications proclaim that Alberta has one of the most competitive business tax environments in North America, with no provincial sales tax, low corporate taxes, and no payroll tax (Alberta Economic Development 2010). The province also makes funds available to

FIGURE 9.1 Members of the team Michael Broadway assembled to advise Brooks on community impacts from IBP's expansion of the Lakeside Processing Plant: Don Stull; Mark Grey, professor of anthropology, University of Northern Iowa; Penney Schwab, executive director, United Methodist Western Kansas Mexican-American Ministries and Health Clinics; and Amy Richardson, district administrator, Nebraska Department of Social Services.

assist developers. In the 1980s, when Cargill built its beef processing facility at High River, about 30 miles south of Calgary, Alberta provided $4 million (Canadian) for the construction of a wastewater treatment plant. It also provided $16 million (Canadian) in grants and loans to Lakeside Packers, located in Brooks, 110 miles southeast of Calgary (Broadway 2001). In 2011, Lakeside received another federal/provincial grant of $1.6 million to upgrade its ground beef production capabilities.

Many Albertans were pleased when IBP purchased Lakeside Packers in 1994 and announced it would double the slaughter capacity and add a boxed beef plant. Fewer live cattle would be shipped to the United States and more valued-added processing would be completed in the province.

When we visited Brooks in September 1996, many of the town's 10,000 residents were unsure what to expect after Lakeside began hiring the first thousand workers for its newly expanded beef plant. To provide guidance, we detailed the social and economic impact of meatpacking plants on small towns in the United States at a public forum. Many in the audience, including the former owner of Lakeside, were skeptical: "Surely, the same things would not happen in Canada." The local newspaper editor, who proudly traces his family roots to the town's early pioneers, openly wondered whether the plant would even open. Nevertheless, we

TABLE 9.1   Likely Social Impacts of a Meatpacking Plant and Recommended Community Responses

Impact	Response
1. Influx of visible minorities and an increase in language and cultural differences	1a. Establish cultural awareness workshops, a diversity committee, and provide ESL services
2. Increase in demand for low-cost housing	2a. Disperse new rental accommodations throughout the community
3. Increase in crime	3a. Establish a community liaison office
4. Increase in homeless persons	4a. Provide a homeless shelter
5. Increase in demand for social services	5a. Create an interagency service-provider group
6. Increase in demand for health care	6a. Hire additional health care professionals and assure the provision of translators

SOURCE: "The Impact of Meatpacking Plants on Small Towns: Lessons to be Learned from the U.S. Experience," workshop presented by Michael Broadway at Heritage Inn, Brooks, Alberta. September 12, 1996.

outlined a set of recommended community responses to the challenges posed by packinghouses based upon two basic premises: social change is inevitable; and communities need to embrace change (see Table 9.1).

We stressed that it would be residents and their elected officials who determined how Brooks responded to the challenges of rapid growth, and we believed that some of the worst community outcomes we had encountered in the United States could be avoided with appropriate planning. Housing shortages in Garden City had been alleviated by constructing large trailer courts, which served to marginalize newcomers and stigmatize them (Benson 1990). Moreover, the concentration of highly mobile persons in trailer parks prevented the development of a sense of a community, and trailer parks became "high crime" areas. To prevent the repetition of these circumstances in Brooks, we recommended dispersal of affordable rental housing throughout the community (see Table 9.1, Response 2a).

To deal with an expected influx of poor people looking for work, we strongly advocated establishing a homeless shelter (Response 4a). Providing shelter, food, and assistance to indigents requires careful coordination between voluntary and governmental agencies (Response 5a). Given the diverse nature of Canada's immigrant stream, we had no way to predict which immigrant groups would end up working in the plant and which language proficiencies would be needed by teachers and other service providers. But once it became apparent where the immigrants were coming from, we proposed that cultural awareness workshops be held for service providers and that Brooks recognize newcomers' contributions by celebrating ethnic holidays and hosting international festivals. To achieve these outcomes, we advised establishing a diversity committee made up of representatives from local government, business, and immigrant groups, which could identify the problems newcomers were experiencing and devise culturally appropriate solutions (Response 1a).

Lakeside's recruitment of young adult single males assured an increase in crime and alcohol-related incidents. But if a community is able to establish clear expectations for behavior and communicate them to newcomers, some criminal activities may be prevented (Response 3a). Although Alberta has a government-funded health care plan for all its citizens, Brooks, like most small towns in rural areas, suffers from a shortage of physicians and nurses. The influx of workers and their families would add to the demand for health care, and we recommended the community hire more health care professionals and professional translators to serve newcomer clients (Response 6a). Implementing such a recommendation is problematic, since Alberta already has programs to encourage physicians and nurses to settle in rural areas. But heavy patient loads, long and unpredictable hours, and the absence of support staff make recruitment difficult.

Finally, based upon the Lexington experience, we recommended formation of a community impact study team, which would consist of representatives from Lakeside, government, and social service providers. Its mandate would be to share information about the newcomers, identify problems in the delivery of services to them, and, where necessary, formulate and coordinate responses. The town council unofficially adopted this recommendation during our visit and appointed one of its own members to chair the study team.

We left town believing we had laid the foundations for a proactive response to the challenges posed by Lakeside's expansion. A follow-up visit, three months after Lakeside began hiring, found a skeptical community—we had predicted social upheaval, and none had occurred! Unfortunately, Brooks was only experiencing the calm before the storm.

A small pool of surplus labor and high turnover led the company's human resources manager to conclude in March 1997 that "we've pretty much exhausted the local labor supplies." And so Lakeside began recruiting nationally, beginning in Newfoundland and Nova Scotia, where the collapse of the Atlantic cod fishery had produced unemployment levels of 30 percent and more in coastal communities (Broadway 2001).

The company established on-site housing for recruits. It designed the housing to provide temporary accommodation, with rent increasing the longer a person stayed. Renters also received meal vouchers for use in the plant's cafeteria. These "benefits" were then deducted from workers' paychecks. When they received their first checks after two weeks on the job, many new employees had little to show for their work.

In less than a decade the trailers became unfit for human habitation and were torn down. The town's subsequent housing shortage was eventually solved by the construction of affordable housing, beginning in 2004, and the collapse of the Alberta oil boom in 2008, which led to outmigration and an increase in housing vacancies (Broadway fieldnotes, March 4, 2011).

The restructuring of Canada's meat industry in the late 1990s—plant closures in cities and the construction of large plants in rural areas—attracted media attention. A Canadian television producer found an article by Michael Broadway on the Canadian meat industry in a Lexus-Nexus search and called

Michael Broadway

FIGURE 9.2 Housing for workers on the grounds of IBP's Lakeside Beef Plant in Brooks, Alberta. The trailers lasted for about a decade before being torn down because of "mold" problems.

to find out what I knew about the Lakeside plant. I said I was conducting a longitudinal study of how Brooks was dealing with the social and economic changes accompanying the plant's expansion and would be going back to the community in January 1998. The producer asked whether I would mind meeting with him and a reporter during my visit. I agreed.

When I returned to Brooks I found it in the throes of many of the predicted social changes. The town council was upset that Brooks was attracting unwanted national attention and I was providing the media with data from my research. Within a week, my working relationship with the town council was severed by the city manager in an e-mail message accusing me of publicly stating that "the town has its head up its ass." Worse was to follow.

A report to the Brooks Community Impact Study Team (Broadway 2001), prepared with the assistance of local social service providers, documented that since the plant expanded in 1996, the town had experienced a 15 percent rise in population; housing shortages; an influx of immigrants from as far away as Iraq, Somalia, Bosnia, and Cambodia; a 200 percent increase in the budget of the Salvation Army for indigent care; a 70 percent jump in the reported crime rate; a 38 percent upswing in the use of the emergency room at the local hospital; and an astounding jump of 820 percent in the demand for one-time transitional assistance payments (welfare) from the Alberta Department of Family and Social Services.

The Brooks study team dismissed the report in a press release, noting, "It is unfortunate that media attention is drawn to our area because of the meatpacking plant, which, in actuality, has caused minimum impacts to our community" (Brooks Bulletin 2000).

BROOKS: "CITY OF A HUNDRED HELLOS"

"Minimum impacts," indeed! Brooks's population rose as immigrants and refugees flocked to town; by 2006 they accounted for 60 percent of Lakeside's employees. But unlike U.S. meatpacking plants that have relied on Latino workers, many of Lakeside's employees were coming from Africa, particularly the Sudan and Somalia. Their arrival strained community relations. In 2005, Lakeside employees went on strike to obtain a union contract. Most strikers were African line workers. Predominantly white clerical and maintenance staff crossed the picket line and tried to get the union decertified. Violent confrontations between picketers and employees ensued and police arrested some picketers for intimidating strike breakers. After three weeks the strike was settled, but not before two Ethiopian line workers died in a car accident on their way home from the picket line. These labor troubles and the rise in value of the Canadian dollar against the U.S. currency undoubtedly contributed to Tyson selling Lakeside to XL Foods, an Alberta-based meat processor, in 2009.

The strike changed Lakeside's labor recruitment strategy. Instead of targeting new immigrants and refugees, the company began to use Canada's Temporary Foreign Worker Program. By 2011, it had hired 700 temporary foreign workers—just under a third of the plant's workforce—from the Ukraine, China, Colombia, Mexico, and the Philippines. Workers recruited under this program cannot change jobs and cannot bring family members. When their two-year contract is up, Lakeside can nominate temporary workers for permanent residency—if it so chooses. This provision is particularly controversial. Critics charge that temporary employees will hesitate to complain about working conditions for fear the company will brand them "troublemakers" and send them home. The prospect of permanent residency and family reunification is powerful inducement for workers to "stick it out." Now the company has lower turnover and absenteeism—in short, a docile workforce (Broadway fieldnotes, March 4, 2011). Lakeside's recruitment of temporary workers from around the world who speak different languages harkens back to strategies used a century ago in Chicago's packinghouses to hamper communications between workers who might be tempted to unionize.

Since the first immigrant and refugee workers and their families began arriving in the late 1990s, the people of Brooks have established an extensive support system to help them. The Support Prevent Educate Counsel is a nonprofit association that promotes healthy families and assists newcomers. Its 35 staff members speak 17 languages and provide programs that emphasize early intervention and developmental screening for immigrant children.

Association staff members visit newcomer families at the end of the school week and help decipher report cards and determine which permission slips to sign. Counselors also provide job search assistance. A staff member explained how he worked with a Chinese man who had been laid off from Lakeside. "First I helped him develop a resume and then I explained how 80 percent of the jobs were never advertized and that he would have to visit potential employers with his resume. I went with him on the first day, and we visited ten employers. The next day I told him he would have to go by himself. A week later he got a job at a tire company; now he knows lots of technical terms and swear words" (Broadway fieldnotes, March 3, 2011).

The association also hosts a Boys and Girls Club, a group for newcomers who practice their English speaking skills, and a women's group that works on craft projects. Yet despite these and other programs, service providers continue to worry: "We just don't know how many people we are failing to reach" (Broadway fieldnotes, March 3, 2011). Isolation is fostered by cultural barriers and geography. Many newcomers live on the town's east side, far from its commercial and service center. Without cars, they remain cut off, and proposals by service providers for a limited bus service have fallen on stony ground.

The diverse origins of its newcomers have meant that traditional communication strategies often prove impractical in Brooks. Many adults lack any knowledge of English, some are illiterate in their own language, and many have never attended school. The proliferation of languages and dialects, estimated at more than 100 in 2006, led the local hospital to subscribe to Language Line, a telephone-based translator service. This service, which requires that both patient and practitioner wear a headset, does not work well for emergency situations requiring decisive intervention. Patients sometimes resort to miming their symptoms, leaving nurses and doctors to guess about their ailments (Broadway fieldnotes, February 5, 2006). Alberta Family and Social Services also contracts with Language Line because it found local translators often to be inaccurate (Broadway fieldnotes, March 4, 2011).

Like other small towns, Brooks has a shortage of doctors, and physicians are frequently unwilling to take new patients. As a result, newcomers end up in the emergency room for routine medical care. In 2009, this chronic doctor shortage meant that expectant mothers had to travel 70 miles down the road to Medicine Hat to deliver their babies (Stanway 2009). This situation lasted for 18 months, during which time Brooks mothers gave birth to more than 300 babies in Medicine Hat, until the local hospital hired a full complement of doctors. For more complicated medical procedures, patients still must travel over 100 miles to Calgary. For the many newcomers without cars, roundtrip bus fare is over $70.

The continuous influx of different newcomer groups means health care workers are constantly asked to participate in different cultural awareness workshops. After a time, "compassion fatigue" sets in. Newcomers' limited ability to speak English presents another barrier to effective health care. This problem is particularly acute for women who require information on reproductive health as well as prenatal and postnatal care.

Differences in cultural attitudes toward wives and children are at the heart of another significant issue for social service providers. The sons and daughters of newcomers are often caught between two "different worlds": the attitudes and behaviors of their peers at school and parental expectations at home. In some instances, this conflict has led parents to say to child welfare staff, "You take care of them." The nearest facility for displaced youths is in Medicine Hat. Reported cases of domestic violence have "significantly increased" among immigrant households. Alberta Child and Family Services staff members attribute the increase to husbands who view wives and children as "their own property, which they can do anything they like with" (Broadway fieldnotes, March 3, 2011).

COMMUNITY STUDY TEAMS: THE IDEAL AND THE REAL

Brooks, Alberta, is not the only town we have encouraged to follow Lexington, Nebraska's example and form a community impact study team. Such teams usually include prominent citizens selected from the clergy, business, government, and providers of health care, education, and social services. Although plant managers or other front office personnel usually serve on such groups, they rarely participate in meaningful ways. As one plant manager put it, "We're in the business of making meat, not providing housing." Companies often make a point of their contributions to local charities, but most of these contributions come in the form of surplus meat or poultry and pledges to United Way from employees. For example, Tyson contributed an impressive $220,025 to the 2010 United Way campaign in Garden City. But of that $220,025, *only 20 percent* ($44,005) came from the company itself; 80 percent came from individual donations by workers (Garden City Telegram 2011).

Impact study teams gather information and provide forums for public discourse, both in their own and in other communities. Members from the Garden City Changing Relations Project team have provided outcomes data in other communities and put counterparts in contact with one another. In Brooks and elsewhere, we have brought along experienced service providers to offer advice in public forums and focused work groups. Such "lateral learning" (Flora et al. 1992:319) is key to successful responses by host communities.

Community impact study teams are vital as a community prepares for the onslaught of change that accompanies a new plant. But having a study team does not guarantee that communities will successfully resolve difficult and often intractable problems. In Brooks, team members were divided between those who thought its function should be limited to information sharing and those who wanted it to have a policy-making role as well. Divisions were so great that the team agreed to bring in an outside mediator to see if some common ground could be found between competing perspectives. Resolution proved impossible, and some social service providers began to meet outside the team and coordinate their own policies (Broadway 2000:44–45).

It is usually not until the deal is done, the ink is dry, and the first spade has been turned on the site of the new plant that we ride into town, brandish our articles and reports from other communities, and tell people "the horse is out of the barn and they are in for one rough ride." The trade-off between economic development and its accompanying social costs is clearly evident to us after almost three decades of research, but it is not always so obvious to communities under consideration for a meatpacking plant. We may raise doubts—and serious ones—in the minds of many, but we are poor competition for the packers' "spin-doctors" and their talk of new jobs and multiplier effects. And we have no corporate jets or expense accounts to underwrite trips to other communities that host company plants.

Only rarely do community members have the chance to consider and debate whether they want a meat or poultry plant in their town. In those instances, we have been invited by citizen groups to present our findings, though never by chambers of commerce or local governments. Our message has rarely been welcome, at least not among local boosters. Plant proposals have been defeated following several hearings in which we have testified (see Crews 2001).

Citizens of host communities are no more of one mind on economic development than on anything else. What Harvey Molotch (1976) called the growth machine—a coalition of individuals and groups that realize economic gain from community growth—thrives when a meat or poultry plant comes to town, even as other aspects of the community suffer.

Just as the local growth machine looks to the packers to infuse its economy with new jobs and tax revenue; local communities have looked to us for magic bullets to dispel the negative consequences associated with hosting a meatpacking plant. Our work is in the tradition of what is often called participatory research (Perez 1997). Although we try to develop a collaborative, alongside-of relationship with communities suitable to a self-help model, most local officials adopt the technical assistance model and assign us to the role of outside experts. They want us to provide them with quick fixes for the problems looming on their horizon. Unfortunately, most problems facing packinghouse communities are long-term and intractable, and broad-based citizen efforts often falter in the face of what one Garden City agency director calls "change fatigue."

Communities have welcomed many of our suggestions, and implemented a number of them, such as establishing homeless shelters, adopting housing codes and zoning ordinances, and creating diversity committees and citizen advisory boards to local governments and agencies. And we have been able to develop collaborative research relationships with local institutions, such as Garden City's Mexican-American Ministries. On a recent visit to Brooks, the former city manager ticked off the list of suggested strategies we provided to the city in 1996 and proudly announced: "I think we have covered them all" (Broadway fieldnotes, March 3, 2011).

As applied social scientists with a longstanding commitment to providing assistance to the communities where we carry out our research, we wish we could speak with authority and confidence about a set of principles and methods that consistently produce desired outcomes. But we have no magic bullets, just warnings that few want to hear. Our prognostications and ongoing research often make chamber boosters and local officials uncomfortable. To take the steps we recommend is to admit the new packing plant they recruited will be a mixed blessing at best; to do nothing risks being overwhelmed by the changes we predict. If the predicted social upheaval does not come promptly, we are accused of crying wolf and dismissed as, to quote Will Rogers, "damned fools a long way from home." But in time the changes do come, leading to unwanted attention from the press and renewed criticism from opponents. And while we nod knowingly as community members tell us our predictions came true, we are invariably humbled and disappointed by the rigidity of the industry and the inability of local communities to do more than mitigate its social and economic costs.

WHAT CAN HOST COMMUNITIES DO, AND WHEN MUST THEY DO IT?

Initially, rural communities are ill prepared to cope with the problems meatpacking and its immigrant workforce bring, since they are usually strapped for resources. And they give new industries tax incentives in exchange for the jobs they promise, further straining already meager resources. Local and state governments are usually eager to respond to increasing demands on physical infrastructure, such as providing roads and sewer systems. Meeting the increasing demands on social infrastructure—social services, health care, education—is another matter. In Canada and the United States, much of this task typically falls to nongovernmental organizations, churches, and volunteer groups. Though details may vary, packinghouse towns all face similar economic, social, and environmental dilemmas. Some have only begun to experience the impact of the industry and its workforce, while others have grappled with these challenges for many years. Next, we review four positive steps communities can use to successfully mitigate negative impacts of meat and poultry processing plants.

1. Look to Other Communities for Guidance and Assistance, and Utilize the Expertise of Experienced Practitioners

Special funds of knowledge already exist in the person of experienced practitioners living in meatpacking communities near and far. Agencies and individuals can seek guidance from those who exemplify "best practices." Health care is a good place to begin.

Headquartered in Garden City, Kansas, Mexican-American Ministries operates full-time primary-care centers in Dodge City, Liberal, and Ulysses, and offers part-time care at smaller sites. Mexican-American Ministries serves the unemployed and underemployed, the uninsured and underinsured, the undocumented, and others unable to access mainstream medical care. Its services include physical examinations and health screening; prenatal and postnatal care;

preventive care; treatment of illness and injury; health education; laboratory tests; prescription assistance; management of chronic conditions; and referrals (see Hackenberg & Kukulka 1995:200–202).

2. Broaden Local Community Participation

Broad-based community participation in the planning process is essential. In reality, participation in planning and development activities in most communities is uneven, and unless great care is taken some constituencies will be excluded from the process. It is especially important not to restrict minority or newcomer interests to a single committee or advisory board.

A number of packinghouse communities have had success with citizen advisory committees to law enforcement, city government, school board, and helping agencies. Mark Grey was a member of the Garden City research team. As founder and director of the Iowa Center for Immigrant Leadership and Integration, headquartered at Northern Iowa University, he has studied and worked with packinghouse towns across Iowa for decades. The Center's publications are valuable resources for communities and agencies facing the challenges of ethnic and linguistic diversity (Grey, Devlin, & Goldsmith 2009; Yehieli & Grey 2005). Grey recommends the creation of "diversity committees," representing a broad array of community agencies and constituencies, including service clubs, helping agencies, institutions of higher education, news media, labor unions, and representatives of major employers. Such committees should be careful to include longtime residents and newcomers from every major ethnic group. Grey (1998:15–16) points out that:

> These communities not only encourage communication between newcomers and the community, but they also can respond constructively to incidents that may heighten distrust…. [They] can coordinate services and avoid duplication of service and save precious resources. They also can identify barriers to existing services and help newcomers overcome these barriers. Just as important, these committees can identify unmet needs and create ways to address them.

3. Invest in Communication

Throughout North America, meat and poultry processing increasingly falls to new immigrants with limited English-language skills who migrate to plants located in rural communities where the vast majority of established residents are monolingual English speakers not used to accommodating linguistic and cultural diversity.

Effective translation and interpretation are pressing needs in packinghouse communities, but these services are usually provided by persons with no formal training in these areas, and, as often as not, with poor writing or verbal skills in one or both of the languages in question. Volunteers, children, support staff pulled off their jobs in an emergency—these are the language brokers most often called upon. Private individuals can limp along "knowing enough to get by" in Spanish, which has become the dominant language on the floors of many meat and poultry plants, or learning a few polite phrases in Burmese or Somali or other newcomer languages. But police, health care providers, schools, and social service agencies need bilingual professional staff.

Recognizing this need and filling it are different matters, however. Bilingual staff in any field are in short supply, and they can demand premium wages. Isolated, rural communities find it exceedingly difficult to attract such professionals, and packinghouse towns such as Brooks, Alberta; Lexington, Nebraska; and Garden City, Kansas, must compete with cities near and far that are eager to attract those with the same skills. Offering higher salaries and signing bonuses have been successful in some locales, but they cause resentment among coworkers who do not qualify for these enhancements. Small towns usually cannot compete with larger communities, and even when they can, new hires often don't stay long.

Grow-Your-Own Programs.   Nearby community colleges or universities could offer scholarships to bilingual high school graduates if they agree to return to teach or otherwise serve their hometowns for a period of time. And having family ties to the community, they would "know what they are getting into."

There are also adults, some with college degrees, who would be eager to return to school to obtain the necessary language or occupational skills to qualify for positions in local agencies. For example, native Spanish speakers might accept scholarships in law enforcement or nursing with an agreement to serve in their home towns for a specified period of time.

Translation.   Garden City, Dodge City, and Liberal, Kansas, each have community colleges, and Brooks has a branch of Medicine Hat College. Tyson's Robards, Kentucky, plant is within a 30-minute drive of two community colleges and two regional universities. Foreign language instructors at colleges or local secondary schools could be enlisted to translate signs, newspaper advertisements, and forms. They could also "back-translate" materials in existing foreign languages to ensure translations are correct. Presently, Mexican Americans with little or no formal training in Spanish do much of the translation in U.S. processing plants and host communities. Mexican Americans may speak Spanish, but often they do not write or read the language well. Limited literacy is also a problem for many native English speakers, and back-translation can help in English usage as well.

All printed matter intended for wide distribution or long shelf life should be professionally translated by a competent professional from English to all other languages spoken by significant numbers of workers or community residents. A second competent professional should translate the document back into English without referring to the original English version. Then, a third literate English speaker familiar with the intent of the document should review the back-translation, note problems, and return the corrected back-translation to the original translator for final revision and publication.

Michael Broadway

FIGURE 9.3 Signs in Spanish, Vietnamese, and English at the Garden City, Kansas, post office.

Reaching Non-English Speakers.   School announcements going home to parents, signs in offices and businesses serving the general public, and announcements in the local media should speak to every major language community in town. The public library should add significantly and regularly to its books and periodicals in these languages.

Brochures welcoming non-English-speaking newcomers and introducing them to local laws, expectations, and services in their native languages can provide an important tool in fostering their adaptation to new cultural circumstances. Such materials may already exist in other communities and should be adapted whenever possible for local use. In 2007, the Garden City chief of police did exactly that. When Somali refugees began arriving from Minneapolis, he requested Somali language materials about curfew and traffic laws from his Minneapolis counterpart, adapted them for use in Garden City, and then made sure they were distributed to Garden City's growing Somali population.

Cultural brokers emerge to provide essential cross-cultural links whenever two or more ethnic or language communities intersect. Identifying and using these natural brokers should be a priority. Sometimes this role can be formalized, as it was in Storm Lake, Iowa, a pork-packing town.

> Storm Lake police sought to overcome communication barriers …
> through the creation of two community service officer positions. One
> position was created for a native Lao speaker and the other for a native
> Spanish speaker. In both cases, these were community outreach officers
> who wore uniforms, but did not carry guns. Their primary purpose was

to establish relations between the newcomer communities and the police and other local services. Because both officers were native speakers and members of the cultural groups they worked with, they were able to establish an immediate rapport. These officers often prevented crime by communicating the community's expectations for behavior. (Grey 1998:21–22)

Storm Lake's police department also worked to prevent officer bias and discrimination by banning the use of derogatory language about ethnic groups and training officers about the cultures of newcomer groups (Ibid.).

4. Recognize and Respect Cultural Differences and Similarities

Culture refers to the collective knowledge and patterns of behavior socially learned and shared by a group of people. Cultural systems shape the behavior of many different types of social groups: nations, organizations, occupations, families, and interest groups. Various cultural forms coexist in the same space, and people belong to more than one cultural grouping at the same time, making the relationship between coexisting cultural systems complex.

National cultures, the ideas and behaviors people share because they were born and raised in a particular country or region, are the most obvious. Several national cultures are invariably represented in packinghouses, and nearby towns rapidly become multicultural and multilingual. This is something their citizens can be proud of.

Don Stull

F I G U R E 9.4 Children from many cultural backgrounds enjoy the Beef Empire Days parade. Beef Empire Days is held each June in Garden City, Kansas.

Work is what brings people to packinghouse towns—and what keeps them there. Meatpacking has always had a tradition of hard, dangerous work and insular corporate cultures. These industry characteristics must be an important consideration in any efforts the community undertakes. Shift work is a good example. Turnover is normally higher on the second (night) shift, which means that new workers are more likely to be placed on this shift. Night work disrupts sleep patterns and daily routines for workers. It can also disrupt families, showing up in indicators such as "latchkey kids" and increased marital discord. Family stress, in turn, contributes to employee turnover.

Shift work is a fact of life for meat and poultry plants and for many other employers as well. Service providers, both in and out of government, must accommodate it. Schools must keep work schedules in mind when arranging parent-teacher conferences; service providers must extend their hours; translators must be available to meet the needs of second-shift workers. Health care providers should offer evening office hours to avoid the more costly practice of clients using the emergency room for routine medical care.

Awareness of, and accommodation to, the needs and cultures of newcomers is necessary if packinghouse towns expect to deal successfully with the challenges they face. But meeting the necessities of newcomers is not sufficient. Planners, policy makers, and service providers must not lose sight of the concerns and the needs of long-established residents. Such forgetfulness, or the appearance of it, is a real danger for communities like Brooks, Lexington, and Garden City, which are stretched to the limit in developing and implementing the services needed by incoming groups.

THE WAY FORWARD

Planning is essential to development. When it involves a broad section of the community, working in a collaborative and participatory manner, planning can create a collective vision. But planning takes time, and consensus is hard to achieve. Plans can be goals in themselves—the final product of an exercise involving professional planners, often brought in from outside. Planning can also intentionally exclude segments of a community and limit community choice.

Community development can mean many different things, and the indicators of its success vary widely—job creation, population retention, increasing the tax base, cleaning up the environment. Different definitions of what people desire will influence the strategies a community chooses. And efforts to influence one outcome—job creation, for example—may have serious consequences for achieving other goals.

Regardless of the desired goals, or the chosen development model, two factors are important to any effort at community development: (1) communities need to look beyond their boundaries for sources of information and remain open to lateral learning; and (2) they need to plan for the future.

Communities are dynamic—they change or they die. But the nature of that change determines the health of communities. Development is more than annual outputs, the number of new jobs, and multiplier effects. It is more complicated than economic forecasters and town boosters are often willing to admit. Planners and politicians should consider not only the benefits of economic development, but also its costs—not just what they should give away to attract new industry, but more importantly, what costs that industry will create for the people of the host community and the state or province after it arrives. If we wish to preserve what we cherish most about our communities, we must place economic development within the larger context of community development. And we must look to other communities and their experiences for signposts toward successful development.

Vibrant local communities are central to the future of rural North America; so are industry and government. Industries have a responsibility to communities that host their facilities—providing jobs is not enough, especially when those jobs come with significant social and economic costs. Governments should do more than lure new business with tax holidays. They should make community development funds available to rural communities, especially those facing rapid growth and increasing ethnic and linguistic diversity. Initial grants can provide transient and low-cost housing, and continuing funding can offset additional drains on the institutions that provide health care, public education, and law enforcement.

Local governments must be willing—and able—to expand physical infrastructure and provide adequate and affordable new housing. They also must attend to increased demands on social infrastructure and ensure adequate and culturally aware services. Schools must provide for expanding enrollments; they must educate diverse student bodies and reach out to parents. Religious leaders must provide guidance during times of rapid change. Charitable and other non-governmental organizations must find ways to stretch their budgets even more, to serve larger clienteles with various and often disparate needs. The media should inform, not inflame. And community members, old-timers and newcomers alike, must learn tolerance, flexibility, and openness to change.

When leaders think first of their community and its overall interests—and when planning and decision making are participatory—towns prosper. When economic interests are first and foremost—and when decision making and planning are concentrated—growth benefits only a few, and community welfare is threatened. The choices we make today shape our communities tomorrow.

10

✳

Not in My Backyard: Community Opposition to the Meat and Poultry Industry

Confined Animal Feeding Operations (CAFOs) have become a national issue. A new hog plant in Utah will produce more animal waste than the animal and human waste created by the city of Los Angeles; 1,600 dairies in the Central Valley of California produce more waste than a city of 21 million people. The annual production of 600 million chickens on the Delmarva Peninsula near Washington, D.C., generates as much nitrogen as a city of almost 500,000 people.

With this emotionally charged salvo, the board of directors of the National Catholic Rural Life Conference called for an immediate moratorium on large-scale livestock and poultry animal confinement facilities on December 18, 1997. The church was not alone in condemning the environmental and social consequences of what has come to be called factory farming. The Consumer Federation of America, the Humane Society of the United States, and EarthSave joined with the National Family Farm Coalition, the National Farmers Union, the Delmarva and Georgia Poultry Justice Alliances, and the National Contract Poultry Growers Association to call for increased regulation of pork and poultry production (National Catholic Rural Life Conference 1997).

The vast majority of animals that provide our meat, dairy, and eggs still live in confined conditions. Opposition to CAFOs is steadily mounting, however. Not only to their stench and pollution, but also to their poor treatment of animals, the increased risks they pose to human health, the loss of independent family farms they portend, and declines in quality of life and property values for those who live near them (Imhoff 2010).

Industry representatives acknowledge problems, but they claim environmental compliance is improving. They argue that confined animal feeding offers the best way to provide consumers with a uniform and inexpensive product, and they support their argument by pointing out that Americans spend less of their disposable income on food than their counterparts in any other nation (Eng 2010).

The poultry industry pioneered modern factory farming, and today most chickens are grown inside massive houses. For every pound of gain, a chicken produces approximately half a pound of dry waste (Poultry Water Quality Consortium 1998). This waste, combined with the rice hulls or wood chips used to line the floors of chicken houses, is called litter. Properly handled, poultry litter is the most valuable of livestock manures and reduces the need for commercial fertilizer (Rasnake, Murdock, & Thom 1991:1). It is high in nitrogen, phosphate, and potash, and is well suited for hay and corn, which require high nutrient levels and a long growing season that allows litter decomposition and nutrient release (Rasnake 1996:1–2). Best of all it is often free for the taking from growers, who must regularly remove it from the floors of their chicken houses and stockpile it until it can be spread on pastures and fields. Some growers remove and spread their own litter; others contract with neighboring farmers for litter removal.

WESTERN KENTUCKY'S TOUR DE STENCH

Depending on its size, a single broiler house produces between 140 and 200 tons of litter each year (Rasnake 1996:1; Stull 2000:157); each breeder house, where hens lay eggs to supply the broiler houses with chicks, generates about 80 tons of litter a year. At this rate, Kentucky's 2,800 broiler houses and 350 breeder houses annually produce between 420,000 and 588,000 tons of chicken litter. Spread on fields at the recommended rate of four tons per acre, this litter fertilizes somewhere between 164 and 206 square miles of Kentucky every year (640 acres per square mile).

Annually disposing of 500,000 tons or more of chicken litter would be a simple matter if chicken houses were spread evenly across Kentucky's 39,732 square miles, but they are not. Poultry processing is concentrated in the western half of the state, and poultry houses are located within a 60–70 mile radius of the plants they supply.

At first, rural western Kentuckians welcomed the poultry industry. It promised new jobs, increased revenues, new markets and premium prices for their corn, and free fertilizer. But they didn't reckon with the smell of chickens and their litter. For poultry companies and their growers it is the smell of money. But for many who live near chicken houses, which are built in complexes ranging from two to 24 houses, it has become the stench of environmental and cultural degradation.

The Robards plant, originally built by Hudson Foods, opened on July 9, 1996. Area residents began voicing concerns before it was even completed (Sebree Banner 1995). Not long after the plant opened, neighbors of its broiler houses were protesting the odor, flies and other vermin, ground water pollution, potential health risks, increased and overweight traffic that damaged roads. Coalitions of property owners went to court to block construction of broiler houses in three counties. The Fiscal Court of Webster County, the county with the most chicken houses, mandated they be at least 600 feet from homes. Eleven days later the poultry company filed suit to block enforcement of the ordinance (Gilkey 1997). Neighbors turned against neighbors; chicken houses were vandalized (McKinley 1998:A1; Associated Press 2002). The "chicken war" was in full swing (Whittington 1997).

The Sierra Club hired Aloma Dew in 1999 to work full-time on its campaign against confined poultry operations in Kentucky. She forged alliances with grassroots organizations and organized conferences on the environmental and socioeconomic consequences of industrial agriculture (Dew 2004).

Dew has led an annual Tour de Stench to raise awareness of the problems associated with industrial poultry production in western Kentucky. The tour was initially designed to raise general awareness of the "problems of health, environment, water and quality of life related to concentration of poultry CAFOs" (Anonymous 2001:1). In all these efforts, she has defended the rights and livelihoods of Kentucky's farmers, even those who have chosen to become poultry growers. In a

Don Stull

F I G U R E 10.1 An anonymous combatant issues a call to arms in western Kentucky's "chicken war," McLean County, Kentucky, 1998.

Don Stull

F I G U R E 10.2 At a stop on the Tour de Stench, a mother and her young children extol the "pleasures" of having broiler houses, which can be seen in the distance, for neighbors.

1999 interview, Dew said, "The farmer is the victim too. Nobody wants to make life harder on farmers…. These corporations are not farmers. They don't care about farmers. They care about the bottom line" (Hutchison 1999:A2).

Nevertheless, chicken farmers, commonly called growers, are part of the poultry industry, and their livelihood is bound to it. Although most farmers consider themselves stewards of their land, they often bitterly oppose environmentalists and their causes. One western Kentucky broiler grower put it this way:

> There are some tree huggers, and the funniest thing is that the firebrands and the tree huggers are mostly above-middle-class housewives with nothing to do on their hands…. These people were socially involved, and they were trying to do the right thing…. But they don't know what the hell they're talking about…. And they're stirring these people up, and they're benefiting from it…. I would rather be an active environmentalist than an environmental activist. Yeah, there are concerns. You can't be running around doing Chicken Little all the time, too. And that's what these people are doing. (Stull interview, November 24, 1998)

Of more immediate concern to growers than so-called tree huggers are their neighbors, who, like them, are country people and often farmers. A grower with four broiler houses characterized his circumstances this way:

> I've had some that supported me, and I've had some that didn't want 'em. I've had some that was really, really against 'em. For the most part, I think there's nine households around mine, and two of 'em was

against 'em and seven of 'em didn't care.... My dad was gonna put four [broiler houses] up and put 'em by mine. And that's when they really got to squealing about it. Didn't like it ... so we decided to move his down here behind this house.... They haven't really given me a whole lot of trouble but I know they didn't like 'em and they didn't want 'em. But now they'll tell you that they're not nearly what they thought they'd be. (Stull interview, November 19, 1998)

THE SIERRA CLUB TAKES ON BIG CHICKEN

On April 22, 2002—Earth Day—the Sierra Club sued Tyson Foods and four of its largest western Kentucky growers, who operated complexes ranging from 16 to 24 broiler houses, citing their operations for emitting excessive levels of ammonia and dust under the federal Superfund law, the Clean Air Act, and the Community-Right-to-Know Act (Lucas 2002:A1; Lovan 2002:A1).

Responding to the lawsuit, Tyson issued a statement regretting the Sierra Club's "attempts to politicize agriculture." "In its misguided lawsuit it wants the public to believe the 7,500 independent farmers who grow chickens for Tyson Foods around the country are running 'factories' and not chicken farms" (Tyson Foods 2002).

The Sierra Club, through its attorney, argued otherwise:

This is all about massive concentrations of chickens. It's not about family farmers. Due to this massive concentration, it is triggering both the reporting requirements for hazardous substances under our toxics laws, and triggering the permit requirements for dust emissions under the Clean Air Act. These emissions—and the reason they are required to report them—are because they threaten public health. (Bruggers 2002:1)

Three of the four farms named by the Sierra Club, including the "Tyson Children" partnership, were owned by out-of-state interests. The suit was settled in 2005 when Tyson agreed to continuously monitor its poultry operations for ammonia emissions for one year and report the results of its findings to the Sierra Club and other plaintiffs. As part of the settlement, Tyson also agreed to spend up to $50,000 to plant trees to screen neighbors from pollution coming from chicken houses, pay all legal fees connected with the case, and compensate the three residents who filed the suit (Mayse 2005).

Scientists from Iowa State University issued a report on chicken house emissions in western Kentucky in 2007. Touted as the most comprehensive study of its kind, the researchers found that two chicken houses emitted over 10 tons of ammonia in one year—levels high enough to cause respiratory harm (Dew 2007).

Hog barns have recently joined chicken houses on the Tour de Stench. In 2005, Tosh Farms announced plans to construct 50 hog barns in Fulton, Hickman, and Carlisle Counties in far-western Kentucky. Located near the state's oldest chicken processing plant, area farmers were already familiar with contract growing.

Headquartered just over the state line in Union City, Tennessee, Tosh Farms was also attracted to Kentucky because it does not charge sales tax on construction materials for barns, has cheap workers' compensation rates, and the region produces a plentiful supply of feed grains. An additional factor, according to critics, is Kentucky's lax enforcement of environmental regulations (Malone 2005).

Not surprisingly, industrial hog production has also raised a stink in western Kentucky. A lawsuit brought by Fulton County residents against the state agency that approved their operating permits described the Tosh Family hog barns as follows:

> Each construction permit sought approval for two animal waste handling facilities, to wit: a "deep pit"—a concrete pit under a swine facility capable of housing 2,490 swine from their arrival weight of 15 pounds until they are ready for slaughter at about 270 pounds. The swine would generate an estimated 1.78 million gallons per year of liquid manure, urine and other swine waste.

In deciding the case, the judge noted that the Kentucky Energy and Environment Cabinet "failed to enforce its own regulatory requirements" when it granted permits for these barns. In doing so, the state did not fulfill its obligation to "protect waterways and the public from excessive nutrients and pathogens and should have considered toxic air emissions" (Bruggers 2009). But the judge did not force the barns to shut down.

In a separate case, a dozen or so neighbors of Fulton County hog barns have sued Tosh Farms claiming its operations have led to oppressive odors and a decline in their property values. To avoid federal waste-discharge regulations, these barns house fewer than 2,500 hogs, the legal definition of a large confined animal feeding operation. If they held more animals, their operator would have to implement a nutrient-management plan to limit impact on surface water. Unlike hog operations that use lagoons, excrement is stored directly beneath these barns, leaving the animals to live on top of their own waste. Fans replace the toxic air in the barn with outside air—unless there is a power outage. Operators empty the underground pit once a year and spray the waste onto or plow it into the ground (Dan 2011).

A FIGHT LOST, A FIGHT TO BE WON:
BIG PIG IN ALBERTA

Kentuckians could not keep concentrated animal feeding out of their state. Elsewhere in North America the fight continues. In western Canada, bountiful supplies of feed grains and sparse rural populations have combined with aggressive business recruitment strategies to make the region a battleground between large-scale animal feeding operations and their opponents.

In 1997 and 1998, rural Alberta municipalities received 471 permitting requests to approve concentrated animal feeding operations. About half the applications were for hog confinement facilities, one-third for cattle feedlots, and the rest for poultry and dairy operations. Sixty percent of the proposals were for new operations; the remainder sought to expand or replace existing ones. Those who oppose confined animal feeding have a difficult task: of the 471 applications, 438 gained approval (Alberta Agriculture, Food and Rural Development 2002).

One such proposal came from Taiwan Sugar Corporation (TSC), a state-owned transnational company based in Taipei. In early 2000, it proposed to build a facility capable of producing 150,000 hogs a year in Foremost, Alberta (pop. 531 in 2001).

Foremost is surrounded by farms and ranches in the County of Forty Mile, in the southeast corner of Alberta. The county covers almost 3,000 square miles and is home to only 3,000 souls, making it a seemingly ideal location. Just in case its permit request was denied, the company also applied to Flagstaff County (pop. 3,697 in 2001), a rural area 100 miles southeast of Edmonton.

Responsibility for approving permits rested with local municipalities at the time of Taiwan Sugar's application. The provincial government encouraged local governments to incorporate the 1995 Code of Practice for the Safe and Economic Handling of Animal Manure into their land use bylaws. The code set standards for the amount of land required for manure disposal, lagoon construction, minimum-distance separation requirements, and other mitigating measures.

Representatives of the company appeared before the County of Forty Mile Municipal Planning Commission in June 2000 to argue that its $42 million (Canadian) investment would create 54 new jobs, provide local farmers with a market for their grain and a source of free manure, and supply Alberta's packers with hogs. Opponents raised concerns about the environmental impact and disputed the company's request to classify the operations as a farm, which would save the company $250,000 a year in property taxes. More than two-thirds of Forty Mile's registered voters signed a petition opposing the plan. The planning commission considered the petition along with a summary of scientific research on the environmental impact of confined hog operations to make its ruling. A month later, the commission denied Taiwan Sugar's planning permission because of the potential for manure to contaminate surface and groundwater, as well as the negative effects of odor from the barns on adjacent property values (Duckworth 2000). Taiwan Sugar appealed the decision (which was later denied) and announced its intention to construct a similar operation in Flagstaff County.

LET THE MATCH RECOMMENCE

Round 1: The Proposal

To grow out 150,000 hogs a year, Taiwan Sugar proposed to place 7,200 sows in 14 barns in five sites near Hardisty in Flagstaff County. The barns were designed to let manure fall through slatted floors before being pumped into a nearby lagoon. The lagoon's high-density polyethylene liner would rest on compacted clay and a leak-detection system, while its negative air-pressure cover would reduce odor. The company would empty each lagoon once a year, allowing for necessary liner repairs. The manure would be spread over 29,400 acres and injected into the soil to reduce runoff and odor. The entire operation would use an estimated 45 million gallons of water a year, provided from wells at one or more of the development sites.

Flagstaff County Development Authority approved the proposal in September 2000, after determining it met requirements as outlined in the county's land use bylaws. In undertaking the review, the county development officer later testified the county had:

> sought to address concerns with respect to odor control, manure storage systems, surface water management, dead animal disposal, pest management, road upgrade, manure management, including soil sampling and tests and land base requirements, record keeping, water sampling and minimum distance separations [and concluded that the development is] compatible with existing land uses in the area.[1]

Round 2: The Appeal

The development authority's decision was immediately appealed by 18 landowners and the Flagstaff Family Farm Promotional Society. The society based its appeal on the grounds that: (1) the lagoons were improperly sited with respect to local groundwater conditions; (2) the development lacked a land base large enough for safe manure disposal; and (3) the barns constituted a danger and/or an annoyance to adjacent landowners, which violated the land use bylaws. A month later, Flagstaff County's Subdivision and Development Appeal Board met to hear the case.

The appeal board consisted of five local farmers. Its chair was a retired provincial government employee with strong ties to the ruling provincial Progressive Conservative Party. Taiwan Sugar, the appeal board, the development authority, and appellants were each represented by legal counsel. Over the course of four days in October 2000, the board listened to more than 920 pages of testimony from engineers, pork industry lobbyists, soil scientists, planners, environmentalists, Taiwan Sugar executives, provincial and county government officials, local citizens, former residents of the area, and Michael Broadway. Legal counsel on all sides agreed that the appeal board's function was to sift through the evidence to determine whether the proposal conformed to Flagstaff County's Land Use Bylaws and Municipal Development Plan. Much of the testimony dealt with technical aspects of the proposal, such as lagoon design and hydrogeological conditions in the vicinity of the barns. But many local residents "deemed to be affected" used the hearings to criticize their elected officials for their role in recruiting Taiwan Sugar.

Round 3: Opening Salvos

Most of the 98 people who spoke at the hearings were against the proposal. A petition presented to the board with 1,222 signatures of local ratepayers also opposed the project.

For Lorraine Davidson, a local farmer, the development was a direct conse-quence of the provincial government's recruiting strategy. Her mother-in-law, Faye, agreed:

> I have viewed with disbelief that our Alberta government would invite
> a foreign government treasury into compete against our pork
> producers.... This is not just a move by a foreign government to use our
> country as a cesspool, while they run the money home to Taiwan....
> It is an assault by corporate hogs on private hog producers.

Taiwan Sugar executive Danny Huang responded, "We are just invite[d] by your people to come over here. I think we have come over here to make friend [sic], not to fight against people or make your people fight together or against each other."

Deep community divisions were also noted by a United Church minister, who characterized the divide as "a conflict between agribusiness and agriculture ... a clash between those who live here and those who just want to do business here.... What is value added to one is devaluation to the other."

Round 4: Factory Farms versus Agriculture

Under Flagstaff County's Municipal Development Plan, "agriculture and provid-ing services to the agricultural community are regarded as the most important forms of development in Flagstaff County." Taiwan Sugar's counsel, citing the plan, argued that "in accordance with generally accepted practices in any provin-cial regs ... these activities may occur 24 hours a day, 365 days a year; and the noise, odors, dust and fumes by the activities will be allowed.... What this sec-tion is saying is inherently farming can be a nuisance but it takes priority."

Opponents cited a different section of the plan: "Landowners should be able to act as they please on their own land as long as or provided neighboring land-owners, business people, residents and future neighbors are not harmed." The provision that any development must not have any harmful effects on neighbors was echoed in the land use bylaws, which gave the county's development authority power to reject any proposal that constitutes "a danger or annoyance to persons."

Round 5: Economic Benefits

The director of Alberta Pork, a marketing organization, supported Taiwan Sugar's proposal because it would increase the supply of hogs and allow packing plants to add "that second shift that they require to make them more cost effi-cient and globally competitive." An eleventh-grader testified that for teenagers, "jobs are few and hard to come by in a small town," but the barns represented an "opportunity to make money." The jobs would be "perfect for any person who has any interest at all in agriculture." A formal endorsement of the project came from the chairman of the Hardisty Economic Development Committee, who noted that "although they did not go looking for TSC," the project offered an opportunity to revitalize "the local economy which is presently quite dismal." A consultant estimated that the 54 full-time jobs provided by the company would generate 26 others. Based upon a study of land sales in a nearby county, he concluded that "a well managed intensive livestock operation will not decrease land values in the proximity in which it is located."

Some local farmers noted that if Taiwan Sugar purchased 45,000 tons of feed grain a year, inventories would fall and thereby boost prices. Farmers would also benefit by having the manure from the barns spread on their land for free, a value they estimated at $25 an acre. Danny Kroetsch, a farmer with a 240-sow farrow-to-finish operation supported the proposal for a different reason:

> People have asked me if I think I will be squeezed out because of the size of TSC. No. In fact I view them as a plus for me and all hog producers because of their knowledge of the Japanese market. These people know that market ... and that can only be seen as a benefit.

Based upon studies conducted in the United States, opponents argued the community would end up absorbing the costs of the operation without receiving any economic benefits. Housing property values would decline in the vicinity of hog barns, and most of Taiwan Sugar's purchases would not come from local businesses. A company consultant reluctantly acknowledged that the larger the operation, the more it spent outside the region. The negative economic consequences of the project were supported by a representative of Canada's National Farmers Union, who noted that while the development would create jobs and a market for feed grains, corporate hog barns "provide significantly fewer of these benefits than the family farms they displace" and "employ fewer people per hog and spend less in their communities than family farm hog producers." The representative concluded: "Transferring hog production from local farm families to corporations such as Taiwan Sugar, Smithfield, and Maple Leaf facilitates and accelerates the extraction of wealth and capital from rural areas."

Round 6: Environmental Issues

Lori Goodrich, president of the Flagstaff County Family Farm Promotional Society, summarized its concerns:

> No one person can tell us that 150,000 pigs will not create odors. No one person can tell us that they will not contaminate our waters. No one person can say that unlined concrete lagoons under the barns will not leak. No one person can tell us that manure pipelines through culverts and across land will not break or separate. It has happened. Don't tell us our land values won't decrease. Who the hell will live beside stinking hog farms?

Taiwan Sugar responded that the sites exceeded the code's recommendation for minimum distance separating CAFOs from neighboring developments and the covers on the lagoons would substantially reduce the odor.

Both sides agreed the lagoons met the code's construction standards, but they differed on the suitability of the proposed sites. A hydrologist, testifying for the appellants, argued that none of the sites were "suitable" in view of the potential for leaks and resulting groundwater contamination, since there were no data on the water table level or movement of groundwater. Taiwan Sugar's experts acknowledged some of the barn sites were in hydrogeological "high risk areas," but any leak in the primary liner would be detected by monitoring wells and contained by the clay liner, giving operators sufficient time to empty the lagoon and make necessary repairs.

Local farmers were also concerned about the amount of water the project would use and its impact upon aquifer levels. Lana and Barry Love testified that their well levels had dropped for the last three years, and that Taiwan Sugar's extraction of another 124,000 gallons a day would only compound the problem. The company responded that it was only proposing to use four times as much water as the Hardisty golf course used to water its fairways and greens, and "in terms of groundwater supply and availability we are not asking to use that much."

Taiwan Sugar estimated the operation would generate 41.3 million gallons of liquid manure. This estimate was not in contention, but opponents disputed the amount and suitability of the land base identified for manure disposal. An agrologist hired by the appellants analyzed the 29,400 acres identified in the proposal for manure spreading and said less than a third of the acreage was suitable because slope and soil characteristics increased potential for runoff and water contamination. Henry Hays, a fifth-generation farmer, voiced the fears of many local people about this aspect of the proposal: "A vast area northwest and west of our house is slated for pig manure. Spring runoff brings water from this area through two County culverts to sloughs adjacent to our house, will pig manure residue end up in our basement?"

Taiwan Sugar said it would comply with the 1995 Code of Practice for the Safe and Economic Handling of Animal Manure: before spreading manure, it would sample the soil to determine the amounts of phosphorous and nitrogen extractable by the crops, to prevent excess amounts running off that would pollute streams and rivers; it would sample manure for nutrient content and adjust the application rate accordingly; and it would cap any abandoned wells. An agrologist would supervise the application and verify compliance with appropriate setbacks from wells, water courses, and property lines. Each landowner would receive a report summarizing the soil sampling plan, the manure content, and application rates. The report would also go to Flagstaff County.

THE DECISION AND ITS AFTERMATH

The board, in reaching its decision, acknowledged that "we are to apply the Land Use Bylaw and any other planning instruments, such as the Municipal Development Plan, as we find them, having regard to proper planning considerations"

(Schorak 2000:17). But after reviewing the evidence and applying the standard, the board disregarded the petition, the concerns expressed over the future of family farms, the potential economic impact of the project, its effect on land values, and the national origin of the developer. Instead, it concluded that "the Land Use Bylaw does contemplate that intensive animal operations may be allowed within the agricultural district.... Based upon the evidence which was before us, the development should be allowed subject to (certain) conditions" (Ibid.:19). Among the conditions added to the permit was a requirement that Taiwan Sugar Corporation pay for persons, appointed or approved by the county, to monitor compliance with the code of practice, and if a breach of the permit did occur, the county could issue a stop order and close the operation.

The conditions added to the permit failed to allay the concerns of many local people, and following the announcement of the board's decision, its chairman was besieged with "hundreds" of angry phone calls from residents (MacArthur 2000). The Family Farm Promotional Society was left with one option, to appeal the decision to the Alberta Court of Appeal. In November 2001, a three-judge panel conducted a full hearing on the appeal and a year later it ruled in favor of the appellants, canceled the planning permit, and referred the matter back to the county's Subdivision and Development Appeal Board. The Flagstaff Family Farm Promotional Society responded with the following statement: "We hope that Taiwan Sugar Corporation will uphold their promise and if the courts turn them down they will leave" (County of Flagstaff Family Farm Promotional Society 2002). The company did leave, and now its only hog operations outside of Taiwan are in Vietnam.

The opposition mounted against Taiwan Sugar Corporation is one of numerous battles fought against concentrated animal feeding operations across the Canadian prairies. The manager of the Alberta Pork Producers Association expressed the industry's frustration with the planning approval system at the appeal hearing:

> We believe that agriculture must be allowed to do business in rural
> areas. We're getting a little frustrated with some of the antics in some of
> the counties that have occurred ... so we'd like to see the province
> come in and induce an act and some regulations and put out some
> standards that we can work with.

The provincial government's efforts to attract investors for industrial animal agriculture and value-added processing to the province have also been frustrated. To resolve this situation, it established a committee to examine how to remove the "uncertainty and controversy" surrounding the approval process. Its April 2001 report recommended that responsibility be taken away from local municipalities and given to a provincial government board. The board would review applications, issue approvals, monitor, and enforce provincewide standards.

Seven months later the provincial legislature gave Alberta's Natural Resources Conservation Board regulatory jurisdiction over concentrated animal feeding operations. It also gave the board power to overturn bans previously enacted by local municipalities (MacArthur 2001). The standards to be used in judging a project's suitability are contained in the 2000 Code of Practice for Responsible Livestock Development and Manure Management developed by Alberta Agriculture, Food, and Rural Development.

The pork industry welcomed change in the approval process, but the president of the Alberta Association of Municipal Districts was disappointed, noting that "land use decisions are properly decided at the local level." After all, communities have to live with the decisions. Lisa Bechthold, a rancher who successfully organized the opposition to Taiwan Sugar in the County of Forty Mile, viewed the new system as a "way to ram the livestock industry down our throats" (Duckworth 2001).

Despite the change in the regulatory environment, the province's hog population declined by over half a million animals between 2002 and 2010 (Canadian Pork Council n.d.). The Canadian prairies are no longer a cheap place to raise hogs, thanks to increases in feed costs and the value of the Canadian dollar, which undercut Canadian pork's ability to compete in its principal export market—the United States.

SAVE OUR JOBS!

Opposition to the meat industry is not restricted to its environmental impact. Public forums, the Internet, books, and journal articles have assured the widespread dissemination of research results on the social and economic impact of meat processing facilities. Sudden population growth, housing shortages, rising demand for social services, and increases in crime have become ammunition for those who oppose new plants. New construction of large processing plants is a rare phenomenon in the second decade of the twenty-first century. North America's meat processors are dealing with a new reality—rising input costs. Food safety has become of paramount public concern in the aftermath of the 1993 Jack-in-the-Box *E. coli* O157:H7 tragedy, the first case of mad cow disease in the United States in 2003, and repeated food recalls related to food-borne illnesses. Meat and poultry companies have been subjected to new regulations and forced to invest in new pathogen-control systems. Added to these costs have been escalating grain prices, which in turn have led to higher meat prices and drops in domestic beef and poultry consumption.

We first became interested in the meat business in the 1980s when the industry was transforming itself from an urban to a rural industry. Over the next two decades, we watched as it expanded into new territories and built new plants. Although industry consolidation has continued in the twenty-first century, its expansion has not. The great recession of 2008 was not kind to the meat and poultry industry. In that year, Tyson Foods closed its beef slaughter facility in Emporia, Kansas, and laid off 1,400 workers. John Morrell closed its Sioux City, Iowa, pork plant in 2010 and terminated 1,500 employees. After JBS acquired Pilgrim's Pride in 2009, it laid off 4,500 poultry workers in Alabama, Arkansas, Louisiana, and Georgia. North of the border, Maple Leaf Foods shut its pork processing plant in Saskatoon, Saskatchewan, in 2007, putting 1,400 employees out of work. In the same year, it laid off 380 workers at a poultry processing plant in Berwick, Nova Scotia, and 100 workers at a Toronto-area processing plant. These plant closures and layoffs reveal an industry struggling to achieve greater efficiency in the face of stagnant growth in domestic meat consumption and growing criticism of its treatment of animals, workers, and the environment.

NOTE

1.   All the quotations dealing with the public hearing are from the official transcripts taken at the Subdivision and Development Appeal Hearing by Snow's Court Reporting, Edmonton, Alberta.

11

✳

Food for Thought

My early interest in meat began at the dinner table. Like everyone else I knew growing up during the 1960s in a small village 20 miles from the center of London, my family's meals revolved around meat. I left for school most days with a "full English breakfast" inside of me—bacon, sausage, bread, and tomatoes fried in bacon grease. Saturday lunch usually consisted of a steak and kidney pie or a casserole filled with bacon, sausage, and liver. On Sundays we would dine on roast meat: lamb, pork, or beef. Mother served leftovers cold during the week or transformed them into shepherd's pie (ground beef covered with mashed potatoes and baked in the oven) or a lamb or beef curry. When we ate Sunday dinner at my grandparents' house, I watched my grandmother drain fat from a roast beef to make gravy and Yorkshire pudding. She poured leftovers into a bowl to cool, and the next day my grandfather would spread the solid fat onto his toast for breakfast. Occasionally, he allowed his grandchildren to sample the delights of "drippings."

My mother always took me with her when she went shopping. We walked the 15 minutes from our home to the center of our village and made the rounds of the local food stores. At the end of the street, across from my elementary school, stood the butcher shop; in its big glass windows carcasses hung from hooks while smaller cuts of meat were neatly displayed and tagged—New Zealand lamb, British beef, Wiltshire ham, Danish bacon. Inside the shop, the butcher, Mr. Groves, stood behind a long wooden table with a small glass front and narrow counter top. He would greet my mother, "How are you today, Mrs. Broadway, lovely weather we are having. And what can I get for you today?"

"A pound of skirt and a quarter of kidney, please," meant our family would be eating steak and kidney pie that evening.

While Mr. Groves deftly cut through bone with a hacksaw or used a razor-sharp knife to trim fat from a skirt steak, I amused myself by making mountains with my toe out of the sawdust spread on the floor to soak up blood. He weighed each cut of meat my mother ordered, carefully wrapped it in white wax paper, wrote its price on the outside, and gave it to the cashier. Mr. Groves's butcher shop had a distinct aroma—a mixture of sawdust, blood, and fresh meat. It was a wonderful smell.

By the 1980s, growing concerns over the harmful effects of red meat were transforming my family's diet. My mother had replaced steak and kidney pie with steak and mushroom pie—and the full English breakfast had become a bowl of cold cereal and two pieces of toast and marmalade. In 1996, I visited my parents with my wife and three children. On a Sunday morning soon after our arrival, my mother asked me to step into the kitchen where my father was standing at the sink peeling potatoes. She announced "Your dad and I have decided we won't be having roast beef for Sunday lunch. We are just not prepared to take the risk, especially for the children." I was shocked, then annoyed! What risk could there possibly be from roast beef? I had fond memories of Sunday family lunches, dining on roast beef, Yorkshire pudding, roast potatoes, Brussels sprouts, and gravy. Now, my parents were telling me that eating beef was risky. What was going on?

Just days before our arrival, the British government announced a "possible link" between meat contaminated with mad cow disease and the recently discovered human affliction: new variant Creutzfeldt-Jacob disease. At the time of the announcement, 10 people in Britain had been identified with this debilitating brain disease for which there is no cure. Eight of the 10 victims had already died. A stroll down to the village newspaper shop confirmed the details of the announcement; a headline blared "It could be worse than AIDS." The article contained predictions that deaths from the disease could reach over 100,000. It was a bad day for the British beef industry and for those of us wanting to eat roast beef.

In 2002, Mr. Groves closed his shop. None of his children wanted to take up his trade, and with no willing buyers my parents lost access to their neighborhood butcher shop. Now, they must travel six miles to the nearest supermarket to buy their meat, where they can choose from an array of neatly packaged portions in the refrigerator section of the meat department. If the store does not have the cut of meat they want, my parents are out of luck. The supermarket does not receive carcasses, nor does it employ skilled butchers to dismember them. Sadly, their grandchildren will no longer be able to gaze in wonder at sides of meat hanging in a shop window or build sawdust mountain ranges as they listen to talk of "a small shoulder of lamb, a loin of pork, or a nice piece of sirloin suitable for roasting," or watch a butcher carefully prepare the meat for their evening meal. No, their grandchildren's meat smells of Styrofoam and cellophane.

BRAVE NEW ANIMAL WORLD

Mad cow disease, or more correctly, bovine spongiform encephalopathy (BSE), epitomizes for many critics all that is wrong with industrial meat production. It is a form of transmissible spongiform encephalopathy (TSE), a degenerative brain disease. Since its discovery in 1986, about 190,000 animals have been diagnosed with BSE worldwide; 97 percent of reported cases have been in Britain (World Organization for Animal Health 2011).

BSE in all likelihood resulted from cattle eating infected animal remains in their feed. Scientists attribute the infectious agent to a very resistant type of protein called a prion. In Britain, the rendering industry took carcass remains from slaughterhouses and turned them into a high-protein cattle feed, produced by cutting up the remains and heating the material to very high temperatures to separate fats from other material. The common products from this process, in addition to animal feed, include tallow, used in soap, and edible fats, used in margarine and cooking fats. The British rendering industry unknowingly contributed to the spread of BSE by exporting high protein animal feed across Europe.

Soon after researchers first identified BSE, the British government established a scientific committee to assess the disease's significance. The committee concluded "there is no evidence that there is any risk to (human) health" (quoted in Washer 2006:460). In reporting this information, British newspapers likened BSE to other food safety issues such as *Salmonella* and *Listeria*, which served to reassure the public that the disease posed no serious health threat. This complacency ended abruptly in March 1996, when the government announced that BSE was the most likely cause of new variant Creutzfeldt-Jacob disease (vCJD), the fatal brain disease that had claimed the lives of eight British citizens. Following the announcement, media accounts gave graphic descriptions of the sufferings of those who had died of vCJD and government advisors predicted an impending epidemic. Television news was filled with images of BSE-infected cows foaming at the mouth, losing their balance, and falling to the ground (McKay 2006). To restore confidence in the British beef industry, the government announced all cattle over the age of 30 months would be slaughtered and removed from the human food chain, because BSE is most commonly found in older cattle.

Meanwhile the press sensationalized the problem. Content analyses of BSE-related articles in British newspapers published at the time of the government announcement found they often misrepresented the link between the disease and human health (Rowe, Frewer, & Sjöberg 2000). Instead of reporting a "possible link" between BSE and vCJD, they often reported it as a "definite link." Also, a study of 425 published newspaper articles in the first nine months of 1996 found that over 63 percent promoted fear of eating meat (Dornbusch 1998).

Academic analyses of BSE have contributed to sensationalism by using emotive language. Forbes (2004: 344) notes that most publication titles used the lurid "mad cow image" followed by "crisis," "disaster," "failure," and "fiasco." Such labels tell readers what to feel before they read the article and reinforce the public impression of BSE as a disaster.

How disastrous was BSE in Britain? Since 1995, 170 persons have died from vCJD (National Creutzfeldt-Jakob Disease Surveillance Unit 2011). To keep BSE from entering the human food chain, the British government oversaw the slaughter of nearly nine million cattle, most by incineration, and spent over five billion pounds to compensate farmers for their losses.

The worldwide ban on British beef exports lasted 10 years. Today, BSE is almost extinct in Britain; the 11 cases reported in 2010 were down from a high of more than 37,000 in 1992 (World Organization for Animal Health 2011). In response to public concern over the disease's impact on food safety, the British government established the Food Standards Agency in 2000 "to protect the public's health and consumer interests in relation to food."

To prevent the spread of BSE, the European Union (EU) implemented a ban on feeding "mammalian processed animal protein" to cattle, sheep, and goats in July 1994. In 2001, the ban was expanded to include all processed animal proteins to all farmed animals (Europa n.d.). To lessen the risk of food-borne illnesses arising from production problems, the EU has implemented a series of measures to improve traceability. These measures are designed to identify where and when contamination occurred, thereby facilitating a speedy recall. Beginning in 2000, all bovines must be identified by ear tags that contain a 12-digit bar code specifying the animal's country of origin, region, herd, and individual identification number. Each animal is also issued a passport listing its individual identification number, date of birth, breed, sex, and mother's identification number. The passport accompanies each animal during transportation and must be updated by each owner until it reaches the slaughterhouse. The meat processor must also maintain the animal's identity, since EU labeling laws require meat to be sold with a reference number that links the product to an individual animal or animals (Bowling et al. 2008).

Despite the EU's mandatory traceability for all food and feed products, the supply chain is only as strong as its weakest link. Days or weeks may pass before the source of food-borne illness outbreaks can be identified, as the deadly 2011

F I G U R E   11.1   A reassuring sign for British beef consumers inside the Handmade Burger Company in Birmingham, England. Outside its billboard advertises "beautifully prepared, handmade chargrilled burgers, using traditionally reared, grass fed, 100% fully traceable prime Scotch beef."

E. coli O104:H4 outbreak in Europe illustrated. This outbreak, which killed 40 people and sickened over 4,000, was first blamed on cucumbers from Spain, before it was later traced to raw sprouts produced on a farm in northern Germany, and finally linked to a shipment of 15,000 kg of contaminated fenugreek seeds that originated in Egypt in 2009 before being widely distributed throughout Europe (CDC 2011; Food Quality 2011).

HOW NOW MAD COW IN THE UNITED STATES?

Bovine spongiform encephalopathy has largely disappeared from the western world's cattle herds since meat and bone meal were banned from cattle feed. In 2010, only 44 cases appeared worldwide. So far just three BSE cases have surfaced in the United States. The first was a Holstein from a Washington State dairy in December 2003. It came from a herd that entered the United States in August 2001 from Alberta. The cow was born in April 1997, before the August 1997 North American ban on ruminant feed containing animal protein (Canadian Food Inspection Agency 2005). Since then governments on either side of the border have introduced progressively more restrictive bans; in 2007, Canada banned cattle parts that could spread bovine spongiform encephalopathy (BSE) from all animal feeds, pet foods, and fertilizers. The removal of so-called specified risk material (the brain, spinal cord, and other tissues that are likely to contain the infective agent if an animal has the disease) from the food chain has added to the industry's costs, since these items have no economic value and have to be safely disposed of.

The second BSE case was in a 12-year-old cow from a Texas herd, which would have been turned into pet food had it not been flagged for BSE testing. Again, because of the animal's age, USDA officials suspected its infection arose from eating contaminated feed before the 1997 ban. The third diseased cow was a ten-year-old "downer" (an animal unable to walk because of injury or illness) found on an Alabama farm in 2006. After a lengthy investigation, researchers attributed this case of mad cow disease to a rare genetic abnormality rather than tainted feed (CDC n.d.).

As of June 2011, only three cases of new variant Creutzfeldt-Jacob disease have ever appeared in the United States. Two of the victims were born in the United Kingdom and most likely contracted BSE there. The third victim was born and raised in Saudi Arabia and had only lived permanently in the United States since 2005, leading researchers to conclude that the person contacted the disease in Saudi Arabia (National Creutzfeldt-Jakob Disease Surveillance Unit 2011). Given this epidemiological history, the risk of anyone contacting vCJD in the United States is virtually zero, while the likelihood of any more animals testing positive for BSE in the United States is also close to zero. So why all the fuss, particularly when other food-borne illnesses are responsible for many more deaths?

When BSE first appeared in Great Britain, journalists and broadcasters frightened people with predictions of devastation and death, using fear to frame events in an entertaining way. Hungry for increased sales and ratings, news media on both sides of the Atlantic have spawned a "cottage industry" of experts "who promote new fears and an expanding array of victims" (Altheide 2002:3). In so doing, they have added BSE to the growing number of what Giddens (1990:133) refers to as "low probability, high consequence risks," which result from globalization and the unintended outcomes of technological innovations. BSE is a product of agricultural industrialization, which in very rare instances has potentially fatal consequences for humans. But given the measures now in place in the European Union and North America, BSE no longer appears to pose an immediate threat to humans. The next section examines other food safety issues arising from industrial meat production.

WHAT'S IN THAT HAM SANDWICH?

Antibiotics are an important weapon in the battle against disease. The widespread use of antibiotics to curtail illness among animals grown in confinement has been blamed for alarming increases in the incidence of human bacterial infections that fail to respond to treatment with these same antibiotics (Angulo et al. 2000). Multidrug resistance in some *Salmonella* bacteria had already grown from 5 to 95 percent by the 1990s (Young et al. 1999).

Concerns first arose about using antibiotics in animal feed soon after the practice began in the 1950s. Critics feared the long-term use of these drugs to promote growth and feed efficiency posed a threat to human health. In the 1970s, the U.S. Food and Drug Administration (FDA) attempted to ban certain agricultural uses of antibiotics, but could not overcome opposition from agribusiness and farm-state legislators. Repeated efforts by the U.S. Congress to ban agricultural use of certain antibiotics since then also have proved unsuccessful.

Despite lack of legislative success, mounting medical evidence links nontherapeutic uses of antibiotics in livestock to antibiotic-resistant bacteria that make it harder to treat infections in humans (U.S. National Research Council 1999). These findings led to an editorial in the *New England Journal of Medicine* urging elimination of antimicrobials in animal feed (Gorbach 2001). In the same issue of the journal, researchers reported that 20 percent of ground meat samples purchased in Washington, D.C., supermarkets contained *Salmonella* and that 84 percent of the isolates were resistant to at least one antimicrobial.

The American Medical Association, American Public Health Association, and American College of Preventive Medicine oppose nontherapeutic use of antimicrobials in animal agriculture. Agriculture and drug lobbies maintain that these concerns are overblown. In 2010, the Food and Drug Administration (FDA) issued nonbinding guidelines that suggested phasing out the use of antimicrobials to promote growth in livestock and using them only to assure animal health. A year later, a coalition of consumer and public interest groups sued the FDA to force it to restrict use of antibiotics in animal agriculture (Institute of Food Technologists 2011).

Escherichia coli is a bacterium commonly found in the lower intestine of warm-blooded animals. Most *E. coli* strains are harmless, but some, most notably *E. Coli* O157:H7, produce a potentially lethal toxin. *E. Coli* O157:H7 was responsible for the deaths of four children who ate contaminated hamburgers at Jack-in-the-Box restaurants in the Seattle area in 1993. In the aftermath of this incident, the USDA's Food Safety and Inspection Service introduced a system for reducing and preventing pathogens on raw products—Hazard Analysis and Critical Control Point (HACCP)—in all federally and state-inspected meat and poultry slaughter and processing plants. HAACP was fully implemented by 2000, but it has not stopped meat contamination. The Food Safety and Inspection Service Web site lists meat recalls since 1996. Most deal with relatively small quantities: West Missouri Beef's 2010 recall of approximately 14,000 pounds of fresh boneless beef that "might" have been contaminated with *E. coli* O157:H7 is typical. It is larger recalls that keep the public on edge, however, such as JBS's 2009 recall of more than 380,000 pounds of beef that "may" have been contaminated with *E.coli* O157:H7.

Despite growing public concern with food-borne illness, food recalls were voluntary until January 2011, when President Barack Obama signed into law the FDA Food Safety Modernization Act. This Act authorizes the Food and Drug Administration and the Department of Health and Human Services to order recalls of tainted foods, increase inspections of facilities that produce or handle food, improve detection of food-borne illness outbreaks, and more closely scrutinize imported foods. Unfortunately, the legislation does not apply to the meat industry. Meat recalls are still initiated by the manufacturer or distributor. Sometimes this occurs at the request of the USDA's Food Safety and Inspection Service, but all recalls are voluntary. If, however, a company refuses to recall its products, the Food Safety and Inspection Service has the legal authority to seize the products (USDA FSIS n.d.).

PLENTY MORE WHERE THAT CAME FROM

Never before have North Americans had so much food to choose from. Most of it is grown and processed under the control of giant transnational corporations that search the globe for cheap and reliable sources of food and feed. The bacon a Peoria schoolboy eats for breakfast might have come from a hog born in Canada and raised in Minnesota. The McDonald's hamburger he eats at lunch could have come from cattle raised in Australia or New Zealand. The chicken fingers he eats at supper most likely came from birds grown in Arkansas on grain imported from Brazil.

Industrialized agriculture's bounty has lowered the cost of food. It has also contributed to "supersized" food portions in restaurants. In 1957, a White Castle hamburger ("The hamburger specialists since 1921") contained just over one ounce of cooked meat. The typical fast food hamburger today contains six ounces (Putnam 1999). McDonald's original hamburger, French fries, and

Michael Broadway

F I G U R E 11.2 White Castle remains part of North America's fast food landscape.

12-ounce cola contained 590 calories (Spake 2002); today's Extra Value Meal—a Quarter Pounder with cheese, large fries, and medium Coca-Cola®—packs in 1,240 calories (McDonalds.com 2011).

The increase in restaurant portion sizes—and loaded with fats, refined sugars, and carbohydrates—has contributed to the explosion in obesity rates among North Americans. In 2007–2009, 24 percent of Canadian and 34 percent of American adults were obese,[1] up 10 percentage points from the 1980s (Shields, Carroll, & Ogden 2011). Childhood obesity has more than tripled, from 6.5 percent in 1980 to 19.6 percent in 2008 for children aged 6 to 11 years (National Center for Chronic Disease Prevention and Health Promotion n.d.).

Not only are the meals we eat in restaurants becoming larger and richer in calories, we also have more to choose from when we shop for food. The average number of items stocked by a typical U.S. supermarket has more than tripled since 1980, from 15,000 to 50,000. In 2010 alone, more than 15,000 new food and beverage items came to market in the United States (Food Institute n.d.). Two-thirds of the new goods are condiments, candy and snacks, baked goods, soft drinks, cheese products, and ice cream novelties (Nestle 2002). Many are hand-held portable foods that encase meat inside tubes, wraps, pockets, and pitas.

The food we take home is more and more "convenient," but it is even more convenient to eat out. Restaurants accounted for about 25 cents of every dollar Americans spent on food in the 1950s; by 2009, they took 49 cents out of every food dollar. In 2011, U.S. restaurants numbered 960,000—one restaurant for every 30 Americans (National Restaurant Association 2011).

The traditional American dining pattern of "three square meals a day" is going the way of the traditional American family of a breadwinning father, a homemaking mother, and their children. More and more Americans are eating throughout the day, a phenomenon referred to as "grazing." Fast food chains and convenience stores have responded with "dashboard dining." A decade ago, Sonic Drive-In began packaging its French fries in round containers so they would conveniently fit in car cup holders (Jolley 2002).

"Fast food culture" has spread around the world. In Asia, for example, KFC (formerly Kentucky Fried Chicken) restaurants are common in Japan, Korea, Malaysia, Thailand, Indonesia, the Philippines, and China. "The Colonel's" move to China is particularly notable. In 2011, China had more than 3,300 KFC restaurants and was opening one new restaurant a day (Yum China n.d.)!

Rising incomes, population growth, and urbanization are behind the world-wide surge in demand for meat and other animal products. Urbanization, result-ing from the transition from an agrarian to industrial-based economy, leads to infrastructure improvements and allows the development of food supply chains. This enables city dwellers to enjoy a more varied diet that is richer in animal proteins and fats than their rural counterparts. This phenomenon is evident throughout most of the developing world, with the exception of sub-Saharan Africa, which experienced little change in per capita meat consumption in the last third of the twentieth century (see Table 11.1). China and Brazil are behind much of the growth in demand for meat in East Asia and Latin America respec-tively, but their consumption levels remain well below those in North America.

China's rapid urbanization and economic growth has led the country to expand its meat production. By 2009, it accounted for nearly half of all the chickens produced worldwide (see Table 11.2). To accommodate this growth China is investing heavily in factory farms. In 2008, the national government provided $350 million to subsidize their development. The provincial govern-ment of Hubei in central China has invested in a 500,000 sow operation—one of the world's largest (Gura 2010).

T A B L E 11.1   Per Capita Meat Consumption (kilograms per year)

Region	1964–1966	1997–1999
World	24.2	36.4
Near East and North Africa	11.9	21.2
Sub-Saharan Africa	9.9	9.4
Latin America and Caribbean	31.7	53.8
East Asia	8.7	37.7
South Asia	3.9	5.3
Industrialized Countries (includes N. America and Europe)	61.5	88.2

1 kilogram = 2.2 pounds
SOURCE: World Health Organization. 2003. Diet, Nutrition and the Prevention of Chronic Diseases. Geneva.

TABLE 11.2 **United States and China Percent Share of World Meat Production, 1994–2009**

	United States		China	
	1994	2009	1994	2009
Beef	21.0	19.0	6.0	10.0
Pork	10.0	10.0	41.0	47.0
Chicken	25.0	20.5	13.0	14.0

SOURCE: FAO (various years) FAO Statistical Yearbook, United Nations.

MEATPACKING AND UNCLE SAM

Since the 1980s, meat and poultry companies have increasingly relied on immigrants to work their slaughter and processing lines. A substantial number of these workers have been unauthorized. In 1997, the Immigration and Naturalization Service (INS) launched an undercover investigation to determine whether Tyson was hiring unauthorized workers at its Shelbyville, Tennessee, chicken plant. Two-and-a-half years and 422 undercover audiotapes, 36 videotapes, and 360,000 pages of subpoenaed documents later, a grand jury indicted six managers and Tyson for: "conspiracy to smuggle illegal aliens into the U.S., provide them with fraudulent work papers and employ them unlawfully for the purpose of commercial advantage and private financial gain" (Tanger 2006:59). After the trial, Tyson fired three of the managers who were caught on tape, another committed suicide, and two pled guilty. They received sentences of one year of probation and fines of $2,100 and $3,100 respectively. The jury excused the company for the illegal acts of its employees because, in the words of Tyson's attorney, the company acted in "good faith" when it hired unauthorized workers and thus was absolved from any criminal liability.

Given the huge expense and monumental failure of its case against Tyson, federal authorities changed tactics and targeted workers rather than employers. In December 2006, more than 1,000 agents from the Immigration and Customs Enforcement (ICE, which replaced the enforcement arm of INS in 2002), some clad in riot gear and carrying assault rifles, descended upon six Swift & Co. meatpacking plants in Colorado, Nebraska, Texas, Iowa, and Minnesota and arrested 1,282 authorized and unauthorized immigrants. The investigation that led to these raids centered on identity theft, specifically the use of false Social Security numbers and "green cards," carried by immigrants who are authorized to live and work in the United States. The arrests and ensuing deportations divided families; some of those arrested had children and spouses who were legal residents or citizens, and these individuals had to decide whether to stay or follow deported family members back to their country of origin (Preston 2006a, 2006b). Months after the raid a newspaper reporter visited Cactus, Texas, where federal officials had netted the largest number of unauthorized workers:

> The streets of this small, isolated city in the Texas Panhandle are virtually empty nowadays, and "For Rent" signs decorate dilapidated trailers and

shabby 1940s-era military barracks that just a few weeks ago were full of tenants. Sales of tortillas and other staples are down. Money wire transactions to Central America have mostly dried up. The "Guatemalas," as local residents call them, are almost all gone, and so are a significant number of Mexican nationals. An estimated 12 to 18 children are now living with only one parent because the other was arrested in a massive immigration raid at the biggest employer in town. (Moreno 2007)

The Swift raids were the largest work-site enforcement operation ever carried out by the federal government, and they reflected a broad change in enforcement policy during George W. Bush's presidency. In the late 1990s, the government fined more than 1,000 employers for hiring unauthorized workers; but by 2004 this number had dropped to just three, and an ICE spokesman admitted the agency no longer fined employers (Finley 2006). In January 2007, ICE arrested 21 workers at Smithfield's Tar Heel, North Carolina, pork plant after the company had provided federal officials with 5,000 employee records. The company terminated another 500 workers because of discrepancies in their job applications (Fears & Williams 2007).

The most significant of ICE's meatpacking raids took place in May 2007 in Postville, in northeastern Iowa, at the site of Agriprocessors Inc., the largest kosher slaughterhouse in the United States. The plant opened in the late 1980s, and orthodox Jews moved to the town to work as kosher butchers. Over the next decade Guatemalan migrants began working at the plant (Duara, Petroski, & Schulte 2008). According to the federal search warrant, immigration officials had filed nearly 700 complaints concerning immigration violations and criminal activity by workers over a two-year period. Close to 400 of the plant's 968 workers were arrested.

Two months after the raid nearly 300 immigrants, mostly Guatemalans and Mexicans, had been convicted of document fraud. Most faced five months in prison and then deportation. With nothing left to lose after their arrests, unauthorized employees described how they were put on the line with no training and forced to work long shifts without overtime or breaks. Federal officials also discovered 20 underage workers, some as young as 13, who put in 12-hour shifts or more, including working through the night and sometimes six times a week (Preston 2008).

Six months after the raid, Agriprocessors filed for Chapter 11 bankruptcy (Olivo 2009). Owned by Aaron Rubashkin, a Hasidic butcher from Brooklyn, Agriprocessors had been frequently cited for violations of state and federal laws governing the environment, labor relations, child labor, and immigration. In the court cases that followed the ICE raid, a plant supervisor was sentenced to three years in federal prison for conspiracy to hire illegal immigrants and aiding and abetting the hiring of illegal immigrants. In 2009, Sholom Rubashkin, plant manager and son of the owner, was convicted in U.S. District Court of fraud and money laundering and sentenced to 27 years in prison. The U.S. attorney chose not to prosecute him on federal immigration violations, and he was acquitted in state court of "knowingly" hiring underage workers. Orthodox Jews from Canada bought the plant at auction in July 2009, and reopened it as Agri Star Meat and Poultry LLC. In 2010, it employed about 600 workers; the newest were Somali refugees (Love 2010).

Worksite immigration raids declined after President Barack Obama took office, and enforcement has centered on employers who knowingly hire unauthorized workers. In 2011, congressional Republicans called for a return to workplace raids (Bennett 2011).

MEAT ME IN COURT

In 1993, 14 current and former employees of IBP's Kansas beef plants filed suit, alleging the company subjected Mexican and Mexican American employees to a "hostile work environment" and "assigned the most difficult and least desirable jobs solely on the basis of their national origin." In 1995, the plaintiffs' attorneys asked us to prepare depositions summarizing our knowledge of IBP's operations in its Finney County, Kansas, plant. Several years later, a federal judge refused to certify a class action lawsuit, requiring each case to be tried individually. In June 1999, on the day the first trial was to begin, attorneys for both sides settled out of court. Terms of the settlement were sealed, but the plaintiffs' lead attorney explained to Michael Broadway that "the workers received more money than they had probably ever seen in their lifetimes," and that her law firm had recovered its costs. But, in her view, the amount of the settlement "was not sufficient to alter IBP's way of doing business."

A lawsuit brought against IBP by employees at its Pasco, Washington, beef plant made it to the U.S. Supreme Court in 2005. The employees demanded payment for the time they spent putting on (donning) and taking off (doffing) work gear. The court ruled in *IBP, Inc. v. Alvarez* that donning and doffing a worker's unique protective gear in company locker rooms was "integral and indispensable," constituting an employee's first and last principal activity of the workday. The court also ruled that the company should compensate workers for the time they spent walking between the locker room and production floor at the beginning and end of the work shift as part of the employees' "continuous workday" (Krakow 2006). The settlement required IBP to pay $11.4 million. The attorneys received $1.9 million, and the remainder went to employees, who received on average $1,886 (National Workrights Institute n.d.). Despite this landmark decision, meat and poultry workers across the country continue to file lawsuits to obtain back pay for time spent donning and doffing. In May 2011, three such lawsuits were set for trial in U.S. District Court in Omaha against Nebraska Beef, Greater Omaha Packing Co., and Tyson Foods (MeatPoultry.com 2011). And so it goes.[2]

NO SUCH THING AS A FREE LUNCH

Industrialized agriculture promises cheap food, but it passes many of its actual costs on to other sectors of the economy, or hides them, in a strategy known as "externalizing costs." Family farms once raised a variety of livestock and incorporated manure into their crop production as parts of a sustainable system; today's factory farms specialize in one or two commodities and rely on large amounts of agrichemicals and petroleum.

Population peaked for many rural counties in the Midwest—America's breadbasket—in the 1930s. Since then, the number of farms has declined by nearly 1.3 million (see Table 11.3). On Canada's prairies, the number of farms peaked in the early 1940s and then declined: in Saskatchewan about 94,000 farms disappeared between 1941 and 2006; Alberta lost 50,000 farms during the same period (Statistics Canada n.d.a).

Small towns were once hubs for local economies, supplying local farmers and in turn depending on their business. Now rural communities, bypassed by corporate farms, are suffering a slow death through out-migration and falling incomes. According to the U.S. Office of Technology Assessment, as farm size increases so does rural poverty (Kimbrell 2002). Family farms still in operation increasingly produce foodstuffs under contract to processors, who determine the final sale price. According to Nolan Jungclaus, an independent producer from Lake Lillian, Minnesota, who testified before the U.S. Senate Agriculture Committee on the effect of packer ownership of livestock, this process is "sucking the lifeblood out of rural communities" (National Farmers Union News 2002).

In desperate attempts to reverse their declining fortunes, local chambers of commerce and, increasingly, economic development officers in state and local governments actively recruit new businesses and industries, offering low or no taxes, free land, "spec" buildings, and other incentives. Small towns have turned to value-added processing of agricultural commodities to create jobs. Meatpacking

TABLE 11.3   Number of Farms in Midwestern States, 1940 and 2009

State	1940	2009	Decline
Ohio	233,700	75,000	158,700
Missouri	256,100	108,000	148,100
Michigan	187,600	55,000	138,600
Illinois	213,400	76,000	137,400
Indiana	184,500	62,000	122,500
Minnesota	197,400	81,000	116,400
Iowa	213,300	93,000	120,300
Wisconsin	186,700	78,000	108,700
Kansas	156,300	66,000	90,300
Nebraska	121,100	47,000	74,100
N. Dakota	74,000	32,000	42,000
S. Dakota	72,500	32,000	40,500
Total	2,096,600	814,800	1,297,600

SOURCE: U.S. Department of Agriculture (USDA), 2002 & 2010 U.S. Statistical Abstract.

and poultry processing accounted for much of rural manufacturing job growth in the United States during the 1980s and 1990s. The state of Arkansas serves as a good example. While running for president in 1992, Bill Clinton boasted of the record number of manufacturing jobs created during his term as governor. What he failed to mention was that most of these jobs were in poultry plants. Arkansas was not alone. Poultry processing became the second fastest growing factory job in the United States and the biggest industry in the South during this period (Horwitz 1994:1; Kwik 1991:14). Beef processing became Nebraska's largest manufacturing employer, accounting for half the state's manufacturing jobs (Ackerman 1991).

But work on meat and poultry lines is physically demanding and dangerous. And packinghouses bring significant social and economic costs to host communities: declining per capita income, housing shortages, increases in population mobility, and rising demands for health care, public safety, education, and indigent care. Employers ignore the added costs that come with their workforces. These externalized costs fall on local residents, who, in addition to paying higher taxes, give of their time and money to support food banks, homeless shelters, and other newcomer services.

ORGANIC AND NATURAL

Rachel Carson's *Silent Spring* (1962) awakened the public to the environmental effects of pesticides, planting the seeds for the organic food movement in the United States. Since then a mounting chorus of critics of industrial agriculture, including Wendell Berry, Wes Jackson, and Michael Pollan, has called for alternatives to industrial agriculture. Thanks to bestsellers such as *Fast Food Nation* and *The Omnivore's Dilemma* and popular documentaries like *Super Size Me* and *Food, Inc.*, a growing number of Americans have become aware of where and how their food is produced. And more and more groups—from production workers and growers to environmentalists and community activists—are challenging the industry giants. What are the viable alternatives to the existing system?

Although still only a tiny part of the total market, consumer demand for organic and "natural" foods is rapidly growing. Coleman's Natural Products Company, Niman Ranch, Laura's Lean Beef, and Applegate Farms raise cattle and poultry on natural grains or grasses without antibiotics or growth hormones. Michael Pollan (2006a:8) has championed what he calls the "pastoral food chain." Describing it as the polar opposite to the "industrial food chain," Pollan claims the pastoral food chain is based on artisanal production, where success depends on higher quality rather than lower price (Ibid.:249). Most of the proselytizing for pastoral food and artisanal production comes from writers who base their arguments on carefully selected examples and anecdotal vignettes about new producers, new restaurants, and new markets. Best known, perhaps, are Michael Pollan's (2006a) praise of Polyface Farm in Virginia and Frances Moore

Michael Broadway

FIGURE 11.3   Organic farm in Westby, Wisconsin.

Lappé and Anna Lappé's (2002) celebration of Alice Waters' Chez Panisse restaurant in Berkeley, California.

Niman Ranch began raising cattle in the early 1970s on 11 acres north of San Francisco using "traditional humane husbandry methods" and "all natural" feeds. Demand for its beef grew, and in the 1990s Niman Ranch used the same principles to raise hogs in Iowa. In 2011, the company suppliers included more than 676 independent farmers and ranchers who "adhere to the strictest protocols and the belief that all-natural, humane and sustainable methods produce the best flavor" (nimanranch.com). "Humane and sustainable methods [and] the best flavor" do not come cheap, however. In 2011, the online purchase price of eight 7 oz. Niman Ranch Tenderloin Filets was $249.95, or $71.00 a pound!

The increasing popularity of organic foods has spawned health-conscious food stores. Founded in 1980, Whole Foods calls itself "the world's leader in natural and organic foods," and it has grown by devouring its competitors, including such smaller regional stores as Bread and Circus, Mrs Gooch's, Fresh Fields, and Wild Oats Markets. By 2011, it operated more than 300 stores across the United States, most located in upscale neighborhoods or close to major universities. Whole Foods has partnered with a third-party nonprofit organization to certify its meat comes from animals not raised in crates or cages that have "enhanced outdoor access." Despite its phenomenal growth, the market Whole Foods serves remains relatively small; in 2010, its sales amounted to $9 billion, which is tiny by comparison with Kroger's $82 billion, Safeway's $40 billion, and the largest food retailer in the world, Walmart, which does not break out its grocery sales from its total U.S. sales of $258 billion (supermarketnews.com).

Arby's, Chipotle Mexican Grill, Chick-fil-A, and Panera Bread Company are among the restaurant chains that have responded to public demand for hormone- and antibiotic-free "natural" foods (Horovitz 2005). Reflecting this trend, a 2010 survey by the firm Context Marketing found 69 percent of respondents willing to pay for "ethically produced" foods. When asked what they meant by "ethical food," more than 90 percent identified three main qualities: protects the environment, meets high quality and safety standards, and treats farm animals humanely.

In response to criticism, the industrial meat industry is beginning to modify how it raises and slaughters animals. Under pressure from consumers, fast food behemoths like McDonald's are insisting on more humane treatment and slaughter of animals. McDonald's now utilizes the services of an Animal Welfare Council for advice on humane animal handling practices. Temple Grandin, world-renowned professor of animal science at Colorado State University, conducts slaughterhouse audits to ensure they meet McDonald's animal handling guidelines. Pressured by Greenpeace, JBS, the world's largest beef processor, signed an agreement with Walmart in June 2009 that promises not to source cattle from deforested areas or from producers who exploit child or slave-like labor (Johnston 2009b).

F I G U R E 11.4 Whole Foods Market in Minneapolis, Minnesota.

VOTING WITH YOUR STOMACH

As a nation, we are at a crucial juncture in how we produce, process, consume, and even think about food. Stretching before us are two alternative futures, according to Tim Lang and Michael Heasman (2004): a dominant productionist paradigm based on corporate agriculture and oligopolistic food industries, and an emerging alternative integrated-ecological paradigm, which produces food locally, naturally, and sustainably on family farms under socially just conditions. Are we doomed to continue to suffer from what Michael Pollan (2006a:2) calls "our national eating disorder," sickened by industrial foods that are bad for our health, the environment, and the people who produce and process them? Or might we be witness to an emerging food future, centered on healthy and sustainable food alternatives (Phillips 2006:47–48)?

Our collective food future will depend upon individual decisions about what we eat and where. Eating at McDonald's or KFC supports transnational corporations and their corporate suppliers; buying locally grown food from a farmers' market and cooking it ourselves supports a more sustainable system of agriculture. Alternatively, local food co-ops, box schemes, and other forms of community-supported agriculture (CSA) offer in-season vegetables, meat, and dairy products from local farms. Even supermarkets may stock local and regional foods and sell natural, grass-fed, free-range, and antibiotic-free meat, responding to sufficient demand for these items. In 2006, Walmart announced to the horror of many in the organic movement that it would begin offering its customers a wide range of organic products, but the price premium would be just 10 percent above conventionally produced items. This restriction suggested to critics that to achieve such an outcome organic producers would have to adopt the economies of scale associated with industrial agriculture, a phenomenon that was already evident with the development of organic concentrated animal feeding operations (Pollan 2006b).

Consumer pressure has already pushed multinational fast-food chains toward healthier menus, and the meat and poultry industry toward better practices in animal agriculture and slaughter. Those of us with a stomach for a fight may wish to lobby Congress to improve access to fresh nutritional food and meat-packing's working conditions.

The Employee Free Choice Act (H.R. 1409; S. 560), introduced in March 2009, is a controversial bill that its sponsors claim will make it easier for unions to organize. Unions are not a panacea for all that ails meatpacking, but they have the potential to ensure that employee concerns over working conditions are addressed and acted upon through contract negotiations. It is no coincidence that the company that revolutionized modern-day meatpacking in the United States—IBP—was virulently anti-union. From its inception, IBP refused to abide by the terms of the existing union master contract, and, thus, began the industry's long decline in wage and working conditions.

The Employee Free Choice Act would let workers choose whether to unionize through secret ballot votes or card checks in which workers obtain union recognition as soon as a majority of employees at a workplace sign union cards. Current law permits management to insist on a secret ballot, which often lets companies campaign for lengthy periods against unionization. Like many reform efforts, it has not received overwhelming support. The bill passed the House in the 111th Congress, but died for lack of sufficient support in the Senate. In 2011, with the Republican takeover of the House of Representatives, the measure remains dead for the 112th Congress.

The Community Gardens Act of 2009 (H.R. 3225) allows, but does not mandate, the USDA to create a grant program to help groups or organizations start, build, and run community gardens. It would encourage healthy lifestyles: make fresh fruits and vegetables more easily available to communities; reduce greenhouse gas emissions; and educate the public on the value of community gardening. This measure also failed in the 111th Congress and faces dim prospects in the 112th Congress.

President Obama's commitment to strengthening local and regional food systems led the USDA to implement *Know Your Farmer, Know Your Food*. This program has no office, no staff, and no budget, just a Web site containing resources such as the location of over 6,500 farmers' markets across the country—a movement that has grown by leaps and bounds since the early 1990s when there were less than 2,000 farmers' markets. But this has not stopped opponents in the U.S. House of Representatives from trying to eliminate the program from the 2011 bill that authorizes USDA spending.

St. Jude is the patron saint of lost causes, and for over a decade he might well have led the charge to get the Preservation of Antibiotics Medical Treatment Act passed. The late Senator Ted Kennedy championed this bill for a decade, and its primary sponsor is the only microbiologist in Congress, Louise Slaughter. Reintroducing this bill in the House of Representatives in 2011, the congresswoman cited an estimate from the Food and Drug Administration that about 80 percent of all antibiotics in the United States are given to animals. If enacted, the proposed bill would forbid the use of antibiotics to facilitate weight gain in animals, a measure that has already been adopted by the European Union and New Zealand (Bottemiller 2011). Although the bill has widespread support among health professionals, it is opposed by the Animal Health Institute, a coalition of pharmaceutical companies and major trade groups.

For those lacking the stomach to lobby Congress, opportunities abound at state and local levels. Land-use regulations dictate agricultural policy and practice "on the ground," and private citizens can influence the outcome of these ordinances. Perhaps the most effective way to regulate animal agriculture is to support stronger rural zoning to limit the number and size of concentrated animal feeding operations, ensure adequate setbacks from neighbors, and protect air and water quality. Paradoxically, in cities and the suburbs, citizens may wish to rescind local ordinances that prohibit modest forms of animal agriculture. Madison, Wisconsin's city council reversed a ban on backyard chickens in 2004 and adopted an ordinance similar to regulations in Seattle, Baltimore, Washington, D.C, and Los Angeles. It allows for up to four egg-laying hens (no roosters) per property, kept in a coop no closer than 25 feet from the nearest neighbor's living quarters. A ban on butchering in the city remains in place. So far about

150 Madison families have taken advantage of the new ordinance (Huffstutter 2009). The Web sites Urbanchickens.org and Backyardchickens.com offer up-to-date information on this growing movement.

Food choices have economic implications; they have moral ones as well. The National Catholic Rural Life Conference has proclaimed an Eaters' Bill of Rights (2002). Each of us has the right to know how our food is grown and processed. We have a right to food that is safe, nutritious, and produced under socially just circumstances, without harming air, water, land—or people. We also have a right to know the country of origin of our food and whether it has been genetically modified.

The Conference advocates policies that "uphold the dignity of family farmers" and opposes the contract-grower system of agricultural production, which makes "serfs of family farmers." It encourages people to support sustainable agriculture and calls on us to purchase locally grown food, use church halls and parking lots for farmers' markets, promote cookbooks that use local produce, and celebrate special days and seasons to widen the connection between food, the land, and spirituality.

THE MEAT AND POULTRY INDUSTRY: HISTORY REPEATED?

When Upton Sinclair wrote *The Jungle* in the early years of the twentieth century, five companies dominated America's meatpacking industry. Livestock producers complained that the Beef Trust conspired to set prices—a claim later supported by a report from the Federal Trade Commission:

> Five great packing concerns of the country—Swift, Armour, Morris, Cudahy, and Wilson—have obtained such a dominant position that they control at will the market in which they buy their supplies, the market in which they sell their products, and hold the fortunes of their competition in their hands.
>
> Not only is the business of gathering, preparing, and selling meat products in their control, but an almost countless number of by-product industries are similarly dominated; and not content... they have invaded allied industries and even unrelated ones. (cited in Skaggs 1986:105–106)

In 1919, the Justice Department indicted the five companies for numerous antitrust violations. In 1920, the five companies agreed to divest themselves of their "vertical business structures" (Skaggs 1986:107).

Now, in the early years of a new century, all that remains of these companies are their names. But in their place a new oligopoly has emerged to dominate the meat industry. In 2008, the top four companies controlled 79 percent of the beef market, 65 percent of the pork market, and 57 percent of the poultry market. Four companies control 36 percent of supermarket food sales (GAO 2009).

In the twenty-first century, the federal governments of the United States and Canada are turning a deaf ear to concerns about monopolistic practices of the giant corporations that control our food. Farmers' and ranchers' complaints about captive supplies and packer ownership of livestock fail to resonate with urban consumers, who are far removed from the *where* and the *how* of food production. Politicians and government officials, whose constituents are increasingly urban, are more likely to curry the favor of powerful agribusiness corporations than listen to the dwindling pleas of small farmers and the small towns that depend on them.

Government in North America is ignoring the fact that our food supply system is controlled by a few corporations. The consequences for our food security, safety, and quality are significant. But viable alternatives exist. All we need do is look among a growing number of producers and providers in North America. Each of us chooses the food we eat, and our choices shape prevailing systems of production, processing, and packaging. The challenge for those concerned about developing a sustainable agricultural system, one that respects land, animals, producers, harvesters, and processing workers is to show consumers the connection between the food they eat and the prevailing industrial production system. Only if we make that connection will more people demand changes in their food and how it is produced. It is to that end that we offer this book.

NOTES

1. The Body Mass Index (BMI) measures overweight and obesity. It is calculated as a weight in pounds divided by the square of a person's height in inches, multiplied by 703. Alternatively, weight in kilograms is divided by the square of a person's height in meters. A BMI between 25 and 29.9 is interpreted as overweight, while 30.0 and above is classified as obese (U.S. Department of Health & Human Services 2001).

2. In June 2011, the Food Safety and Inspection Service ruled that meat, poultry, and egg processing facilities must pay USDA inspectors for donning and doffing hardhats, hearing protectors, and work-related equipment, and for walking to and from their inspection station at the beginning and ending of each shift and before and after lunch (Meat&Poultry Staff 2011).

References

Ackerman, Pam. 1991. "All Across Nebraska, Beef Is Big Business." *Lexington* (Nebraska) *Clipper*, May 29.

Adams, Andy. 1903. *The Log of a Cowboy: A Narrative of the Old Trail Days.* Boston: Houghton Mifflin.

Ahmad, Shajia. 2010. "Emmaus House Seeks City Assistance." *Garden City* (Kansas) *Telegram*, December 22.

Alberta Agriculture, Food, and Rural Development. 2000. *Code of Practice for Responsible Livestock Development and Manure Management.* Edmonton: Alberta Agriculture.

———. 2002. *Loss and Fragmentation of Farmland.* Edmonton: Alberta Agriculture.

Alberta Economic Development. 2010. *Highlights of the Alberta Economy.* Edmonton: Alberta Economic Development.

Albrecht, Stan L. 1982. "Commentary." *Pacific Sociological Review* 25: 297–306.

Altheide, David L. 2002. *Creating Fear: News and the Construction of Crisis.* New York: Aldine de Gruyter.

Alvesson, Mats. 1995. *Cultural Perspectives on Organizations.* Cambridge, UK: Cambridge University Press.

American Meat Institute. n.d. "The Market Works: Don't Dismantle Progress." http://www.meatfuelsamerica.com/ GIPSA (November 6, 2010).

Anderson, Ken. 2010. "Swiss Will Decide If Animals Should Have Lawyers." *Brownfieldagnews.com*, February 19. http://www.ellinghuysen.com/ news/articles/98074.shtml (February 22, 2010).

Angulo, F., K.R. Johnson, R.V. Tauxe, and M.L. Cohen. 2000. "Origins and Consequences of Antimicrobial Resistant Nontyphoidal Salmonella: Implications for the Use of Fluoroquinolones in Food Animals." *Microbial Drug Resistance* 6:77–83.

Animal Agriculture Alliance. 2010. "Activists Share Anti-Agriculture Agenda at Conferences." Animalagalliance.org, August 16. http://www.ellinghuysen.com/ news/articles/106040.shtml (August 17, 2010).

Animal Studies Group. 2006. "Introduction." *Killing Animals.* Urbana: University of Illinois Press.

Animal Welfare Approved. 2010. "Antibiotics in Farming: Has Tyson Shot Itself in the Foot?" January 25. http://www.animalwelfareapproved.org/2010/01/25/antibiotics-in-farming-has-tyson-foods-shot-itself-in-the-foot (November 19, 2010).

Annis, Robert C., and Bill Ashton. 2010. *Immigration to Rural Canada Responding to Labour Market Needs and Promoting Welcoming Communities*. Paper presented at Metropolis Prairie Meeting, Winnipeg, Manitoba, Canada, September 17.

Anonymous. 2001. "Tour de Stench." April 20. Typescript, 2 pp. Authors' files.

Associated Press. 2000. "Kentucky Poultry Production Up 13,000 Percent." *The Gleaner* (Henderson, Kentucky), June 25.

———. 2002. "Chicken Farmers Increasing Vigilance." *Courier & Press* (Evansville, Indiana), October 22.

———. 2005. "Teen's Name Change Criticizes KFC." *The Gleaner* (Henderson, Kentucky), December 31.

———. 2011. "Obama Signs Food-Safety Bill." January 7. http://www.foodsystemsinsider.com.html (January 7, 2011).

Austin, Lisa. 1988. "Rich Potential for Kansas Carries Risk." *Wichita* (Kansas) *Eagle-Beacon*, September 11:1A, 10A–11A.

Ávila, Henry J. 1997. "The Mexican American Community in Garden City, Kansas, 1900–1950." *Kansas History* 20:23–27.

Bach, Robert. 1993. *Changing Relations: Newcomers and Established Residents in U.S. Communities: A Report to the Ford Foundation by the National Board of the Changing Relations Project*. New York: Ford Foundation.

Barrett, James R. 1987. *Work and Community in the Jungle: Chicago's Packinghouse Workers, 1894–1922*. Urbana: University of Illinois Press.

Bennett, Brian. 2011. "Republicans Want a Return to Workplace Immigration Raids." *Los Angeles Times*, January 27.

Benson, Janet E. 1990. "Good Neighbors: Ethnic Relations in Garden City Trailer Courts." *Urban Anthropology* 19:361–386.

Bjerklie, Steve. 1993. "A Fine Scattering of Genes: Poultry Breeders Meet New Needs With New Birds." *Meat&Poultry* 39(2):18–24.

———. 2007. "Animal Instincts: What Does the Public Really Think About Animal Welfare?" MeatPoultry.com, November 17. http://www.ellinghuysen.com/news/articles/61251.shtml (December 12, 2007).

Blanchard, Leola Howard. 1989. *Conquest of Southwest Kansas*. Garden City, KS: Finney County Historical Society. (First published in 1931.)

Block, Ben. 2008. "More Companies Discontinuing Farm Animal Confinement." Worldwatch Institute, April 7. http://www.worldwatch.org/node/5689 (August 21, 2010).

Boggs, Donald L., and Robert A. Merkel. 1984. *Live Animal Carcass Evaluation and Selection Manual*, 2nd ed. Dubuque, IA: Kendall Hunt.

Bowers, Douglas E. 2000. "Cooking Trends Echo Changing Roles of Women." *Food Review* 23(1):23–29.

Bowler, Ian. 1985. "Some Consequences of the Industrialization of Agriculture in the European Community." In *The Industrialization of the Countryside*. Michael Healey and Brian W. Ilbery, eds., pp. 75–98. Norwich, UK: Geo Books.

———. 1992. "The Industrialization of Agriculture." In *The Geography of Agriculture in Developed Market Economies*. Ian Bowler, ed., pp. 7–31. Harlow, UK: Longman.

Bowling, M.E., D.L. Pendell, D.L. Morris, Y. Yoon, K. Katoh, K.E. Belk, and G.C. Smith. 2008. "Identification and Traceability of Cattle in Selected Countries Outside North America." *The Professional Animal Scientist* 24:287–294.

Boyens, Ingeborg. 2001. *Another Season's Promise: Hope and Despair in Canada's Farm Country*. Toronto: Penguin.

Broadway, Michael J. 1990. "Meatpacking and Its Social and Economic Consequences for Garden City, Kansas, in the 1980s." *Urban Anthropology* 19:321–344.

———. 1991. "Economic Development Programs in the Great Plains: The Example of Nebraska." *Great Plains Research* 1:324–344.

———. 1995. "From City to Countryside: Recent Changes in the Structure and Location of the Meat and Fish Processing Industries." In *Any Way You Cut It: Meat Processing and Small-Town America*. Donald D. Stull, Michael J. Broadway, and David Griffith, eds., pp. 17–40. Lawrence: University Press of Kansas.

———. 2000. "Planning for Change in Small Towns or Trying to Avoid the Slaughterhouse Blues." *Journal of Rural Studies* 16:37–46.

———. 2001. "Bad to the Bone: The Social Costs of Beefpacking's Move to Rural Alberta." In *Writing Off the Rural West: Globalization, Governments, and the Transformation of Rural Communities*. Roger Epp and Dave Whitson, eds., pp. 39–52. Edmonton: University of Alberta Press and Parkland Institute.

———. 2007. "Meatpacking and the Transformation of Rural Communities: A Comparison of Brooks, Alberta, & Garden City, Kansas." *Rural Sociology* 72:560–582.

Broadway, Michael J., and Donald D. Stull. 1991. "Rural Industrialization:

The Example of Garden City, Kansas." *Kansas Business Review* 14(4):1–9.

———. 2006. "Meat Processing and Garden City, KS: Boom and Bust." *Journal of Rural Studies* 22:55–66.

Broadway, Michael J., Donald D. Stull, and Bill Podraza. 1994. "What Happens When the Meat Packers Come to Town?" *Small Town* 24(4):24–28.

Brooks Bulletin. 2000. "Michael Broadway Report Says Lakeside Expansion Created Social Problems in Brooks." October 11.

Brooks, J. 1988. *Here's the Beef: Underreporting of Injuries, OSHA's Policy of Exempting Companies from Programmed Inspections Based on Injury Records, and Unsafe Conditions in the Meatpacking Industry*. Washington, DC: U.S. Government Printing Office.

Bruggers, James. 2002. "Sierra Club Vows Suit Over Chicken Farms and Dust They Produce." *Courier-Journal* (Louisville, Kentucky), February 5:1–3.

———. 2009. "Judge Rules Western Kentucky Hog Farm Permits Need Reworking." *Courier-Journal* (Louisville, Kentucky), November 16.

Bucklaschuk, Jill. 2008. *Settlement: Considerations for Temporary Foreign Workers in Brandon and Area*. Discussion Paper Number 2. Rural Development Institute, Brandon University, Manitoba, Canada.

Bullard, Bill. 2010. "Farm Bill Comments: Implementation of Regulations Required Under Title XI of the Food Conservation and Energy Act of 2008: Conduct in Violation of the Act, RIN 0580-AB07." Comments to the Grain Inspection, Packers and Stockyards Administration, USDA. November 22. Billings, MT: Ranchers-Cattlemen Action Legal Fund, United Stockgrowers of America (R-CALF USA).

Bureau of Labor Statistics. 2010. "Occupational Employment and Wages, May 2010: Meat, Poultry, and Fish Cutters and Trimmers." http://www.bls.gov/oes/current/oes513022.html (May 24, 2011).

———. n.d.a. "Databases, Tables, and Calculators by Subject: Manufacturing: Average Hourly Earnings of All Employees." http://data.bls.gov.cgi-bin/surveymost (May 24, 2011).

———. n.d.b. "Occupational Injuries and Illnesses in the United States by Industry." Washington, DC: U.S. Government Printing Office.

Burke, Garance. 2010. "Lawmakers Probe Lax Enforcement of Animal Rules." Associated Press, March 12. http://www.ellinghuysen.com/news/articles/99010.shtml (March 12, 2010).

Burt, Jonathan. 2006. "Conflicts Around Slaughter in Modernity." In *Killing Animals*. The Animal Studies Group, pp. 120–144. Urbana: University of Illinois Press.

Campa, Arthur. 1990. "Immigrant Latinos and Resident Mexican Americans in Garden City, Kansas: Ethnicity and Ethnic Relations." *Urban Anthropology* 19:345–360.

Canadian Food Inspection Agency. 2005. *Canada's Feed Ban*. http://www.gov.pe.ca/photos/original/af_feedbanE.pdf (July 1, 2011).

Canadian Pork Council. n.d. "Statistics: Description of Canadian Hog Farms." http://www.cpc-ccp.com/statistics-farms-e.php (March 28, 2011).

———. 2009. *Strategic Transition Plan: The Canadian Hog Industry's Plan for Success*. Ottawa, Canada.

Canfax. 2001, 2010. *Statistical Briefer*. Calgary, Alberta, Canada.

Carlisle, Vanessa. 2010. "American, Urban, and Vegan: An Interview." Bikyamasr.com, August 19. http://www.ellinghuysen.com/news/articles/106172.shtml (August 19, 2010).

Carson, Rachel. 1962. *Silent Spring*. Boston: Houghton Mifflin.

Carter, Tom. 2010. *Housing Strategies for Immigrants in Rural Southern Manitoba*. Rural Development Institute, Brandon University, MB, Canada.

Center for American Progress; OMB Watch. 2004. *Special Interest Takeover: The Bush Administration and the Dismantling of Public Safeguards*. Washington, DC: Reece Publishing.

Centers for Disease Control (CDC). n.d. "BSE (Bovine Spongiform Encephalopathy, or Mad Cow Disease)." http://www.cdc.gov/ncidod/dvrd/bse/ (June 5, 2011).

———. 2011. "Investigation Update: Outbreak of Shiga Toxin-Producing E. coli O104 (STEC O104:H4) Infections Associated with Travel to Germany." http://www.cdc.gov/ecoli/2011/ecoliO104 (July 1, 2011).

Channelnewsasia.com. 2011. "Brazil Issues US$1.2b in Fines on Beef Companies." April 15. http://www.channelnewsasia.com/stories/afp_world_business/view/1122928/1/.html (April 15, 2011).

Chite, Ralph. 2008. *Farm Bill Budget and Costs: 2002 vs. 2007*. Congressional Research Service, Order Code RS22694. Washington, DC: U.S. Government Printing Office.

Clemen, Rudolf Alexander. 1923. *The American Livestock and Meat Industry*. New York: Ronald Press Company.

Cohen, Laurie P. 1998. "Meatpacker Taps Mexican Labor Force: Thanks to Help from an INS Program." *Wall Street Journal*, October 15.

Context Marketing. 2010. "Ethical Food." http://contextmarketing.com/sources/feb28-2010/ethicalfoodreport.pdf (October 5, 2011).

County of Flagstaff Family Farm Promotional Society. 2002. *Alberta Court of Appeal Decision*. Flagstaff County, Alberta, Canada.

Crews, Joel. 2001. "Not in My Backyard: Community Resistance Hinders New Plant Construction Projects." *Meat&Poultry* 47(2):24–26, 28–29, 80.

Cultural Relations Board, City of Garden City, Kansas (CRB). 2001. "Changing Relations: Newcomers and Established Residents in Garden City, Kansas, 1990–2000." Unpublished manuscript, 34 pp. Authors' files.

Dale, Edward Everett. 1965. *Cow Country*. Norman: University of Oklahoma Press. (First published in 1942.)

Dan. 2011. "The Tour de Stench." Watershed Media Blog, March 22. http://watershedmedia1.blogspot.com/2011/03/tour-de-stench.html (April 24, 2011).

Davidson, Alan. 1999. *The Oxford Companion to Food*. New York: Oxford University Press.

DeGrazia, David. 2002. *Animal Rights: A Very Short Introduction*. New York: Oxford University Press.

DeGruson, Gene, ed. 1988. *The Lost First Edition of Upton Sinclair's The Jungle*. Memphis, TN: Peachtree Publishers.

Dew, Aloma. 2004. "With Liberty and Justice for All—Environmental Justice and Big Chicken in Kentucky." *Sustain* 10:48–50.

———. 2007. "Poultry Operations Emit Unhealthy Levels of Ammonia According to New Study: Sierra Club and Medical Professionals Express Concern." http://www.sierraclub.org/environmentallaw/lawsuits/docs/pressrelease.pdf (April 23, 2011).

Dhuyvetter, Kevin C., Jennifer Graff, and Gerry L. Kuhl. 1998. *Kansas Beef Industry Economic Trends*. Manhattan: Kansas State University Agricultural Experiment Station.

Domina, David A., and C. Robert Taylor. 2010. "Restoring Economic Health to Beef Markets." August 25. Lincoln, NE: Organization for Competitive Markets.

Donham, Kelley J., Steven Wing, David Osterberg, Jan L. Flora, Carol Hodne, Kendall M. Thu, and Peter S. Thorne. 2007. "Community Health and Socioeconomic Issues Surrounding Animal Feeding Operations." *Environmental Health Perspectives* 115:317–320.

Dornbusch, Donald. 1998. "An Analysis of Media Coverage of the BSE Crisis in Britain." In *The Mad Cow Crisis*. Scott C. Ratzan, ed., pp. 138–152. New York: New York University Press.

Drabenstott, Mark. 1998. "This Little Piggie Went to Market: Will the New Pork Industry Call the Heartland Home?" *Federal Reserve Bank of Kansas City Economic Review* 83(3):79–97.

Duara, Nigel, William Petroski, and Grant Schulte. 2008. "Claims of ID Fraud Lead to Largest Raid in State History." *Des Moines* (Iowa) *Register*, May 12.

Duckworth, Barbara. 2000. "Alta. Community Says No Thanks to Sow Barn." *Western Producer* (Saskatoon, Saskatchewan), July 20.

———. 2001. "Alberta's ILO Policy Gets Mixed Reviews." *Western Producer* (Saskatoon, Saskatchewan), July 12.

Eckholm, Erik. 2010. "Farmers Lean to Truce on Animals' Close Quarters." *New York Times*, August 11. http://www.nytimes.com/2010/08/12/us/12farm.html?_r=2&th&emc=th (August 12, 2010).

The Economist. 2002. "Oh, Temptation: Fast-Food Lawsuits." August 3.

Edmonds, Scott. 2002. "Action Urged on U.S. Farm Subsidies." *Toronto Globe and Mail*, May 21.

Eisnitz, Gail. 1997. *Slaughterhouse: The Shocking Story of Greed, Neglect and Inhumane Treatment Inside the U.S. Meat Industry*. Amherst, NY: Prometheus Books.

Ellis, Shane. 2009. "State of the Beef Industry 2009." http://beefmagazine.com/BEEF_SOI_2009.pdf (January 6, 2011).

Eng, Monica. 2010. "The Costs of Cheap Meat." *South Florida Sun-Sentinel*, September 24. http://www.sun-sentinel.com/health/ct-met-cheap-protein (September 24, 2010).

Europa. n.d. "Food Safety: From Farm to Fork." http://ec.europa.eu/food/food/biosafety/tse_bse/feed_ban_en.html (July 1, 2011).

FAOSTAT n.d. "Export Commodities by Country." http://faostat.fao.org/site/342/default.aspx (November 30, 2010).

Farley, Stephanie. 2009. "Officials: Bonanza BioEnergy Holding Its Own in Tough Economy." *Garden City* (Kansas) *Telegram*, January 27.

Farm Animal Welfare Council. 2003. *Report on the Welfare of Farmed Animals at Slaughter or Killing, Part 1: Red Meat Animals.* London: FAWC.

Fearnley-Whittingstall, Hugh. 2007. *The River Cottage Meat Book.* Berkeley, CA: Ten Speed Press.

Fears, Darryl, and Krissah Williams. 2007. "In Exchange for Records, Fewer Immigration Raids." *Washington Post*, January 29.

Fesperman, Dan, and Kate Shatzkin. 1999. "The New Pecking Order: The Plucking of the American Chicken." *Baltimore Sun*, February 28. http://sunspot.net/content/storyserver (March 13, 1999).

Fiddes, Nick. 1991. *Meat: A Natural Symbol.* London: Routledge.

Fink, Leon. 2003. *The Maya of Morgantown: Work and Community in the Nuevo New South.* Chapel Hill: University of North Carolina Press.

Finley, Bruce. 2006. "Managers Who Hire Undocumented Are Seldom Punished as Workers Are." *Denver Post*, December 17.

Flora, Cornelia, Jan L. Flora, Jacqueline D. Spears, and Louis E. Swanson, with Mark B. Lapping and Mark Weinberg. 1992. *Rural Communities: Legacy & Change.* Boulder, CO: Westview.

Food & Water Watch. 2010. *Factory Farmed Hogs in North Carolina, Fact Sheet.* Washington, DC.

Food Institute. n.d. "Food Institute Research Resources." http://www.foodinstitute.com/research.cfm (May 30, 2011).

Food Quality. 2011. "European *E. Coli* Outbreaks Could Recur: Seeds Widely Distributed, Difficult to Recall." http://www.foodquality.com/details/article/1304505 (July 26, 2011).

Forbes, Ian. 2004. "Making a Crisis Out of a Drama: The Political Analysis of BSE Policy Making in the UK." *Political Studies* 52:342–357.

Forero, Juan. 2011. "Brazilian Company JBS Dominates World Beef Industry from Farm to Fork." *Washington Post*, April 14. http://www.washingtonpost.com/world/from-farm-to-fork.html (April 15, 2011).

Foruseth, Owen J. 1997. "Restructuring of Hog Farming in North Carolina: Explosion and Implosion." *Professional Geographer* 49:391–403.

Friedland, Dani. 2011. "Brazilian Beef May Have Largest Carbon Footprint: Study." *Meatingplace*, March 8. http://www.meatingplace.com (March 8, 2011).

Friends of the Earth. 2010. *From Forest to Fork: The U.K.'s Contribution to Deforestation in Brazil.* London: Friends of the Earth.

Fyksen, Jane. 2010. "Animal Ag in Cross-hairs Over Antibiotic Use, Health Group Wants Ban, Veterinarians Don't." *AgWeekly*, July 22. http://www.ellinghuysen.com/news/articles/104931.shtml (July 23, 2010).

Garden City (Kansas) *Telegram*. 2011. "Thank You for Creating Opportunities and Inspiring Hope for a Better Tomorrow." Finney County United Way. January 29:B6.

Gearing, Fred. 1979. "Microanalysis and Action Anthropology." In *Currents in Anthropology: Essays in Honor of Sol Tax*. Robert Hinshaw, ed., pp. 391–408. The Hague: Mouton.

Gibson, Craig D. 1998. "Managing Your Poultry Business: Impacts of Income Tax, Debt Payment, and Retirement Planning." 21-page typescript accompanying presentation at the Hopkins County Extension Office, Madisonville, Kentucky, November 9. Authors' files.

Giddens, Anthony. 1990. *The Consequences of Modernity*. Cambridge, UK: Basil Blackwell.

Gilkey, Sam. 1997. "Mega-Livestock Issues in News Since May." *The Messenger* (Madisonville, Kentucky), September 2:1A, 3A.

Gorbach, Sherwood. 2001. "Antimicrobial Use in Animal Feed—Time to Stop." *New England Journal of Medicine* 345:1202–1203.

Gordon, John Steele. 1996. "The Chicken Story." *American Heritage* 47(5):52–67.

Gouveia, Lourdes, and Donald D. Stull. 1995. "Dances With Cows: Beef-packing's Impact on Garden City, Kansas, and Lexington, Nebraska." In *Any Way You Cut It: Meat Processing and Small-Town America*. Donald D. Stull, Michael J. Broadway, and David Griffith, eds., pp. 85–107. Lawrence: University Press of Kansas.

———. 1997. *Latino Immigrants, Meat-packing, and Rural Communities:*

A Case Study of Lexington, Nebraska. JSRI Research Report No. 26. East Lansing: Julian Samora Research Institute, Michigan State University.

Government Accountability Office (GAO). 2005. *Worker Safety and Health: Safety in the Meat and Poultry Industry, While Improving Could Be Further Strengthened*. GAO-05-96. Washington, DC: U.S. Government Printing Office.

———. 2009. *Agricultural Concentration and Agricultural Commodity and Retail Food Prices*. http://www.gao.gov/new.items/d09746r.pdf (August 18, 2011).

Grandin, Temple. 2006. *Thinking in Pictures: My Life with Autism*, expanded edition. New York: Vintage Books.

———. and Catherine Johnson. 2010. *Animals Make Us Human: Creating the Best Life for Animals*. Boston: Mariner.

Green, George Norris, and Jim McClellan. 1985. "Sick Chickens." *Southern Exposure* 13(5):48–55.

Green, Hardy. 1990. *On Strike at Hormel: The Struggle for a Democratic Labor Movement*. Philadelphia: Temple University Press.

Grey, Mark. 1995. "Pork, Poultry and Newcomers in Storm Lake, Iowa." In *Any Way You Cut It: Meat Processing and Small-Town America*. Donald D. Stull, Michael J. Broadway, and David Griffith, eds., pp. 109–128. Lawrence: University Press of Kansas.

———. 1998. *Handbook for Creating Sustainable Multiethnic Food-Producing Communities*. Ames: Iowa State University Extension.

———. 1999. "Immigrants, Migration, and Worker Turnover at the Hog Pride Pork Packing Plant." *Human Organization* 58:16–27.

———. 2000. "'Those Bastards Can Go To Hell!' Small-Farmer Resistance to Vertical Integration and Concentration in the Pork Industry." *Human Organization* 59:169–176.

Grey, Mark, Michele Devlin, and Aaron Goldsmith. 2009. *Postville, U.S.A.: Surviving Diversity in Small-Town America*. Boston: Gemma.

Griffith, David. 1995. "*Hay Trabajo*: Poultry Processing, Rural Industrialization, and the Latinization of Low-Wage Labor." In *Any Way You Cut It: Meat Processing and Small-Town America*. Donald D. Stull, Michael J. Broadway, and David Griffith, eds., pp. 129–151. Lawrence: University Press of Kansas.

Gura, Susanne. 2010. "Industrial Livestock Production and Biodiversity." In *The Meat Crisis*. Joyce D'Silvia and John Webster, eds., pp. 57–79. Washington, DC: Earthscan.

Gurian-Sherman, Doug. 2008. *CAFOs Uncovered: The Untold Costs of Confined Animal Feeding Operations*. Cambridge, MA: Union of Concerned Scientists.

Gutierrez, David. 2008. "Tyson Foods Injects Chickens with Antibiotics Before They Hatch to Claim 'Raised Without Antibiotics.'" NaturalNews.com, November 9. http://www.naturalnews.com/024756.html (November 19, 2010).

Hackenberg, Robert A., David Griffith, Donald Stull, and Lourdes Gouveia. 1993. "Creating a Disposable Labor Force." *Aspen Institute Quarterly* 5(2):78–101.

Hackenberg, Robert A., and Gary Kukulka. 1995. "Industries, Immigrants, and Illness in the New Midwest." In *Any Way You Cut It: Meat Processing and Small-Town America*. Donald D. Stull, Michael J. Broadway, and David Griffith, eds., pp. 187–211. Lawrence: University Press of Kansas.

Hage, Dave, and Paul Klauda. 1989. *No Retreat, No Surrender: Labor's War at Hormel*. New York: William Morrow.

Haley, Mildred, Elizabeth A. Jones, and Leland Southard. 1998. "World Hog Production: Constrained by Environmental Concerns." *Agricultural Outlook* AGO-249:15–19.

Harris, Marvin. 1985. *Good to Eat*. New York: Simon & Schuster.

Haspel, Tamar. 2006. "With a Little Prodding, Meat Eaters Are Developing a Conscience." *The Record*, August 15. http://www.ellinghuysen.com/news/articles/37603.shtml (August 15, 2006).

Healthy Choice. n.d. "Fresh Mixers." http://www.healthychoice.com/products/fresh-mixers.html (November 5, 2010).

Heffernan, William D. 1984. "Constraints in the U.S. Poultry Industry." *Research in Rural Sociology and Development* 1:237–260.

Hoelle, Jeffrey. 2011. "Convergence on Cattle: Political Economy, Social Group Perceptions and Socio-economic Relationships in Acre, Brazil." *Anthropology News* 52(1):38.

Hofstrand, Don. 2008. "Domestic Perspectives on Food versus Fuel." *AgMRC Renewable Energy Newsletter*, July. http://www.agmrc.org/renewable_energy/biofuelsbiorefining_general/domestics_perspectives_on_food_versus_fuel.cfm (October 2, 2010).

Holmberg, Allan R. 1958. "The Research and Development Approach to the Study of Change." *Human Organization* 17:12–16.

Horovitz, B. 2005. "Fast-Food 'Natural' Takes Wing on Safety Fears." *USA Today*, February 4:1B.

Horowitz, Roger. 1997. *Negro and White Unite and Fight! A Social History of Industrial Unionism in Meatpacking, 1930–1990*. Urbana: University of Illinois Press.

———. 2006. *Putting Meat on the American Table: Taste, Technology, Transformation.* Baltimore: Johns Hopkins University Press.

———. 2008. "'That Was a Dirty Job!' Technology and Workplace Hazards in Meatpacking over the Long Twentieth Century." *Labor* 5(2):13–25.

Horowitz, Roger, and Mark J. Miller. 1999. *Immigrants in the Delmarva Poultry Processing Industry: The Changing Face of Georgetown, Delaware, and Environs.* JSRI Occasional Paper No. 37, The Julian Samora Research Institute. East Lansing: Michigan State University.

Horton, Rachel A., Steve Wing, Stephen W. Marshall, and Kimberly A. Brownley. 2009. "Malodor as a Trigger of Stress and Negative Mood in Neighbors of Industrial Hog Operations." *American Journal of Public Health* 99:S610–S615.

Horwitz, Tony. 1994. "9 to Nowhere: Blues on the Chicken Line." *Wall Street Journal*, December 1:A1, A8–A9.

Hoy, Jim. 1997. "The Flint Hills of Kansas." *Range* 5(2):4–7.

Hubbert, Sarah. 2009. "HSUS Uses Growing Litigation Department to Target Agriculture." *Beef Issues Quarterly* 1(1):28–29.

Huffstutter, P.J. 2009. "Backyard Chickens on the Rise Despite Neighborhood Clucks." http://articles.latimes.com/2009/jun/15/nation/na-chicken-economy15 (June 17, 2011).

Human Rights Watch. 2004. *Blood, Sweat, and Fear: Workers' Rights in U.S. Meat and Poultry Plants.* New York: Human Rights Watch.

Humane Society of the United States. 2010. "World's Largest Cruise Lines Hatch New Animal Welfare, Sustainability Initiatives." August 11. www.ellinghuysen.com/news/articles/105893.shtml (August 13, 2010).

Hutchison, Slone. 1999. "McLean County Residents Voice Poultry Complaints." *The Gleaner* (Henderson, Kentucky), September 14:A2.

Ikerd, John. 1998. "Sustainable Agriculture, Rural Economic Development, and Large-Scale Swine Production." In *Pigs, Profits, and Rural Communities.* Kendall M. Thu and E. Paul Durrenberger, eds., pp. 157–169. Albany: State University of New York Press.

Imhoff, Daniel. 2010. *The CAFO Reader: The Tragedy of Industrial Animal Factories.* Berkeley, CA: Watershed Media.

Institute of Food Technologists. 2011. "Group Sues FDA to Limit Use of Antibiotics in Animal Agriculture," June 8. http://www.ift.org (June 14, 2011).

Iowa Beef Processors. 1989. *Cumulative Trauma Disorders.* Dakota City, NE: Iowa Beef Processors.

Jiménez, Tomás R. 2010. *Replenished Ethnicity: Mexican Americans, Immigration, and Identity.* Berkeley: University of California Press.

Johnston, Tom. 2008. "Bad Behavior." *Meatingplace*, February: 12–18.

———. 2009a. "Downer." *Meatingplace*, February: 10–18.

———. 2009b. "JBS Signs Sustainability Pact with Wal-Mart." Meatingplace.com, June 26. http://www.meatingplace.com/MembersOnly/WebNews (June 26, 2009).

Jolley, Chuck. 2002. "The Next Big Thing." *Meat&Poultry* 48(3):14.

Jones, Dena. 2008. *Crimes Without Consequences: The Enforcement of Humane Slaughter Laws in the United States.* Washington, DC: Animal Welfare Institute.

Kansas Beef Council. n.d. "Compliments of Cattle." Promotional brochure. Authors' files.

Kay, Steve. 1997. "The Nature of Turnover: Packers Attempt to Reverse Financial Gain." *Meat&Poultry* 43(9):30–33.

Keeton, Kara. 2010. "Something to Crow About: Kentucky Chicken Producers Challenge Equine as Top Earning Agribusiness Sector." *The Lane Report.* Lexington, KY: Lane Communications Group.

Kilman, Scott. 2003. "Poultry in Motion: With Invention, Chicken Catching Goes High-Tech." *Wall Street Journal,* June 4. http://www.mindfully.org/Technology/2003/Chicken-Catching-Machine4jun03.htm (October 21, 2004).

Kimbrell, Andrew. 2002. "Seven Deadly Myths of Industrial Agriculture." In *The Fatal Harvest Reader.* Andrew Kimbrell, ed., pp. 3–36. Washington, DC: Island Press.

Koeleman, Emmy. 2010. "Animal Welfare Now a Global Issue to Consider." Vetsweb.com, July 20. http://www.ellinghuysen.com/news/articles/104751.shtml (July 20, 2010).

Kopperud, Steve. 2009. "'Humane' Principles Not Standardized." *NCBA Issues Update,* January–February: 13–15.

Krakow, Mary M. 2006. "Donning and Doffing, Walking and Waiting: Paid or Unpaid Time?" Fredrikson and Byron, P.A. http://www.fredlaw.com/articles/employment/empl_0601_mmk.html (June 6, 2011).

Krause, Kenneth R. 1991. *Cattle Feeding, 1962–89: Location and Feedlot Size.* Commodity Economics Division, Economic Research Service, U.S. Department of Agriculture. Agricultural Economic Report No. 642.

Kwik, Phill. 1991. "Poultry Workers Trapped in a Modern Jungle." *Labor Notes* 146:1, 14–15.

Lamb, Russell L., & Michelle Beshear. 1998. "From the Plains to the Plate: Can the Beef Industry Regain Market Share?" *Federal Reserve Bank of Kansas City Economic Review* 83(4):49–66.

Lamphere, Louise, ed. 1992. *Structuring Diversity: Ethnographic Perspectives on the New Immigration.* Chicago: University of Chicago Press.

Lang, Tim, and Michael Heasman. 2004. *Food Wars: The Global Battle for Mouths, Minds, and Markets.* London: Earthscan.

Lappé, Frances Moore, and Anna Lappé. 2002. *Hope's Edge: The Next Diet for a Small Planet.* New York: Penguin Putnam.

Lappé, Frances Moore, Joseph Collins, and Peter Rosset. 1998. *World Hunger: Twelve Myths.* New York: Grove Press.

Lawrence, John, Glenn Grimes, and Marvin Hayenga. 1998. "Production and Marketing Characteristics of U.S. Pork Producers, 1997–98." Staff Paper No. 311, Economics Department, Iowa State University.

Lobo, Philip. 2009. "A Review of International Animal Welfare Systems." *NCBA Issues Update,* March–April–May: 15–16.

Long, Victoria Sizemore. 1991. "Tyson Food Empire Had Its Start Between Fruit-Hauling Seasons." *Kansas City Star,* June 25:D–30.

Lovan, Dylan T. 2002. "Group Plans to Sue Chicken Farms." *The Gleaner* (Henderson, Kentucky), February 6:A1, A11.

Love, Orlan. 2010. "Two Years after Agriprocessors Raid, Postville Is Flush with New Optimism." *The Gazette* (Iowa City, IA), May 12.

Lucas, John. 2002. "Suit Targets Poultry Firm, Its Growers." *The Gleaner* (Henderson, Kentucky), April 23:A1, A12.

Lyman, Howard. 1998. *Mad Cowboy*. New York: Simon & Schuster.

MacArthur, Mary. 2000. "Alberta Mega Barn Approved." *Western Producer* (Saskatoon, Saskatchewan), December 7.

———. 2001. "ILO Board Can Overturn Local Bans." *Western Producer* (Saskatoon, Saskatchewan), November 29.

MacDonald, James M. 2008. *The Economic Organization of U.S. Broiler Production*. Washington, DC: USDA Economic Information Bulletin No. 38.

MacLachlan, Ian. 2001. *Kill and Chill: Restructuring Canada's Beef Commodity Chain*. Toronto: University of Toronto Press.

Malone, James. 2005. "Hog Farms Booming in State." *Courier-Journal* (Louisville, Kentucky), August 22.

Mancino, Lisa, and Constance Newman. 2007. *Who Has Time to Cook?* Washington, DC: USDA Economic Research Report No. ERR-40.

Marcus, Erik. 2005. *Meat Market: Animals, Ethics, and Money*. Ithaca, NY: Brio Press.

Marsh, Bill. 2010. "A Hen's Space to Roost." *New York Times*, August 15:WK3.

Martin, Larry, Zana Kruja, and John Alexiou. 1998. *Prospects for Hog Production and Processing in Canada*. George Morris Centre, University of Guelph, Ontario, Canada.

Matheny, Gaverick, and Cheryl Leahy. 2007. "Farm-Animal Welfare, Legislation, and Trade." *Law and Contemporary Problems* 70:325–358.

Mayse, James. 2005. "Tyson Foods Agrees to Monitor Level of Ammonia Emissions." *Messenger-Inquirer* (Owensboro, Kentucky), January 28.

McDonalds.com 2011. "McDonald's USA Nutrition Facts for Popular Menu Items." http://nutrition.mcdonalds.com/nutritionexchange/nutritionfacts.pdf (June 16, 2011).

McKay, Robert. 2006. "BSE, Hysteria and the Representation of Animal Death: Deborah Levy's Diary of a Steak." In *Killing Animals*, pp. 146–169. Urbana: University of Illinois Press.

McKinley, Morgan G. 1998. "Vandalism Takes Financial Bite." *The Messenger* (Madisonville, Kentucky), July 23:A1, A3.

Meat&Poultry Staff. 2011. "Donning-Doffing for Inspectors to Be Compensable." June 13. http://www.meatpoultry.com/News/NewsHome/Regulatory/2011 (June 14, 2011).

MeatPoultry.com. 2011. "Donning and Doffing Lawsuits Set for Trial Next Week." April 27. http://www.meatpoultry.com/News/NewsHome/Business/2011/4/Donning-doffing lawsuits to start next week.aspx (June 7, 2011).

Mellon, Margaret, Charles Benbrook, and Karen Lutz Benbrook. 2001. *Hogging It: Estimates of Antimicrobial Abuse in Livestock*. Cambridge, MA: Union of Concerned Scientists.

Merchant, James A., Alison L. Naleway, Eric R. Svendsen, Kevin M. Kelly, Leon F. Burmeister, Ann M. Stromquist, Craig D. Taylor, Peter S. Thorne, Stephen J. Reynolds, Wayne T. Sanderson, and Elizabeth A. Chrischilles. 2005. "Asthma and Farm Exposures in a Cohort of Rural Iowa Children." *Environmental Health Perspectives* 113: 350–356.

Miller, Marlys. 2008. "Animal Rights' Gives Lobbying as Much Attention as Animal Care." *Pork Magazine*, July 31. http://www.ellinghuysen.com/news/articles/72871.shtml (July 31, 2008).

Mirabelli, Maria C., Steve Wing, Stephen W. Marshall, and Timothy C. Wilcosky. 2006. "Race, Poverty and Potential Exposure of Middle School Students to Air Emissions from Confined Swine Feeding Operations." *Environmental Health Perspectives* 114:591–596.

Molotch, Harvey. 1976. "The City as a Growth Machine." *American Journal of Sociology* 82:309–330.

Moreno, Ivan. 2008. "Beef Industry, Animal Rights Groups Duel." Associated Press, February 19. http://www.ellinghuysen.com/news/articles/64964.shtml (February 19, 2008).

Moreno, Sylvia. 2007. "Texas Meat-packing Town Nearly Emptied by Immigration Raid." *Washington Post*, February 11.

Morrison, John M. 1998. "The Poultry Industry: A View of the Swine Industry's Future?" In *Pigs, Profits, and Rural Communities*. Kendall M. Thu and E. Paul Durrenberger, eds., pp. 145–154. Albany: State University of New York Press.

National Catholic Rural Life Conference. 1997. "An Immediate Moratorium on Large-Scale Livestock and Poultry Animal Confinement Facilities." A Statement from the Board of Directors of the National Catholic Rural Life Conference, December 18 (e-mail: November 29, 2001).

———. 2002. "Ethics of Eating." http://www.nrclc.com/card01backtext.html (August 2, 2002).

National Cattlemen's Beef Board. 2009. "Critical Analysis of Livestock's Long Shadow." http://www.explorebeef.org/CMDocs/ExploreBeef/FactSheet_LivestocksLongShadow.pdf (November 7, 2010).

National Center for Chronic Disease Prevention and Health Promotion. n.d. "Childhood Obesity." http://www.cdc.gov/HealthyYouth/obesity (May 30, 2011).

National Creutzfeldt-Jakob Disease Surveillance Unit. 2011. "CJD Statistics." http://www.cjd.ed.ac.uk/figures.htm (June 14, 2011).

National Farmers Union News. 2002. "Farmers Union Members Testify on Negative Impacts of Livestock Concentration." *National Farmers Union News* 49(8):3.

National Hog Farmer. 2007. "North Carolina Keeps Swine Lagoons." July 26. http://nationalhogfarmer.com/news/newsflash/north-carolina-swine-lagoons/index.html (April 13, 2011).

National Restaurant Association. 2011. *Pocket Factbook*. http://www.restaurant.org/pdfs/research/2011forecast_pfb.pdf (June 5, 2011).

National Workrights Institute. n.d. *Class Actions: A Look at the Record*. http://workrights.us/wp-content/uploads/2011/02/Class-Action-PDF.pdf (June 6, 2011).

Nestle, Marion. 2002. "The Soft Sell: How the Food Industry Shapes Our Diets." *Nutrition Action Newsletter* 29(7):11.

Newkirk, Ingrid. 2009. *The PETA Practical Guide to Animal Rights*. New York: St. Martin's Griffin.

Nocera, Joe. 2008. "A Case of Abuse, Heightened." *New York Times*, March 8. www.ellinghuysen.com/news/articles/65961.shtml (March 10, 2008).

North Carolina Department of Agriculture & Consumer Services. 2010. *Agricultural Statistics*. Raleigh, North Carolina.

Nunes, Keith. 1999. "The Jungle Revisited: How Far Has This Industry Come?" *Meat&Poultry* 45(12):16–20.

Olivo, Antonio. 2009. "Immigration Raid Leaves Damaging Mark on Postville, Iowa." *Los Angeles Times*, May 12.

Opler, Morris. 1945. "Themes as Dynamic Forces in Culture." *American Journal of Sociology* 5:198–206.

Pacelle, Wayne. 2010. "Animals." In *Gristle: From Factory Farms to Food Safety*. Moby with Miyun Park, eds., pp. 33–51. New York: New Press.

Pearce, Fred. 2004. "Brazil's Beef Trade Wrecks Rainforest." *New Scientist* 182:14–15.

Perez, Carlos A., ed. 1997. "The Colors of Participation." *Practicing Anthropology* 19(3):2–35.

Personick, M.E., and K. Taylor-Shirley. 1989. "Profiles in Safety and Health: Occupational Hazards of Meatpacking." *Monthly Labor Review* 112(1):3–9.

PETA. n.d. "The Case for Controlled-Atmosphere Killing." www.PETA. org (August 2, 2010).

Phillips, Lynne. 2006. "Food and Globalization." *Annual Review of Anthropology* 35:37–57.

Pollan, Michael. 2006a. *The Omnivore's Dilemma: A Natural History of Four Meals*. New York: Penguin.

———. 2006b. "Wal-Mart Goes Organic: And Now for the Bad News." http://michaelpollan.com/articles-archive/wal-mart-goes-organic-and-now-for-the-bad-news (July 1, 2011).

Portes, Alejandro, and Jósef Böröcz. 1989. "Contemporary Immigration: Theoretical Perspectives on Its Determinants and Modes of Incorporation." *International Migration Review* 23:606–630.

Poultry Water Quality Consortium. 1998. *Poultry Water Quality Handbook*, 2nd ed. expanded. Chattanooga, TN: Poultry Water Quality Consortium.

Preston, Julia. 2006a. "U.S. Raids 6 Meat Plants in ID Case." *New York Times*, December 13.

———. 2006b. "Immigrants' Families Figuring Out What to Do After Federal Raids." *New York Times*, December 16.

———. 2008. "After Iowa Raid, Immigrants Fuel Labor Inquiries." *New York Times*, July 27.

Putnam, Judy. 1999. "U.S. Food Supply Providing More Food and Calories." *Food Review* 22(3):2–12.

Quinones, Sam. 2007. "A Soccer Season in Kansas." In *Antonio's Gun and Delfino's Dream: True Tales of Mexican Migration*, pp. 219–279. Albuquerque: University of New Mexico Press.

Raab, Amy. 1997. "From Sagebrush to Slaughterhouse." *Range* 5(1):18–20.

Ramsey, Doug, and John C. Everitt. 2001. "Post-Crow Farming in Manitoba: An Analysis of the Wheat and Hog Sectors." In *Writing Off the Rural West: Globalization, Governments and the Transformation of Rural Communities*. Roger Epp and Dave Whitson, eds., pp. 3–20. Edmonton: University Press of Alberta and Parkland Institute.

Rasnake, Monroe. 1996. *Broiler Litter Production in Kentucky and Potential Use as a Nutrient Source*. AGR-168. Lexington: University of Kentucky College of Agriculture, Cooperative Extension Service.

Rasnake, Monroe, Lloyd Murdock, and William O. Thom. 1991. *Using Poultry Litter on Agricultural Land*. AGR-146. Lexington: University of Kentucky, College of Agriculture, Cooperative Extension Service.

Reeve, Agnesa. 1996. *Constant Frontier: The Continuing History of Finney County, Kansas*. Garden City, KS: Finney County Historical Society.

Report of the Policy Commission on the Future of Farming and Food. 2002. "Farming and Food: A Sustainable Future." http://www.cabinet-office.gov.uk/farming (February 1, 2002).

Rifkin, Jeremy. 1992. *Beyond Beef: The Rise and Fall of the Cattle Culture*. New York: Penguin.

Riggs, Mike. 2010. "PETA Blames Meat-Eaters for Deepwater Oil Explosion." *The Daily Caller*, May 3. http://www.ellinghuysen.com/news/articles/101433.shtml (May 7, 2010).

Rowe, Gene, Lynn Frewer, and Lennart Sjöberg. 2000. "Newspaper Reporting of Hazards in the UK and Sweden." *Public Understanding of Science* 9:59–78.

Royal Society for the Prevention of Cruelty to Animals. 2009. "Vote for Your Animal-Friendly Supermarket." August 11. http://www.ellinghuysen.com/news/articles/89612.shtml (August 14, 2009).

Sacks, Oliver. 1995. *An Anthropologist on Mars: Seven Paradoxical Tales*. New York: Alfred Knopf.

Salter, Jim. 2007. "Hardee's to Buy Eggs, Pork from Cage-Free Suppliers." Associated Press, September 27. http://www.ellinghuysen.com/news/articles/58013.shtml (September 27, 2007).

Salvage, Bryan. 2008a. "Largest Beef Recall in History Has Industry Reeling." MeatPoultry.com, February 19. http://www.ellinghuysen.com/news/articles/64964.shtml (February 19, 2008).

———. 2008b. "Poultry Industry Adopts 'Statement of Ethical Principals'" [*sic*]. MeatPoultry.com, July 21. http://www.meatpoultry.com/news/headline_stories_print.asp?ArticleID=95150 (July 28, 2008).

Sandburg, Carl. 1916. "Chicago." In *Chicago Poems*. New York: Henry Holt and Company.

Sara Lee Corp. n.d. "Feeling the Glow Yet?" http://jimmydean.com/products/scrambled-eggs-with-bacon-and-cheese-diced-apples-seasoned-hash-browns.aspx (November 5, 2010).

Saslow, Rachel. 2010. "An Interview with Animal Scientist Temple Grandin." *Washington Post*, April 6. http://www.ellinghuysen.com/news/articles/100147.shtml (April 7, 2010).

Schiffman, Susan, Elizabeth A. Miller, Mark S. Suggs, and Brevick G. Graham. 1995. "The Effect of Environmental Odors Emanating from Commercial Swine Operations on the Mood of Nearby Residents." *Brain Research Bulletin* 37:369–375.

Schlosser, Eric. 2001. *Fast Food Nation: The Dark Side of the All-American Meal*. New York: Houghton Mifflin.

Schoenborn, Sara. 2010. "Pew Campaign, Health Care Without Harm Push for End of Overuse of Antibiotics in Animal Ag." *AgWeekly*, July 22. http://www.ellinghuysen.com/news/articles/104931.shtml (July 23, 2010).

Schorak, Paul. 2000. "Decision of the Subdivision and Development Appeal Board of Flagstaff County: Re: Development Permit No. 00-25." Sedgewick, Alberta, Canada.

Sebree (Kentucky) *Banner*. 1995. "Tuesday Meeting Held to Clarify Construction of Area Chicken Houses." July 20:1–2.

Seibert, Gale. 1989. "Class Lecture for Meat and Carcass Evaluation," Garden City (Kansas) Community College, January 31. Authors' files.

Shields, Margot, Margaret D. Carroll, and Cynthia Ogden. 2011. *Adult Obesity Prevalence in Canada and the United States*. NCHS Data Brief No.56. Hyattsville, MD: National Center for Health Statistics.

Shipman, Pat. 2010. "The Animal Connection and Human Evolution." *Current Anthropology* 51:519–538.

Sinclair, Upton. 1962. *The Autobiography of Upton Sinclair*. New York: Harcourt, Brace & World.

———. 1985. *The Jungle*. New York: Penguin. (First published in 1906.)

Singer, Peter. 2002. *Animal Liberation*. New York: Ecco. (First published in 1975.)

Skaggs, Jimmy M. 1986. *Prime Cut: Livestock Raising and Meatpacking in the United States, 1607–1983.* College Station: Texas A&M University Press.

Smedman, Lisa. 2008. "Slaughterhouse Deaths Reminiscent of Auschwitz." *Vancouver Courier*, August 27. http://www.ellinghuysen.com/news/articles/74597.shtml (September 5, 2008).

Smith, Rod. 2011. "HSUS, UEP Reach Agreement to Transition to Colonies." *Feedstuffs*, July 7. http://www.feedstuffs.com (July 7, 2011).

Smith, Wesley J. 2010. *A Rat Is a Pig Is a Dog Is a Boy: The Human Cost of the Animal Rights Movement.* New York: Encounter Books.

Smithfield. n.d. "The Smithfield Food Family of Companies." http://www.smithfieldfoods.com/investors/view.aspx (November 6, 2010).

Snow, Richard F. 1996. "Letter from the Editor: Chicken Feed." *American Heritage* 47(5):5.

Spake, Amanda. 2002. "A Fat Nation." *U.S. News & World Report* 133(7):40–47.

Specter, Michael. 2003. "The Extremist: The Woman Behind the Most Successful Radical Group in America." *The New Yorker*, April 14:52–67.

Statistics Canada. n.d.a. "Canadian Statistics." http://www.statcan.ca/english/Pgdb (January 10, 2011).

———. n.d.b. "Total Pigs on Census Day 2006, Manitoba, Saskatchewan." http://www.statcan.gc.ca/pub/95-629-x/6/4124468-eng.htm (April 13, 2011).

Stinnett, Chuck. 1996a. "Chicken Litter." *The Gleaner* (Henderson, Kentucky), August 24:A9.

———. 1996b. "Poultry Company Chief: Production Here to Escalate." *The Gleaner* (Henderson, Kentucky), October 24:A1, A10.

Stith, Pat, and Joby Warrick. 1995. "Murphy's Law: For Murphy, Good Government Means Good Business." *The News & Observer* (Raleigh, North Carolina), February 22. http://www.pulitzer.org/archives/5897 (April 5, 2011).

Storck, Ann Bagel. 2007. "Humane Nature: It's Not Just Talk." *Meatingplace*, March:52–54.

Strange, Marty, and Chuck Hassebrook. 1981. *Take Hogs, for Example: The Transformation of Hog Farming in America.* Walthill, NE: Center for Rural Affairs.

Striffler, Steve. 2002. "Inside a Poultry Processing Plant: An Ethnographic Portrait." *Labor History* 43:305–313.

Stull, Donald D. 1990. "'I Come to the Garden': Changing Ethnic Relations in Garden City, Kansas." *Urban Anthropology* 19:303–320.

———. 1994. "Knock 'Em Dead: Work on the Killfloor of a Modern Beefpacking Plant." In *Newcomers in the Workplace: Immigrants and the Restructuring of the U.S. Economy.* Louise Lamphere, Alex Stepick, and Guillermo Grenier, eds., pp. 44–77. Philadelphia: Temple University Press.

———. 2000. "Tobacco Barns and Chicken Houses: Agricultural Transformation in Western Kentucky." *Human Organization* 59:151–161.

———. 2009. "Tobacco Is Going, Going … But Where?" *Culture & Agriculture* 31:54–72.

Stull, Donald D., Janet E. Benson, Michael J. Broadway, Arthur L. Campa, Ken C. Erickson, and Mark A. Grey. 1990. *Changing Relations: Newcomers and Established Residents in Garden City, Kansas.* Final report to the Ford Foundation's Changing Relations Project Board, Binghamton, New York, February 5. Institute for Public Policy and Business Research Report No. 172. Lawrence: University of Kansas.

Stull, Donald D., and Michael J. Broadway. 1990. "The Effects of Restructuring on Beefpacking in Kansas." *Kansas Business Review* 14(1):10–16.

———. 2008. "Meatpacking and Mexicans on the High Plains: From Minority to Majority in Garden City, Kansas." In *Immigrants Outside Megalopolis: Ethnic Transformation in the Heartland*. Richard C. Jones, ed., pp. 115–133. Lanham, MD: Lexington Books.

———. 2010. "What's Meatpacking Got to Do with Worker and Community Health?" In *Meat, Medicine and Human Health in the Twentieth Century*. David Cantor, Christian Bonah, and Matthias Dorries, eds., pp. 77–94. London: Pickering & Chatto.

Stull, Donald D., Michael J. Broadway, and Ken C. Erickson. 1992. "The Price of a Good Steak: Beef Packing and Its Consequences for Garden City, Kansas." In *Structuring Diversity: Ethnographic Perspectives on the New Immigration*. Louise Lamphere, ed., pp. 35–64. Chicago: University of Chicago Press.

Swaka, Alison, and Bill Kerr. 2010. "Challenging US Country of Origin Labelling at the World Trade Organization: The Law, the Issues and the Evidence." Canadian Agricultural Trade Policy and Competitiveness Research Network. http://ageconsearch.umn.edu/ bitstream/95806/2/Commissioned Paper 2010-01 Sawka and Kerr.pdf (July 30, 2011).

Symes, David, and Terry Marsden. 1985. "Industrialization of Agriculture: Intensive Livestock Farming in Humberside." In *The Industrialization of the Countryside*. Michael Healey and Brian W. Ilbery, eds., pp. 99–120. Norwich, UK: Geo Books.

Tanger, Stephanie, E. 2006. "Enforcing Corporate Responsibility for Violations of Workplace Immigration Laws: The Case of Meatpacking." *Harvard Latino Review* 9:59–90.

Taylor, C. Robert, and David A. Domina. 2010. *Restoring Economic Health to Contract Poultry Growing*. Report for the Joint U.S. Department of Justice and U.S. Department of Agriculture/ GIPSA Public Workshop on Competition Issues in the Poultry Industry, May 21, Normal, AL. Lincoln, NE: Organization for Competitive Markets.

Thompson, Paul B. 2008. "The Opposite of Human Enhancement: Nanotechnology and the Blind Chicken Problem." *Nanoethics* 2:305–316.

Thu, Kendall, Kelly Donham, Randy Ziegenhorn, Stephen Reynolds, Peter S. Thorne, Peryasamy Subramanian, Paul Whitten, and Jason Stookesbury. 1997. "A Control Study of the Physical and Mental Health of Residents Living Near a Large Swine Operation." *Journal of Agricultural Safety and Health* 3:13–26.

Tietgen, Gwen. 2005. "Perkins Makes City History." *Garden City* (Kansas) *Telegram*, April 15.

Troughton, Michael J. 1986. "Farming Systems in the Modern World." In *Progress in Agricultural Geography*. Michael Pacione, ed., pp. 93–123. London: Croom Helm.

Tyson Foods. n.d. "Tyson's Live Production Teams Span Nine Counties." In *Growing the Future*, 12-page advertising insert in several Western Kentucky newspapers, July 1999.

———. 2002. "Statement of Tyson Foods, Inc. Regarding Sierra Club Lawsuit." http://www.tysonfoodsinc. com /corporate/news/viewNews. asp?article=966 (August 2, 2002).

———. 2009. *Fiscal 2009 Fact Book*. http://www.tysonfoods.com/~/ media/Corporate/Files/Download/ Request-Tyson_2009_Fact_Book. ashx (January 10, 2011).

Ulack, Richard, Karl Raitz, and Gyula Pauer. 1998. *Atlas of Kentucky*. Lexington: University Press of Kentucky.

United Food and Commercial Workers. n.d. "Injury and Injustice—America's Poultry Industry." www.ufcw.org/press_room/fact_sheets_and_back ground/poultry (February 21, 2011).

University of Wisconsin Health Institute. n.d. "County Health Rankings Snapshot 2010: Finney County, Kansas." http://www.countyhealthrankings.org/kansas/finney (February 12, 2011).

U.S. Census Bureau. 1913. *Thirteenth Census of U.S. Taken in Year 1910, Volume 1, Population 1910: General Report and Analysis*. Washington, DC: U.S. Government Printing Office.

U.S. Census Bureau. 1914. *Thirteenth Census of U.S. Taken in Year 1910, Volume 4, Population 1910: Occupation Statistics*. Washington, DC: U.S. Government Printing Office.

———. 1984. *1982 Census of Agriculture, North Carolina*. Washington, DC: U.S. Government Printing Office.

———. 2011. *2010 Statistical Abstract of the United States, Per Capita Consumption of Major Food Commodities*. http://www.census.gov/compendia/statab/2011/tables/11s0213.pdf (July 30, 2011).

U.S. Court of Appeals, 6th District. 2010. *Alton T. Terry v. Tyson Farms, Inc.* Appeal from the U.S. District Court for Eastern District of Tennessee at Winchester. No. 08-00003—Harry S. Mattice, Jr., District Judge. Argued: March 4, 2009. Decided and Filed: May 10, 2010.

U.S. Department of Agriculture (USDA). 2009. *2007 Census of Agriculture, North Carolina*. Washington, DC: U.S. Government Printing Office.

USDA Economic Research Service. n.d. "Rural Population and Migration." http://www.ers.usda.gov/Briefing/Population (October 2, 2010).

———. 2010. "Food CPI and Expenditures." http://www.ers.usda.gov/Briefing/CPIFoodAndExpenditures/Data/Expenditures_tables/table1.html (October 27, 2010).

USDA Food Safety and Inspection Service. n.d. "FSIS Food Recalls." http://www.fsis.usda.gov/factsheets/FSIS_Food_Recalls/index.asp (July 1, 2011).

USDA Grain Inspection, Packers and Stockyards Administration (GIPSA). 2010. *2009 Annual Report Packers and Stockyard Program*. Washington, DC: U.S. Government Printing Office.

USDA National Agricultural Statistics Service. n.d. "Data and Statistics: Quick Stats 2.0." http://quickstats.nass.usda.gov (July 30, 2011).

———. 1999a. *1997 Census of Agriculture: United States Summary and State Data Volume 1, Geographic Area Series Part 51*. Washington, DC: U.S. Government Printing Office.

———. 1999b. *1997 Census of Agriculture, North Carolina*. Washington, DC: U.S. Government Printing Office.

———. 2010. "Kentucky Agricultural Statistics 2009–2010 Bulletin." http://www.nass.usda.gov/Statistics_by_State/Kentucky (January 17, 2011).

U.S. Department of Health and Human Services, Public Health Service, Office of the Surgeon General (USDHHS). 2001. *The Surgeon General's Call to Action to Prevent and Decrease Overweight and Obesity*. Washington, DC: U.S. Government Printing Office.

U.S. Department of Labor, OSHA Office of Communications. "2001 Statement of Assistant Secretary Charles N. Jeffress on Effective Date of OSHA Ergonomics Standard." http://www.osha.gov/pls/oshaweb/owadisp.show_document?p_table=NEWS_RELEASES&p_id=1368.

U.S. Environmental Protection Agency. 2008. "New Requirements for Controlling Manure, Wastewater from Large Animal Feeding Operations." http://yosemite.epa.gov/opa/admpress.nsf/dc57b08b5acd42bc852573c90044a9c4/eafce2ca2b2eedea852574f300607fef!OpenDocument (March 23, 2011).

U.S. National Research Council. 1999. *The Use of Drugs in Food Animals: Benefits and Risks*. Washington, DC: National Academy Press.

Van Arsdall, Roy N., and Henry C. Gilliam. 1979. "Pork." In *Another Revolution in U.S. Farming?* Lyle P. Schertz, ed., pp. 190–254. Washington, DC: USDA.

Vialles, Noelie. 1994. *Animal to Edible*. Cambridge, UK: Cambridge University Press.

Ward, Fay E. 1989. *The Cowboy at Work: All About His Job and How He Does It*. Norman: University of Oklahoma Press. (First published in 1959.)

Warren, Wilson J. 2007. *Tied to the Great Packing Machine: The Midwest and Meatpacking*. Iowa City: University of Iowa Press.

Washer, Peter. 2006. "Representations of Mad Cow Disease." *Social Science & Medicine* 61:457–466.

Waterkeeper Alliance. 2010. "Groups Serve Notice of Intent to Sue North Carolina Industrial Hog Facility for Violations of Clean Water Act and Resource Conservation and Recovery Act." http://www.waterkeeper.org/ht/a/GetDocumentAction/i/20975 (March 23, 2011).

Webb, Walter Prescott. 1981. *The Great Plains*. Lincoln: Bison Books, University of Nebraska Press. (First published in 1931.)

Whittington, Janet. 1997. "'Chicken War' Is Heating Up." *The Messenger* (Madisonville, Kentucky), August 19:1A, 3A.

Wilcox, Mike. 2008. "Let Piglets Keep Their Balls!" *Radio Netherlands Worldwide*, October 17. http://www.ellinghuysen.com/news/articles/76586.shtml (October 20, 2008).

Williams, William H. 1998. *Delmarva's Chicken Industry: 75 Years of Progress*. Georgetown, DE: Delmarva Poultry Industry.

Wing, Steve, Dana Cole, and Gary Grant. 2000. "Environmental Injustice in North Carolina's Hog Industry." *Environmental Health Perspectives* 108:225–231.

Wing, Steve, and Susanne Wolf. 2000. "Intensive Livestock Operations, Health, and Quality of Life Among Eastern North Carolina Residents." *Environmental Health Perspectives* 108:233–238.

Wood, Anita. 1988. *The Beef Packing Industry: A Study of Three Communities in Southwestern Kansas*. Final Report to the Department of Migrant Education. Flagstaff, AZ: Wood and Wood Associates.

World Organization for Animal Health. 2011. "Geographical Distribution of Countries That Reported BSE Confirmed Cases Since 1989." http://www.oie.int/animal-health-in-the-world/bse-specific-data (June 14, 2011).

Wrangham, Richard. 2009. *Catching Fire: How Cooking Made Us Human*. New York: Basic Books.

Yehieli, Michele, and Mark A. Grey. 2005. *Health Matters: A Pocket Guide for Working with Diverse Cultures and Underserved Populations*. Yarmouth, ME: Intercultural Press.

Young, Richard, Alison Cowe, Coilin Nunan, John Harvey, and Liz Mason. 1999. *The Use and Misuse of Antibiotics in U.K. Agriculture*. Bristol, UK: Soil Association.

Yum China. n.d. "Yum." http://www.yum.com/company/china.asp (May 30, 2011).

Zane, J. Peder. 1996. "It Ain't Just for Meat; It's for Lotion." *New York Times*, May 5:E5.

Index

Information in figures and tables is indicated by *f* and *t*. Information in footnotes is indicated by n after the page number and preceding the note number.